BLM

The Making of a
New Marxist Revolution

BLM

MIKE GONZALEZ

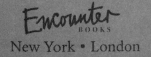

Encounter
BOOKS

New York • London

First American edition published in 2021 by Encounter Books,
an activity of Encounter for Culture and Education, Inc.,
a nonprofit, tax-exempt corporation.
Encounter Books website address: www.encounterbooks.com

Manufactured in the United States and printed on
acid-free paper. The paper used in this publication meets
the minimum requirements of ANSI/NISO Z39.48–1992
(R 1997) (*Permanence of Paper*).

FIRST AMERICAN EDITION

LIBRARY OF CONGRESS CATALOGING-IN-PUBLICATION DATA

Names: Gonzalez, Mike, 1960– author.
Title: BLM: The Making of a New Marxist Revolution / by Mike Gonzalez.
Other titles: Black Lives Matter: The Making of a New Marxist Revolution
Description: First American edition. | New York: Encounter Books, 2021.
Includes bibliographical references and index.
Identifiers: LCCN 2021013984 (print) | LCCN 2021013985 (ebook)
ISBN 9781641772235 (hardcover) | ISBN 9781641772242 (ebook)
Subjects: LCSH: Black lives matter movement—United States.
Black power—United States—History.
Black lives matter movement—Philosophy. | African American radicals.
Civil rights movements—United States. | African Americans—Politics and government.
Classification: LCC E185.615 .G66 2021 (print) | LCC E185.615 (ebook)
DDC 323.1196/073—dc23
LC record available at https://lccn.loc.gov/2021013984
LC ebook record available at https://lccn.loc.gov/2021013985

Interior page design and composition by Bruce Leckie

1 2 3 4 5 6 7 8 9 20 21

To my sister Lucy

CONTENTS

INTRODUCTION

On January 6, 2021, the holy day of the Epiphany, a few hundred supporters of Donald Trump occupied the Capitol building while Congress met to certify the votes of the 2020 election. The representatives of the people had to be whisked to safety while the protesters marauded through some of the most sacrosanct halls of our nation's democracy. Trump, then in his last days as president, was instantly accused and convicted of inciting the crowd by the press, the Democrats, and even some members of his adopted Republican Party. Trump had indeed spoken to the rioters minutes earlier, in front of the White House, some 3.6 miles from Capitol Hill. "I know that everyone here will soon be marching over to the Capitol building to peacefully and patriotically make your voices heard," he told them. He also said, "If you don't fight like hell, you're not going to have a country anymore."[1] For that, the House of Representatives impeached the president two weeks later, the first time in U.S. history that a president had been twice impeached. Trump was later acquitted by the Senate.

The January 6 attack certainly was disturbing. An unruly mob of buffoons had invaded the people's house and threatened America's elected representatives, sending a signal to the nation and the world that something wasn't quite right with the country. This was, moreover, a political attack.

The attackers did something else that was shameful: they gave some political leaders an excuse not to be frank about the Black Lives Matter organizations and their leaders, a group of Marxists who do not just want to defund the police, empty the prison system, and eliminate the courts, as bad as that in itself would be. I myself saw this at a May 26, 2021 hearing of the House Subcommittee on Civil Rights and Civil Liberties in which I testified about Black Lives Matter. My mere mention of the damage BLM had wrought made two members of the Squad, Rep. Ayanna Pressley (Massachusetts) and Rep. Rashida Tlaib (Michigan) livid. BLM's leaders seek to dismantle "the organizing principle of this society"—words spoken by the main founder of BLM, as I will explain in this book. Unfortunately, the Capitol attackers validated a long-standing, stubborn liberal axiom that "right-wing" militancy was a much greater threat than the left-wing version. This reflexive but false belief had been used again and again over the previous seven years to prevent any reasonable discussion of where the BLM organizations wanted to take America. The January 6 attack handed the liberal establishment something to hang on to and use to deflect attention from the real existential danger posed by BLM.

As it was, politicians had already found it impossible to criticize Black Lives Matter because the concept that black lives matter is so unimpeachable. Who could be against black lives mattering? Rancid racists do exist and always will. But Americans by and large are not racist, and they do want justice and equality among the races. This is indeed the reason that the BLM organizations, which are committed to radically changing the way of life of the freest, most prosperous society on earth, use the BLM label. Other labels, such as Red Ideas Matter or Dismantling the Family Matters, wouldn't have worked, though they would more truly represent organizations that advocate policies that make it more difficult for all individuals to succeed and thus close racial gaps.

Making this conversation harder to have is, ironically, the most important impact the Capitol attackers are likely to have on society. Other than that, the groups said to have been involved have very little power over our lives. For all the awful symbolism of the attack, those groups—the Proud Boys, the Boogaloo Bois, the Three Percenters, QAnon—do not have a political action committee, bills in Congress, millions of dollars in hand, a curriculum being disseminated to the country's 14,000 school districts, a sycophantic media that acts as a press agent, or the cultural cachet that lets BLM partner with the musical *Hamilton*. Nor do they have economic and foreign policy views, or an academic discipline that underpins their ideas. As this book will inform you, BLM has all these things. It is already changing your life. The January 6 attack, for all the media apoplexy that accompanied it, is already being forgotten, which is why pundits keep bringing it up again and again and calling it an "insurrection."

BLM had already changed society when the Capitol was occupied. America on January 5, 2021 was unrecognizable from a year earlier—in everything from sports to office work to school curricula to legislation—and what happened a day later gave us an emboldened left that felt it had the moral upper hand and a reason to stop, cancel or jail anyone daring to stand athwart BLM and yell "stop." The left, and its supporters in the press, immediately seized the moment to cry that an "insurrection" or even a "coup" had been attempted. For months after January 6, a media that had been openly supportive of the 2020 mayhem minutely analyzed what they ludicrously built up to be the equivalent of 9/11 and Pearl Harbor. Unreported went the fact that January 6 was not the first time the Capitol had been attacked, and that the three previous acts of aggression—including terrorists shooting at congressmen point blank from the House visitors' gallery—were all perpetrated by leftists who were later released from prison by Democratic presidents.[2]

When Rep. Maxine Waters urged BLM protesters to become even more bellicose in the streets prior to the announcement of the verdict on Derek Chauvin—the police officer who eventually (April 20, 2021) was found guilty of killing George Floyd—the media and all the other institutions controlled by the left simply looked the other way. Waters, a radical who represents a district that covers South Los Angeles, told the protesters, "We gotta stay on the street, we've got to get more active, we've got to get more confrontational, we've got to make sure that they know that we mean business." The parallels with what Trump said could not have been more blunt (except that Waters did not tell her audience to remain peaceful). The judge overseeing Chauvin's trial, Peter Cahill, called Waters's comments "abhorrent" and "disrespectful to the rule of law and the judicial branch," and he warned that they could be used to overturn the verdict.[3] But how did the left, so outraged three months earlier, react? Crickets. Waters was not impeached.

WHICH INSURRECTION?

The United States was confronted with an insurrection, but was it on January 6 or during the seven months that preceded it? Eleven days after the January 6 riot, as America was still sifting through the aftermath, NPR aired an interview with Army Lt. Gen. Mark Hertling in which he described what an insurrection is. "If you take the definition out of the military's doctrinal manual, it says something like it's an ongoing uprising and an organized uprising that uses both violent and nonviolent means to overthrow an existing government or to wrest away aspects of government control." The manual, he added soberly, "continues by saying that it often counts on government security forces—meaning the police, the military—to overreact, which then brings more proponents of the insurgency because they believe the government institutions are faltering. All of those contribute to an insurgency."

NPR's interviewer, Lulu Garcia-Navarro, pressed Lt. Gen. Hertling on whether he thought January 6 constituted an insurgency, and he answered, "I do, Lulu.... We're seeing some of the same in U.S. society right now, and they all go by names. I mean, you could recite the Proud Boys, QAnon, the Three Percenters. You can go down the list. Each one of them have different desires and different objectives, and they are sucking the population, because of other factors like disinformation and misinformation from the government, into their aggrievement. And that's what's troubling."[4]

Except that, if you truly follow what he says the manual says, the assault on our Capitol—more operetta than high drama—hardly fills the bill. It was stomach-churning to see a grown man with bison-horned headgear and tattoos parade around the Capitol, or another with his feet on the desk of the Speaker of the House. But the riot was neither "an ongoing uprising" nor "organized" in the true sense of the word. It is even debatable that it sought to overthrow an existing government. The left and the press have eagerly exaggerated all these traits, overegging the "command and control" aspects, which journalists repeated as if they were military experts, in the belief that it will hand them the moral upper hand. They could then expect to use this advantage to ram through their preferred policies. If they were honest with themselves and others, however, they would have admitted all those things about the events that took place in the long turbulent year that had just concluded.

America in 2020 had had its Year of Living Dangerously. It faced an all-out assault on all its institutions, structures and systems, and haunting scenes worthy of Peter Weir's 1982 film by that name. The death of George Floyd, a forty-six-year-old black man, at the hands of a white Minneapolis policeman, Derek Chauvin, on May 25 touched off months of protests, riots, and looting. Whatever drugs may have been coursing through his veins, George Floyd was murdered; there was no justification for what Chauvin did.

There was also no justification for BLM's use of this tragedy, however. Within days of Floyd's death, portions of many American cities from coast to coast and border to border became scenes of marches and street shutdowns during the day and destruction at night. The protests, which could degenerate into violent intimidation of city dwellers and in over six hundred cases into outright riots, were organized by Black Lives Matter organizations that promise racial equality but preach Marxism, transgender ideology, "queer affirmation," and so on. Mobs brought down statues, broke into stores—both large retailers and small mom-and-pops—and looted merchandise. Diners at outdoor restaurant tables were harassed by marauding BLM activists into chanting their slogans. And it all happened in the middle of a pandemic. Within days of the start of the violence, vandals had caused the loss of at least nineteen lives and somewhere between $1 billion and $2 billion in damage, "marking it as the costliest civil disorder in U.S. history," according to the Insurance Information Institute.[5]

By late June, things had gotten so serious that the Australian academic David Kilkullen, a leading expert in the British counter-insurgency in Malaya in the 1950s and the man who conceptualized and monitored George W. Bush's successful surge in Iraq in 2008, wrote that the United States was in a state of what the Central Intelligence Agency's *Guide to the Analysis of Insurgency* calls "incipient insurgency." Although the moment did not meet all the conditions of insurrection, Kilkullen wrote, the CIA's definition of incipient insurgency "encompasses pre-insurgency and organizational stages."[6] The CIA manual itself describes how a sense of injustice is manipulated at this stage.

> During the preinsurgency stage, insurgents identify and publicize a grievance around which they can rally supporters. Insurgents seek to create a compelling narrative—the story a party to an

armed struggle uses to justify its actions in order to attain legitimacy and favor among relevant populations. Specific indicators that insurgents are seeking to mobilize the population around a grievance might include:

- Emergence of websites or the circulation of flyers, pamphlets, DVDs, or other promotional materials that generate popular discussion of the grievance.
- Media articles or opinion pieces on the issue.
- Espousal of the grievance by legitimate political or social organizations.
- Demonstrations or protests in which the issue plays a prominent rallying role.[7]

The BLM-induced violence of 2020 included all these characteristics. Through the use of repeated exaggerations, the BLM leaders and organizations manipulated a sense of injustice and, just as important, a sense of white guilt that has been building since the 1960s. It was meant, moreover, to overthrow an existing constitutional order, to dismantle "the organizing principle of this society," in the words of the top leader of the Black Lives Matter organizations that directed and coordinated the insurgency. It resulted in the reprehensible loss of lives and property, and precipitated the changes in everyday life in America that BLM leaders sought.

When Major League Baseball returned to a restless nation in August, it became clear to what degree things were not back to normal. Opening Day, delayed by months because of the COVID-19 pandemic, was a pageant to racial self-flagellation. Teammates locked arms while announcers repeated platitudinal incantations about "systemic racism" in America. That this was happening to the pleasant National Pastime—one of the most integrated areas of American life after the valiant Jackie Robinson broke the color line, and a sport that hitherto had escaped the self-inflicted racial wounds of the NFL and the NBA—was ominous. Our schools, our offices, our legislatures, everything from the sublime and sacred such as our churches, to the mundane such as our fraternities and sororities, succumbed to an obsession with all things race following the protests and riots.

The ghoulish tragicomedy of the Capitol riots will not affect our lives in the same manner, except by accelerating the changes that the BLM mayhem induced. Heather Mac Donald got it right, as usual, when she wrote two days later that the January 6 attack "will give even more fuel to the ongoing desecration of our heritage by the Left, a desecration that will prove more momentous than what occurred on Wednesday."[8]

WHAT REALLY HAPPENED IN 2020

The George Floyd protests that led to widespread changes in American life were not spontaneous events. The American population (and people in other parts of the world) did not suddenly rise up in righteous anger, take to the streets, and demand not just that police departments be defunded, but that all of our supposedly racist structures, institutions, and systems be overhauled. The 12,000 or so demonstrations and 633 related riots identified in September 2020 by Princeton's U.S. Crisis Monitor took organizational muscle.[9] The hold on institutions from the classroom to the ballpark required ideological commitment.

That muscle and commitment were provided by the various Black Lives Matter organizations that have sprung up throughout the United States, and later in Canada, Europe, and the rest of the world. The leaders and activists of these organizations make savvy use of social media to spread their message and organize the marches, sit-ins, statue-tumblings, and riots. They seized on the video showing George Floyd's suffering to unleash nationwide the insurgency that Kilkullen described. They have exaggerated the real problems that do exist in society, to the point that teenagers in the freest country on earth repeat zombielike that "people are hurting" and that we need systemic change, and use the real fear of social cancelation or loss of livelihood to chill dissent by those who understand what's going on.

Given the level of transformation these organizations have already wreaked on their country, it behooves Americans to ask who their leaders are and what they intend to do. As the CIA manual puts it, "An ideal insurgent leader displays charisma, the flexibility to balance ideology with the need to be inclusive and leverage local grievances, and an ability to engender loyalty and maintain group unity."[10] It is important to understand the people who fill this role for BLM.

Simply put, the women (for they are mostly women) at the helm of these groups are self-avowed Marxist-Leninists. Their flagship issue is police and prison reform. They equate what they would call "mass incarceration" to the issue of slavery in the nineteenth century. The breakdown of the "carceral state" is their new abolitionist movement. Behind the prison and police reform façade, however, lies a deep ideological commitment to abandoning our free-market and liberal democratic system and to remaking America along Marxist lines. For years, these leaders have been immersed in the dark bog of international communism, associating with the most radical groups and individuals from Oakland to Berlin to Caracas. What they seek for America is a future where natural rights such as those to speech, conscience, or property would be curtailed or even eliminated.

The top leaders are Alicia Garza, Patrisse Cullors, and Opal Tometi, three African American lesbians whose long-standing ties to domestic Marxist revolutionaries and links with international groups that seek revolution in Asia, Latin America, and Europe will be revealed in this book. There are many others. They have ties to 1960s white radicals who saw in the plight of black Americans an opportunity to launch a revolution that would overthrow the government and refashion the American system, in the way the governments of the tsars, Chiang Kai-shek, and Fulgencio Batista were overthrown by revolutionaries; the centuries-old cultures of Russia, China, and Cuba were laid waste; and the everyday life of the people changed forever. The black community hadn't seen such a radical set of leaders since Huey Newton, Bobby Seale, and Eldridge Cleaver were running the Black Panthers in the late 1960s and extolling the killing of cops and other whites (and in the case of Cleaver, the rape of white women), and Stokely Carmichael was gallivanting around the globe embracing every communist dictator from Cuba to North Vietnam to Algiers.

Both the insurgency of the 1960s and the one today came at a time when the country's elites had seemed to fail, though in the present case the perception that elites had gotten their positions of power through fraudulent means could be found among Americans of both left and right. One big difference now is that far-left organizations have been able to use pervasive social media to radicalize, activate, and organize the young, from teenagers to millennials. Another big difference is that unlike the Panthers, who instilled fear in most Americans because the media reported on their activities and agenda fairly and the FBI investigated them, BLM is free to act with impunity and has the organizing muscle to alter our lives.

ABSENCE OF MEDIA VETTING

The background and agenda of the BLM organizers are unknown to many good Americans who pitched Black Lives Matter signs on their lawns or wore facemasks or shirts emblazoned with the slogan to church on Sunday in the summer of 2020, and still do so today—or worse, engaged in ritualistic self-denunciations like those extracted by Mao's Red Guards. The media did not report on the organizing behind the protests, or did so only with caveats and subterfuge. Not only did the media not reveal the steadfast dedication of Garza, Cullors, and Tometi to Marxist ideology— something that was demonstrable and easily documented—but it denied these attachments. PolitiFact, a self-described media "fact checker," ran a specious report in which it quoted only professors who said that calling the BLM leaders Marxist was a misrepresentation if not a racist dog whistle. "These days, Marxism usually means analyzing social change through an economic lens, with the assumption that the rich and the poor should become more equal," PolitiFact's Tom Kertscher deceitfully wrote. Sure, the BLM leaders may say they are Marxist, Kertscher added, "but the movement has grown and broadened dramatically. Many Americans, few of whom would identify as Marxists, support Black Lives Matter, drawn to its message of anti-racism."[11]

The last part is no doubt true, but only because "journalists" such as Kertscher report the facts in such deceptive ways, or don't report them at all. One can say that the media did not cover the BLM organizations as much as covered *for* them. Those journalists or outside experts who dared to report on BLM, trying to expose their ties and intentions and the extent of the damage from the disturbances, or the editors who published op-eds not in keeping with the new dogma, were summarily fired or disciplined in public. (I myself was publicly flagellated by the *New York Times* and *Axios* after pointing to ties between BLM and pro-Maoist groups, as will be seen in chapter 6.) Or, when journalists did report what the BLM leaders were saying, as when the *New Yorker*'s David Remnick quoted Alicia Garza being callous about the wanton property destruction, it was to side with them. Garza told Remnick, "I am not going to spend my time telling people to go home. ... We don't have time to finger-wag at protesters about property. That can be rebuilt. Target will reopen. The stores will reopen. That's assured." In response, Remnick wrote that "the human capacity for patience and endurance, in the face of blatant injustice, is not without limits. The ballot also has its limits."[12]

Nor can the various levels of government be of much help. We know too well that multiple Democratic mayors and governors refused to use their police force, let alone the National Guard, to quell the riots and looting in their towns, and rejected help from the federal government. Mayor Ted Wheeler of Portland typified that approach when he reacted to President Trump's offer of sending federal law enforcement officials to the city to help quell the mayhem caused nightly by BLM and Antifa activists: *No, thanks* was his answer. "Tens of thousands of Portlanders have peacefully protested and marched for the noble cause of fixing our broken criminal justice system," Mayor Wheeler wrote in a letter to President Trump on August 28, 2020. "They are part of the proud progressive tradition of Portlanders fighting for justice—from racial justice to economic justice to environmental justice."[13] When rioters were arrested, "rogue prosecutors" who had been elected in several cities with far-left money tossed out their cases and released the rioters.

The government is also very limited in what it can do in terms of gathering intelligence on First Amendment–protected activities, such as the right to demonstrate. Whereas the CIA is largely free to collect information on foreign actors who may threaten our way of life, its domestic counterparts, such as the Federal Bureau of Investigation or the Director of National Intelligence (DNI), are prevented by statutes and rules (including Executive Order 12333) from doing the same among U.S. citizens or permanent resident aliens. J. Edgar Hoover's FBI certainly did investigate communists in the 1930s, 1940s, and 1950s, and the anti-war and civil rights era radicals in the 1960s, through the use of wiretaps, break-ins, and other means of intelligence gathering. But today, the First and Fourth Amendments prohibit much of the domestic surveillance work that would have been necessary to know how much of the 2020 protests were organized by a tight-knit group of Marxists. We don't save the liberal democracy village by letting others destroy the liberal democracy village. But have we left ourselves without adequate protection? The changes that the leaders of the BLM organizations want would erode or extinguish our liberties. This presents a conundrum. Any conservative who may be tempted to think that those constitutional protections leave us vulnerable must balance that very real concern with the equally valid consideration of what an unleashed FBI could do to conservative movements freely carrying out constitutionally protected activity.

As a result, there is no place in the federal government—not in the Justice Department, the Department of Homeland Security, the FBI, or the DNI—where one can find out how much the 2020 protests, and all the deep societal changes that have followed in their wake, were the work of a network of groups whose leaders are committed to implementing a communist blueprint in the United States. PolitiFact's Tom Kertscher is completely right in saying that many Americans who reject communism support Black Lives Matter. When my well-meaning neighbors put up lawn signs that both praise BLM and declare "silence is violence," they don't get the contradiction. They don't know what they don't know.

THIS BOOK

This book exists to fill the void in public awareness. If journalists will not report on the real nature of the Black Lives Matter organizations and their leaders, and if the federal government cannot gather information on First Amendment–protected activities, this book will attempt to correct the record and analyze all the aspects of what transpired in 2020, as well as the historical forces that led up to those events. It will explain that, while only the deranged can take issue with the sentiment that black lives matter, the agenda of the organizations that have astutely appropriated that slogan is far different. This is important for Americans to learn—before they agree to a wholesale change of everything around them.

Any book, essay, or op-ed that touches on the subject of the plight of black Americans, and the use of it by those who want to change society, must recognize and explore the real suffering of black Americans. It must answer the question of whether the United States is institutionally, structurally, or systemically racist, as these are the reasons the activists give for seeking to transform all of its institutions and structures, and indeed the American system itself (i.e., the way everything works). In my view, the answer is a clear no. I write as someone who has resided at least a year in seven countries in Asia, Europe, and Latin America (and has spent weeks or months in many more), and I can compare and contrast. Moreover, it is dangerous to pretend that America is systemically racist, as that belief inexorably creates an urge to change the entire system. As this book will demonstrate, the relationship is inverse. For the leftist radicals of the 1960s, the lust to transform America came first, and then those who sought this change latched on to the black struggle as the vehicle best suited to those ends. "Wars like Vietnam came and went, but it was only the brewing revolution of American blacks, JJ [Weatherman leader John Jacobs] prophesied, that had the potential to destroy the country," writes Bryan Burrough about the leaders of the Weather Underground in *Days of Rage*, a history of 1960s radicals.[14] Or as O'Brien warned Winston Smith in George Orwell's *1984*, "Power is in tearing human minds to pieces and putting them together again in new shapes of your own choosing."

Black Americans themselves have not sought to overthrow the country's system or to tear it up. Quite the contrary: they have demanded their rightful place in it. From Frederick Douglass to

Martin Luther King, they used the Constitution itself to show it was their right to have such a place. In fact, they have been knocking on the national door and asking to be full participants for centuries. Sometimes the door has remained shut, sometimes it has been slammed in their faces. Before the civil rights movement, which finally removed all legal obstacles to full black participation, the door opened and closed by turns. The infliction of untold suffering on blacks provides the darkest pages of this country's history, just as the struggle for their rights and full acceptance in society has provided the most hopeful chapters in America's experiment as a self-ruling, constitutional republic.

The story obviously starts with the Founding. Chapter 1 will tackle the myth at the heart of BLM and the entire woke movement, that the founding documents and the Founders themselves perpetuated slavery. Is that the case? Or is it rather the case that, as Lincoln held, the founding generation fully expected the Spirit of '76 to soon wash away slavery, and that white Southerners agreed and then went out of their way to quash that spirit?

After a harrowing civil war fought to end it, one which took the lives of more than 600,000 people—360,222 of them white Northerners who fought on the anti-slavery side—there was a ray of hope, and an opportunity missed. The promise of Reconstruction was abandoned in the 1870s, and then came the era of *Plessy v. Ferguson* (1896) with its doomed "separate but equal" doctrine (presaging what many woke Americans today seem to pursue). Jim Crow laws followed, and blacks became for all intents and purposes a separate caste—which is exactly what Justice John Marshall Harlan tried to prevent when he stood as the single dissenter in the *Plessy* decision and wrote, "In the eye of the law, there is in this country no superior, dominant, ruling class of citizens. There is no caste here."[15]

Given this history, it is hardly surprising that our foreign enemies have repeatedly tried to exploit these divisions—most recently in the attempts by the ISIS caliphate to recruit blacks, and the more ham-fisted use of our internal divisions by the People's Republic of China. But the most intense of these efforts was carried out by the USSR right after its founding in 1917. The Soviets' campaign to enlist blacks in their schemes to touch off revolution in the U.S. homeland was sustained for decades and highly sophisticated. It attracted some big names, such as the poet Langston Hughes, who despaired of America ever giving its black citizens a fair chance. Such efforts to subvert America racially will continue as long as our divisions continue, which means they will be around for a long time. Chapter 2 will take a brief look at our enemies' attempts to widen and deepen our divisions. Many black intellectuals gravitated toward Marxism, either in response to Soviet entreaties or because they internalized the belief (shared today by Garza, Cullors, and Tometi) that capitalism is inherently racist. Among these black Marxists one can count, sadly, some of the best minds of black America, including first-rate intellectuals such as W. E. B. Du Bois, James Baldwin, Langston Hughes, and Chandler Owen (who became a Republican in the 1920s and went on to write speeches for President Eisenhower).

Yet by far the biggest attempt to use black resentment to foment revolution in the United States came in the 1960s, and this time it was not a foreign power that started it. Revolutionary governments from Havana to Algiers were happy to give support, but the movements covered in chapter 3, whose leaders have had a huge impact on our would-be revolutionaries today, were started by Americans, both black and white. In the first case, propelled by the all-important concept of Black Power, there were the Black Panthers and the Black Liberation Movement, which evolved into the Black Liberation Army. Their leaders were charismatic men and women such as Huey Newton, Bobby Seale (who founded the Black Panthers), Eldridge Cleaver, Angela Davis, JoAnne Chesimard, and Stokely Carmichael, who was born in Trinidad and moved to the Bronx as a child. They instilled fear in America's leaders, but most importantly, they manipulated white guilt.

Former Black Panthers and Black Liberation Army figures who are still alive, such as, respectively, Angela Davis and JoAnne Chesimard (now known as Assata Shakur and living in exile in Havana), are important intellectual influences on the BLM leaders. On the set of *Democracy Now!* in 2017, Alicia Garza gushed to Angela Davis, "I also want to say, you are one of my greatest teachers. I have a bookshelf full of your writings."[16]

The white revolutionaries of the 1960s, many of them members of the Weather Underground—designated by the FBI as a domestic terrorist organization—have had a direct influence on the BLM leaders, not only as intellectual forces, but more importantly as funders and trainers on how to organize for social causes and use civil action to effect radical societal transformation. The Weathermen were interesting because they were exclusively white, from upper- and middle-class families. Back then, as today, their main interest was to find young volunteers to join the revolutionary struggle, for whom the Weathermen would act as the revolutionary vanguard. For this reason, chapter 3 devotes a great deal of attention to them. Eric Mann, for example, a former member of the Weather Underground and the founder of the Labor/Community Strategy Center in Los Angeles, trained Cullors for ten years, well before she helped Garza and Tometi launch the #BlackLivesMatter hashtag in 2013. Mann served eighteen months in prison for assault and battery, and he remains committed to overthrowing the American system and achieving world revolution through organizing people like Cullors.[17] The purpose of his Labor/Community Strategy Center, which he calls the "Harvard of Revolutionary graduate schools," is "to build an anti-racist, anti-imperialist, anti-fascist united front," Mann told students at the University of California, San Diego in 2008.[18] Nor is Mann the only link between BLM and the Weathermen. We should therefore understand the Weathermen, and what their goals were at their inception and remain to this day.

After learning what formed their thinking, we will delve into who the leaders of BLM are in chapter 4. Patrisse Cullors, Alicia Garza, Opal Tometi, Melina Abdullah, Ash-Lee Woodard Henderson, and all the other major leaders of BLM organizations—such as the Movement for Black Lives, the Black Lives Matter Global Network, the Black Futures Lab, and so on—cannot properly be described as progressives. They are Marxist to the core, sometimes with Leninism thrown in for good measure. They don't hide it; only the media hides it. Their attachment to anti-capitalist causes, to organizations domestic and international that explicitly seek to remake the world and achieve global revolution, predates the deaths of Trayvon Martin in Sanford, Michael Brown in Ferguson, Freddie Gray in Baltimore, Breonna Taylor in Louisville, and certainly George Floyd in Minneapolis. These women are not muscle for hire; they didn't have late-in-life epiphanies that moved them from mundane suburban lifestyles to radical causes; they are not grifters who have found an easy way to make a buck by activating online young people seeking purpose in their lives. No, Garza, Cullors, and the others are committed revolutionaries—they have studied their subject, and by all appearances they believe in the Marxist canon.

Yet even with the benefit of media malpractice, the BLM organizations and their leaders would not have been able to achieve the success they saw in 2020 had not some of the wealthiest families in America, as well as some of the most profitable corporations, stepped up to finance their activity. Chapter 5 will be dedicated to that old Watergate adage, "Follow the money." Inexplicably, the Buffetts, the Rockefellers, and the Gateses—not to mention Nike, Amazon, and Gatorade—have joined the Soros family and the Tides Center in financing BLM. With some of these families we may be witnessing a sort of "third-generation syndrome," in which the creativity and risk taking of the first generation have been completely replaced by guilt. In the case of Fortune 500 corporations, it is easier to understand: they may be buying peace and using virtue signaling as a marketing tool. Their embrace of wokeness following the summer of 2020 extended beyond financing Marxist outfits, to carrying out "anti-racism" trainings that were inspired by critical race theory, and promoting BLM in other ways.

We can easily see how people in authority were intimidated if we look at what happened when the FBI tried to do something, which will be the subject of chapter 6. In a 2017 intelligence assessment, the bureau warned that what it called "Black Identity Extremists" could create havoc within the United States, and therefore it needed to investigate. The Congressional Black Caucus and other liberal groups and journalists swung into action, applying pressure on the bureau to desist from the idea. In a letter to Director Christopher Wray, the Black Caucus—which at the time had only one Republican among its forty-nine House members—raised the specter of J. Edgar Hoover, who, as one of the founders of the FBI in 1935 and its first director until his death in 1972, did much to protect America from communist infiltration. "As you're no doubt aware, the FBI has a troubling history of utilizing its broad investigatory power to target black citizens," the caucus wrote.[19] The effort by the Black Caucus had the intended chilling effect. The investigation was defanged. In testimony to the U.S. Senate on July 23, 2019, Wray told Senator Cory Booker of New Jersey, "We don't use the term black identity extremism anymore."[20]

Fear of criticizing the BLM organizations drew attention to Antifa, short for Anti-Fascist. Criticizing Antifa presented less of a risk than criticizing groups that bore the name Black Lives Matter, and therefore became the "safe space" for the less than courageous who still wanted to appear to be doing something. Antifa therefore merits some attention, and it will also be covered in chapter 6, even though I believe that it carried much less organizational muscle than BLM.

The sweeping changes that began in 2020 and loom larger in 2021 find their philosophical genesis in theories that took over the universities decades earlier, which go loosely under the banner of critical race theory, a grandchild of the critical theory of the so-called Frankfurt School. Critical theory directly produced critical legal theory in American law schools, and critical legal theory inspired other academics to create critical race theory. Like its predecessors, CRT submits all previous norms, traditions, and institutions to relentless criticism. This constant disparagement is intended to weaken the foundations of society, the better to replace them. All three theories deny the existence of metaphysical truth, let alone transcendent truth. Instead of absolute truth and established historical fact, CRT sees only competing narratives that are all equally subjective. Such a view denies that what has happened (history) actually happened; it therefore ignores Aristotle's famous dictum that "this alone is lacking even to God, to make undone things that have once been done."[21] According to CRT, what has been taught as the American Way is nothing but white supremacy.

In chapter 7, I will focus on critical race theory and its leading proponents: writers such as Derrick Bell, Kimberlé Crenshaw, and Richard Delgado. The protests of 2020 may have purportedly been about the deaths of George Floyd and Breonna Taylor, but in fact were just a street-level manifestation of these noxious academic theories. Listen to Garza, Tometi, and Cullors speak, and you realize every word is the result of CRT, which thus informs the BLM curricula.

Reading this book will not be an exercise in despair, however. What the activists seek does not need to be our reality. If the year 2020 saw our cities torn apart and our institutions begin to transform rapidly, it also saw many Americans wake up to wokism, as it were. The final chapter of this book will be devoted to solutions: What can everyday Americans and their leaders do to make sure that our universities do not become madrassas where anti-Americanism is taught, where future generations are filled with grievances and the desire to redesign society? How can we be courageous in our personal lives without risk of losing our livelihood and our place in society? Lawfare, long a tool of the left, will need to be part of the answer. Companies must feel the real risk of lawsuits if they insist on putting their employees through the workplace harassment of anti-racism training. We must also look for ways to reform the police. If we are going to have a national conversation on police, it should start with police unions, indeed all public-sector unions, including those for teachers. The final chapter will examine how we as a nation can become a more perfect union.

BLM

CHAPTER 1

THE FOUNDING V. SLAVERY

On an August day in 1834, in a Maryland farming stable not far from Chesapeake Bay, Frederick Douglass, then a teenager, held off his sadistic master, Edward Covey. For months, Covey (to whom Douglass had been loaned for a year) had tyrannized Douglass, then around age sixteen, at a whim. At one point, Douglass decided to fight back, and on that morning he did. As he recounted twenty-one years later,

> I was resolved to fight, and, what was better still, I was actually hard at it. The fighting madness had come upon me, and I found my strong fingers firmly attached to the throat of my cowardly tormentor; as heedless of consequences, at the moment, as though we stood as equals before the law. The very color of the man was forgotten.

Douglass then added, with characteristic humility,

> Well, my dear reader, this battle with Mr. Covey—undignified as it was, and as I fear my narration of it is—was the turning point

in my "life as a slave." It rekindled in my breast the smouldering embers of liberty; it...revived a sense of my own manhood. I was a changed being after that fight. I was nothing before; I WAS A MAN NOW. It recalled to life my crushed self-respect and my self-confidence, and inspired me with a renewed determination to be A FREEMAN.[1]

For the six months that Douglass remained with Covey, the latter left him alone, not laying a hand on him again. After he gained his freedom, Douglass went to work on his mind, closely studying our nation's founding documents, and went on to become the nation's most famous abolitionist, one whose counsel was sought by journalists and presidents alike. His calls for Americans to live up to the promises of the Founders, to interpret the Constitution "as it ought to be interpreted," and therefore end slavery, proved how welcome the guarantees of the Founding were to abolitionists.

The Douglass-Covey face-off represented a small, personal turning point for America's foremost abolitionist, one he complemented later with his self-education. The first half of the nineteenth century was to be the theater of other, larger points of inflection, though these, sadly, were intended to prevent Douglass's liberating moment and consequent education from being replicated on a mass scale across the young country. The Revolutionary War had brought hope and real change not just to the lives of the white former colonists but also to the lives of both slaves and freedmen. The Spirit of '76 was indomitable: it led to manumissions, the expansion of the voting franchise to freedmen, and the general feeling that slavery would soon be a thing of the past.

Slave owners and other racists noticed that, too, however, and their apprehension grew. As the historian C. Bradley Thompson writes, the abolitionist movement in the North "based its moral philosophy on the principles of the Declaration." Eventually, therefore, "proslavery thinkers came to realize that the greatest intellectual obstacle to promoting slavery in the United States was the Declaration of Independence and its psychic hold on the minds of ordinary Americans, including patriotic Southerners."[2] This understanding gave them a choice between the Declaration and slavery. They chose the latter and sealed their fate.

This process began in earnest a decade or so before the Douglass-Covey fight, when slave states started to reverse the advances of the Spirit of '76. Some of slavery's proponents, such as John C. Calhoun, one of the most prominent politicians in the first half of the nineteenth century, saw Jefferson's inclusion of the American ideal that "All men are created equal" as a false and even dangerous proposition. In the place of individual equality, Calhoun foreshadowed today's identity politics by promoting permanent interest groups. Calhoun did not invent factions; James Madison had warned against them as a disuniting force. One difference is that Calhoun and today's BLM left, rather than fearing factions, embrace them as the natural order of things. For them, factions lack a base in transcendent truths and natural rights, but represent relativistic values, as Harry Jaffa brilliantly demonstrated in a 2001 essay.[3]

Still other nineteenth-century slavery apologists, such as Abraham Lincoln's rival Stephen Douglas, differed with Calhoun, but in their case, they said that the Founders never intended to include blacks. Lincoln—and Douglass—disagreed with both these views, and believed the Founders and their documents, however imperfect, as all earthly things are, were principled and worth treasuring.

This period is important to cover because the leaders of the Black Lives Matter organizations actually agree with Stephen Douglas and the writer of the Supreme Court's *Dred Scott* decision. In the pursuit of a political project to transform America, they must tarnish her institutions, traditions, and ideals, because those stand in the way of what they want to do. Alicia Garza, Opal Tometi, Patrisse Cullors, and the writers of the 1619 Project, particularly its architect, Nikole Hannah-Jones, therefore end up, ironically, siding with Douglas and spurning Douglass. In order to understand this, we must examine the record.

ACTS, COMPROMISES, AND DECISIONS

Some of the most noteworthy nineteenth-century turning points leading history away from the promise of '76 were the attempts by slave states to expand the scourge of slavery to the new territories that were becoming states to the west. Slavery's proponents had started counting votes in the Senate very closely. Population growth, both through native births and immigration, was taking place in the north, so soon these free states had comfortable majorities in the House of Representatives. The Senate became the last bulwark against eventual abolition. The desperation was so great that Southerners at one point in the 1850s even envisioned buying the island of Cuba from Spain in order to gain one more slave state.[4] Madrid refused to sell, and the exercise came to nothing, but it shows the length to which the proslavery leaders were willing to go.

One of the major turning points was the Missouri Compromise of 1820, which admitted that territory to the Union as a slave state and Maine as a free one, and prohibited slavery in any of the territories west of Missouri or above the latitude of 36°30'. Another was the Kansas-Nebraska Act of 1854, which repealed the latitudinal prohibition of the Missouri Compromise and allowed settlers of a territory to have the "popular sovereignty" to decide whether slavery would be allowed.

The backlash against liberty had begun slowly at first, a quarter century after the Declaration was signed. Some of the states that had ratified the Constitution, those in the South, started passing laws and enacting codes that denied all black Americans, not just slaves, the ability to enjoy the rights protected by the Constitution. South Carolina led the way in 1800, passing a new act that extended to freedmen a previous, though rarely enforced, ban on slaves gathering together to learn how to read or write. The legislature declared that "assemblies of slaves, free negroes, mulattoes... met together *for the purpose of* MENTAL INSTRUCTION, in a confined or secret place, &c., &c., are declared to be an unlawful meeting."[5] As historian Christopher Frank Lee explains, the South Carolina legislature "did not prohibit education, per se, but they did not want groups of blacks meeting out of the public eye."[6] Worse was to come.

About a quarter century later, states did start outright forbidding free blacks from learning to read and write. In 1823, "Mississippi also outlawed teaching any black person, free or enslaved, and Georgia did the same in 1829."[7] Alabama followed suit in 1833. Its Slavery Code of that year held that "Any person who shall attempt to teach any free person of color, or slave, to spell, read or write, shall upon conviction thereof by indictment, be fined in a sum of not less than two hundred fifty dollars, nor more than five hundred dollars." The codes also held that any freeman who wrote a pass for a slave would be administered thirty-nine lashes.[8]

As for the slaves, not only was their freedom extinguished but also the new codes spelled out in detail how all their liberties, no matter how small, were to be trampled upon. Leaving the plantation where they lived was forbidden to any slave without a "pass, or some sort of letter or token" from his or her owner. No slave was to "keep or carry any gun... or any other weapon whatsoever." No person was allowed to buy, sell, or give to or receive anything from a slave "without the consent of the master," and any owner who allowed his slave to transact freely would be fined $50, a goodly sum back then. Slaves were prohibited from owning dogs, horses, or even mules. Hogs could be kept under some circumstances. It was unlawful, too, for more than five male slaves "with or without passes" to assemble any place off their owner's plantation. Violations of these laws would result in either lashes on the bare back or branding of the face or chest.

The U.S. Supreme Court's *Dred Scott* decision of 1857 is in a league of its own as far as turning the country away from freedom. Chief Justice Roger Taney declared parts of the Missouri Compromise to be in violation of the Fifth Amendment and affirmed not only that black Americans were not citizens but also that they could never be, whether free or enslaved. Blacks, wrote Taney in what has been identified by all accounts as the worst decision in Supreme Court history, were not included in the Declaration's assertion that all men are created equal; they were not members "of the political community formed and brought into existence by the Constitution of the United States."[9]

Dred Scott was a slave from Missouri whose owners had taken him to Illinois, a free state, and to Wisconsin, a free territory. Upon their return to Missouri, he attempted to buy his freedom, but his owners refused. Thereupon he sued to prove that, as a former resident in free areas, he was free. The decision that bears his name, more than any of the other turning points, made war inevitable. It established a rival constitutional order at odds with the one of 1787. Within a handful of years, Lincoln had been elected, most of the slave states had seceded, and Americans were at each other's throats over slavery.

Because BLM's leaders today oddly share Taney's view that the Declaration and the Constitution excluded blacks, it is best to review the most famous passage in *Dred Scott*, in order to observe how close it comes to what our woke elements in the early twenty-first century think happened:

In the opinion of the court, the legislation and histories of the times, and the language used in the Declaration of Independence, show, that neither the class of persons who had been imported as slaves, nor their descendants, whether they had become free or not, were then acknowledged as a part of the people, nor intended to be included in the general words used in that memorable instrument.

It is difficult at this day to realize the state of public opinion in relation to that unfortunate race, which prevailed in the civilized and enlightened portions of the world at the time of the Declaration of Independence, and when the Constitution of the United States was framed and adopted. But the public history of every European nation displays it in a manner too plain to be mistaken.

They had for more than a century before been regarded as beings of an inferior order, and altogether unfit to associate with the white race, either in social or political relations; and so far inferior, that they had no rights which the white man was bound to respect; and that the negro might justly and lawfully be reduced to slavery for his benefit.... This opinion was at that time fixed and universal in the civilized portion of the white race. It was regarded as an axiom in morals as well as in politics, which no one thought of disputing, or supposed to be open to dispute.[10]

One lawyer who vehemently disagreed with Taney—and with Garza and Hannah-Jones today—was Lincoln, who in a speech in Chicago in 1857, after the Supreme Court had issued its decision, said it was "based on assumed historical facts which are not really true."[11] Lincoln then quoted at length from Justice Benjamin Robbins Curtis's meticulous dissent in the 7–2 decision. Curtis's argument that blacks had indeed formed part of the compact that created the United States was so persuasive that Taney actually went back and added eighteen pages to his controlling decision in a vain attempt to rebut Justice Curtis's arguments. The part that Lincoln quoted from the Curtis dissent in the Chicago speech was this:

> That Constitution was ordained and established by the people of the United States, through the action, in each State, of those persons who were qualified by its laws to act thereon, in behalf of themselves and all other citizens of that State. In some of the States, as we have seen, colored persons were among those qualified by law to act on this subject. These colored persons were not only included in the body of *"the people of the United States,"* by whom the Constitution was ordained and established, but in at least five of the States they had the power to act, and doubtless did act, by their suffrages, upon the question of its adoption.[12]

What Lincoln and Justice Curtis meant is that not only were the estimated 60,000 freedmen who lived in the thirteen states when the Constitution was ratified in 1788 "counted on a par with whites," for the purpose of apportionment, as the Hillsdale College historian David Azerrad puts it, but also they voted in elections and to adopt the Constitution, if they met the property and tax qualifications. "It is a little known fact of American history that black citizens were voting in perhaps as many as 10 states at the time of the founding (the precise number is unclear, but only Georgia, South Carolina, and Virginia explicitly restricted suffrage to whites)," writes Azerrad.[13] All they had to do was meet the property and tax qualifications, and in fact they did exercise the franchise.

The two opposing views clearly came to the fore in 1858, in the third debate between the two candidates vying for the Illinois Senate seat, Lincoln and the man who eventually won, the proslavery Stephen Douglas. Douglas agreed with Taney's view, maintaining that the American government "was made on the white basis...by white men, for the benefit of white men." Douglas, whose position was that blacks were inferior beings, incapable of self-government, added that "in my opinion the signers of the Declaration had no reference to the negro whatever when they declared all men to be created equal. They desired to express by that phrase, white men, men of European birth and European descent." Lincoln held the opposite view. "In the way our fathers originally left the slavery question, the institution was in the course of ultimate extinction, and the public mind rested on the belief that it was in the course of ultimate extinction," said Lincoln. "When this government was originally established, nobody expected the institution of slavery would last until this day."

Lincoln's view that the founding generation expected that the contagion of liberty would soon make slavery wither away can be seen, for example, in George Washington's response to Methodist leaders who asked him in 1785 to sign an emancipation petition. He agreed with them, he told them, and was supportive of expanding to Virginia the anti-slavery legislation being passed in other states and would even let the Virginia legislature know. But he warned them that there were still obstacles in Virginia, and "it would be dangerous to make a frontal attack on a prejudice which is beginning to decrease." Washington added, "Time, patience and enlightenment, and it will be overcome."[14]

Two years later, we again see this expectation in the comments at the Constitutional Convention in Philadelphia by the anti-slavery Connecticut delegate Oliver Ellsworth, that "slavery in time will not be a speck in our country." The reason for not getting rid of slavery right then and there can be seen in the debate over the importation of slaves, which in a compromise was allowed to continue until 1808. "If we do not agree on this middle & moderate ground," said Ellsworth again, "we should lose two States, with such others as may be disposed to stand aloof, should fly into a variety of shapes & directions, and most probably into several confederations and not without bloodshed." So of course the Convention did compromise with slavery, so it would not lose Georgia and South Carolina. But, as Princeton University historian Sean Wilentz wrote in the *New York Times* in 2015, the Convention was a resounding defeat for the proslavery side, which wanted the odious practice written into the national charter. Wilentz wrote:

> Yes, slavery was a powerful institution in 1787. Yes, most white Americans presumed African inferiority. And in 1787, proslavery delegates to the Constitutional Convention in Philadelphia fought to inscribe the principle of property in humans in the Constitution. But on this matter the slaveholders were crushed. James Madison (himself a slaveholder) opposed the ardent proslavery delegates and stated that it would be "wrong to admit in the Constitution the idea that there could be property in men." The Constitutional Convention not only deliberately excluded the word "slavery," but it also quashed the proslavery effort to make slavery a national institution, and so prevented enshrining the racism that justified slavery.[15]

Seventy-one years later, Lincoln lay the fault for the retrogression at the feet of "Douglas and his friends," the proslavery forces who had broken the Founders' prohibition on expanding slavery to new territories, stated in the Northwest Ordinance of 1787, and now pretended to make slavery "national and perpetual."[16]

BLM'S VIEW

In this key debate—not just the one that took place between Lincoln and Douglas in 1858, but the one on the same matter that continues to this day—Alicia Garza, Patrisse Cullors, Opal

Tometi, Nikole Hannah-Jones, and the entire woke complex in academia, the media, and other culture-making institutions, believe that Stephen Douglas, not Lincoln, was right, which means to them *Dred Scott* must have been, in fact, correctly decided. To them, America's founding documents did not include blacks. Alicia Garza, the founder and in many ways the top leader of Black Lives Matter, spoke for many when she told University of Missouri students in 2016 that "in the Constitution, we are only three-fifths of a person. The people vowing to protect the Constitution are vowing to protect white supremacy and genocide."[17] A year earlier, she told a group in Cambridge, Massachusetts, that "Black people and the conditionality of our humanity is written into our constitution."[18] The Black Lives Matter curriculum being taught to children across the country encourages students to think that the phrase "we the people" in the preamble of the Constitution refers only to white men.[19] BLM at School, the educational branch of BLM, distributes to educators the writings of Howard Zinn and James Loewen, as well as the curriculum of the 1619 Project, which are dedicated to smearing the Founders. The curriculum teaches that "protections for slavery were embedded in the founding documents; enslavers dominated the federal government, Supreme Court and Senate from 1787 through 1860." Not even the Thirteenth Amendment—which abolished slavery!—escapes a clubbing. The curriculum also spreads filmmaker Ava DuVernay's idea that the Thirteenth Amendment's words making involuntary servitude possible "as a punishment for crime whereof the party shall have been duly convicted" is what has created BLM's imaginary "from slavery to mass incarceration" pipeline.[20]

Indeed, the entire philosophical framework supporting Black Lives Matter bases itself on the notion that the Founders were at best hypocrites and at worst seeking to cement slavery. Nikole

Hannah-Jones, the architect of the 1619 Project, which seeks to put race at the center of everything in America, wrote in the project's foundational essay that "Our Declaration of Independence, approved on July 4, 1776, proclaims that 'all men are created equal' and 'endowed by their Creator with certain unalienable rights.' But the white men who drafted those words did not believe them to be true for the hundreds of thousands of black people in their midst."[21] The Boston University activist Ibram X. Kendi, for his part, believes that what happened in 1776 was a declaration of "white American independence," and chides Jefferson because he "never made the anti-racist declaration: all racial groups are equal." In his 2019 best seller, *How to Be an Antiracist*, Kendi denounces "A color-blind Constitution for a White-supremacist America." Groups and permanent group interests—Calhoun's idée fixe—are, again ironically, also what seems to matter most to Kendi and others on the left.[22]

The case for Calhoun foreshadowing today's identity politics was made most recently, and best, by the 1776 Commission that President Trump put in place in late 2020, which President Biden revoked on his very first day in office (revoking it was a demand by BLM).[23] It is important to understand Calhoun's thinking, for, as the Commission's executive director, Matt Spalding, said to me in an email, the woke today may get their history from Taney and Douglas, "but they get the political science from Calhoun." To quote from an earlier, unpublished version of the Commission's report, which was shortened in the published report for reasons of space:

> Like modern-day proponents of identity politics, John Calhoun championed diversity. Resisting the common American identity that follows from the Declaration's principle of equality, he argued that the American polity was not a real community. It was reducible to diverse majority and minority groups. Like modern-day

proponents of identity politics, Calhoun saw these groups as more or less permanent, products of their particular historical circumstances. Like modern-day proponents of identity politics, Calhoun was concerned that the talk of achieving unity through rational deliberation and political compromise was a façade. In reality, majority groups would use the political process to oppress minority groups. In Calhoun's America, respect for each group demanded that each hold a veto over the actions of the wider community. But Calhoun's argument justified why some groups must outrank others, and provided the means to enforce those hierarchies.

Calhoun's categories, like those of the entire BLM and critical race theory project (there will be more on this in chapter 7), are based on immutable characteristics—in his case, race, and today, not only race but also national origin, sex, disability status, etc., rather than volitional interests, which is how Madison saw interest group politics. The woke today want to base policy on race—as we see in the farming bill that was included in the Biden stimulus bill of March 2021, which forgave loans for black farmers. Part of the reason that the woke complex today dismisses the Constitution, in fact, is that, as it has been written and amended, it stands in the way of many of the things they want to do, from instituting group rights and racial privileges to suppressing the rights to speech, property, and conscience.[24] This was the key question that led to the Civil War: the Southern states, taking their cue from Calhoun, believed the Constitution permitted slavery, agreeing with today's woke. Lincoln and Douglas believed it didn't. The difference was resolved on the field of battle.

That today's woke see the Constitution as a bothersome impediment, pretty much as Woodrow Wilson and the Progressives did in their day, was made stark to me during a debate of my own on NPR's program *On Point* on March 8, 2021, with Georgetown professor of African American studies Robert Patterson. Every time I told him that President Joe Biden's new push for equity (a buzzword for unequal treatment of individuals by government in order to attain racial parity) was unconstitutional and that he, Patterson, couldn't do all the things he wanted to do, he bristled. At one point, unsurprisingly, he blurted out that the Constitution held that he, a black man, was only three-fifths human, and he therefore implied it was illegitimate. This issue goes to the heart of the constitutional crisis America is traversing in the third decade of the twenty-first century. A good portion of those on the extreme left believe (or say they believe) that our national compact—the document that spells out how the country is to be *constituted*—is dishonest and therefore illicit. Thus, we violate the Constitution of 1787 daily and live now with a rival one, cobbled up together from attitudes, tacitly accepted practices, and legal decisions that find loopholes to approve racial preferences in everything from university admissions to government contracts. The other rival constitution is unwritten, like the British one, and the tension it produces has given us the dangerous regime politics that we saw play out in 2020 and on January 6, 2021.[25]

Patterson's and Garza's view that the so-called three-fifths clause of the Constitution proclaimed that the lives of black Americans were worth only a portion of those of whites is widely shared, and typical of the mistakes in historical analysis that students are taught today. "Equating enslaved Blacks to three-fifths of all other (White) persons matched the ideology of racists on both sides of the aisle," writes Kendi in *Stamped from the Beginning*.[26] The clause, however, was actually an antislavery measure, proposed by the abolitionist James Wilson and insisted upon by representatives of free states who wanted to limit the power of the slave states. It was the slave state leaders who wanted to count their slaves fully for the purposes of apportioning seats in the House of Representatives, so that they could more easily maintain and expand slavery. I explained this to Patterson, adding that the clause had been proposed by the abolitionist James Wilson, to no avail, of course.

Azerrad rightly comments on how ironic it is that

> many Americans who are resolutely opposed to racism unwittingly agree with Chief Justice Roger Taney's claim in Dred Scott.... In this view, the worst Supreme Court case decision in American history was actually correctly decided. Such arguments have unsettling implications for the health of our republic. They teach citizens to despise their founding charter and to be ashamed of their country's origins. They make the Constitution an object of contempt rather than reverence. And they foster alienation and resentment among African-American citizens by excluding them from our Constitution.[27]

This resulting alienation is a feature, not a bug, of the criticism. The twenty-first-century Americans who make arguments similar to Taney's understand full well that promoting the false view that the Founders and Framers viewed blacks as inferiors, who were excluded from the original contract, will delegitimize the United States. They mean to make the Constitution and the Founding project objects of contempt, to more easily tear down the entire structure and put something different in its place. It is a central argument of this book that BLM and similar institutions prioritize overhauling the U.S. system over doing anything to improve the lives of black Americans; otherwise, they would endorse the individual effort and striving that would better black lives. That, however, would mean joining the system, not wrecking it and replacing it.

DOUGLASS'S VIEW

Frederick Douglass took the opposite view. In his famous July 4 oration of 1854, Douglass said,

> I differ from those who charge this baseness on the framers of the Constitution of the United States. It is a slander upon their memory, at least, so I believe.... Fellow-citizens! there is no matter in respect to which, the people of the North have allowed themselves to be so ruinously imposed upon, as that of the pro-slavery character of the Constitution. In that instrument I hold there is neither warrant, license, nor sanction of the hateful thing; but, interpreted as it ought to be interpreted, the Constitution is a GLORIOUS LIBERTY DOCUMENT. Read its preamble, consider its purposes. Is slavery among them? Is it at the gateway? or is it in the temple? It is neither.[28]

Douglass's admiration for the founding documents and their ideals naturally extended to the economic way of life upon which the commercial republic was based, which means that he did not have much truck with the socialism espoused today by the leaders of Black Lives Matter. Garza, for example, told an audience during a gathering of Left Forum, an international Marxist group, that "it's not possible for a world to emerge where black lives matter if it's under capitalism, and it's not possible to abolish capitalism without a struggle against national oppression."[29] This is a consistent message for Garza. In 2015 she told the *SF Weekly* that "Black lives can't matter under capitalism. They're like oil and water."[30]

Douglass faced similar crowds, as socialism, having just been born, was ascendant in the mid-nineteenth century among some American intellectuals. At the thirteenth annual meeting of the Rhode Island Anti-Slavery Society, in November 1848 (the year the *Communist Manifesto* was published), Douglass grew angry when he heard a communist drawing the same comparison we hear today between ownership of humans and the ownership of capital. Douglass wrote that the Marxist speaker "strangely enough went on in an effort to show that wages slavery is as bad as chattel slavery," according to the author Damon Root, who quotes Douglass as adding, "The attempts to place holding property in the soil—on the same footing as holding property in man, was most lame and impotent. And the wonder is that anyone could listen with patience to such arrant nonsense."[31]

Not all proslavery forces agreed with Taney and Douglas that the Founders had excluded black people. John C. Calhoun recognized that the ideals of the Founding documents were a direct threat to what he and others called their "peculiar institution," a benign term meant to conceal its horrors. Calhoun, speaking on the floor of the Senate in 1848, decried

> the dangerous error I have attempted to expose, that all men are born free and equal, as if those high qualities belonged to man without effort to acquire them, and to all equally alike, regardless of their intellectual and moral condition. The attempt to carry into practice this, the most dangerous of all political error, and to bestow on all, without regard to their fitness either to acquire or maintain liberty...has done more to retard the cause of liberty and civilization, and is doing more at present, than all other causes combined.[32]

Calhoun excoriated the Founders, and Jefferson above all, for introducing the idea of liberty for all.

> While it is powerful to pull down governments, it is still more powerful to prevent their construction on proper principles.... We now begin to experience the danger of admitting so great an

error to have a place in the declaration of our independence. For a long time it lay dormant; but in the process of time it began to germinate, and produce its poisonous fruits. It had strong hold on the mind of Mr. Jefferson, the author of that document, which caused him to take an utterly false view of the subordinate relation of the black to the white race in the South; and to hold, in consequence, that the former, though utterly unqualified to possess liberty, were as fully entitled to both liberty and equality as the latter; and that to deprive them of it was unjust and immoral.[33]

The ideal that all men are created equal, complained Calhoun, "was inserted in our Declaration of Independence without any necessity. It made no necessary part of our justification in separating from the parent country, and declaring ourselves independent."[34]

THE EFFORT TO THWART THE FOUNDING

The fact that these ideals were so dangerous to slavery and all forms of tyranny is the reason we see, in the early decades of the nineteenth century, the persistent effort to obstruct the expansion of liberty that blacks were enjoying, especially freedmen. If the argument that blacks were unqualified to possess liberty needed to be made, then there could be no distinction between slaves and freedmen. Because today's left singles out the Declaration and Constitution, and Jefferson, Madison, Washington, and all the other Founders, as the culprits, as enabling slavery, it is important to examine the record of what actually took place in the nation's first years.

The Founding had led to hope; it had set slavery, as Lincoln said, on the course of extinction (which is why men such as Calhoun found it so dangerous). Free blacks, especially, enjoyed more rights in the aftermath of the Revolution than they had earlier, or would later in the century that followed. Even in South

Carolina, one of the most proslavery states in the South, the situation improved for a time. Whereas in 1740, the colony had passed a "Negro Act," in which section two declared that "color is prima facie evidence, that the party bearing the color of the Negro, mulatto or mestizo, is a slave"—in other words, that a free black person was a contradiction in terms—the Revolution provided some relief.[35]

Writing about the period between the Revolutionary War and the start of the nineteenth century, Christopher Frank Lee explains that, in South Carolina,

> After the war the Assembly renewed some of the existing laws controlling slaves, but from 1783 to 1799 passed only one new law restricting slave behavior. That law prevented shopkeepers from dealing with slaves not having a ticket from their master. In contrast, the Assembly passed one surprising law. They not only freed, they enfranchised a slave woman along with her child because her husband had courageously served during the war as a spy for Governor Rutledge.[36]

Even after the slave revolt of 1791 in Haiti had left thousands of white French colonists dead, causing fear of slave revolts throughout the New World, Lee writes that in South Carolina

> a number of measures to control slaves were introduced but not passed. For the most part, it was the Senate which blocked this legislation.... Later they postponed or rejected bills to restrain emancipation and to compel ship captains to give bond not to carry off Negroes. Overall the postwar era was not a time of harsh legal repression for slaves despite the Haitian Revolution.[37]

Citing research done by the historian Robert Olwell, another historian at the University of South Carolina, David W. Dangerfield, writes that 53 percent of the manumissions that took place in South Carolina between 1737 and 1785 came in the last ten years "and were undoubtedly influenced by the 'importance of the Revolution.'" Even if evidence that many of the manumitted slaves were of lighter skin does suggest also a secondary motive—that the slaveowner was manumitting one of their own children or another relative—it was also true that "a shortlived wave of late colonial-era manumissions were inspired by Enlightenment ideology that influenced some slaveowners to offer freedom to their slaves in the spirit of American liberty."[38]

In his 1857 Chicago speech, Lincoln remarked that Taney had assumed that the lives of blacks were improving, but "This assumption is a mistake. In some trifling particulars, the condition of that race has been ameliorated; but, as a whole, in this country, the change between then and now is decidedly the other way; and their ultimate destiny has never appeared so hopeless as in the last three or four years."[39]

Lincoln recalled the important point that free blacks had the right to vote—which means that, by inference, many must have voted for the delegates sent to the Constitutional Convention, and to the ratification conventions held later in the new states, and therefore had very much been part of the original covenant. This is all the more the case as some of the states in 1787 and 1788 momentarily suspended the property qualifications, allowing all free male citizens twenty-one or above to vote.[40] But, as Lincoln noted, this right to vote had now been taken away from free blacks.

> In two of the five States—New Jersey and North Carolina—that then gave the free negro the right of voting, the right has since been taken away; and in a third—New York—it has been greatly abridged; while it has not been extended, so far as I know, to a single additional State, though the number of the States has more than doubled. In those days, as I understand, masters could,

at their own pleasure, emancipate their slaves; but since then, such legal restraints have been made upon emancipation, as to amount almost to prohibition. In those days, Legislatures held the unquestioned power to abolish slavery in their respective States; but now it is becoming quite fashionable for State Constitutions to withhold that power from the Legislatures. In those days, by common consent, the spread of the black man's bondage to new countries was prohibited; but now, Congress decides that it will not continue the prohibition, and the Supreme Court decides that it could not if it would. In those days, our Declaration of Independence was held sacred by all, and thought to include all; but now, to aid in making the bondage of the negro universal and eternal, it is assailed, and sneered at, and construed, and hawked at, and torn, till, if its framers could rise from their graves, they could not at all recognize it. All the powers of earth seem rapidly combining against him.[41]

All these turning points that so outraged Lincoln—taking away from free blacks the right to vote or even to learn how to read, the ability to extend slavery to the new territories and states, the restraints on emancipation—were then the result of the fear of liberty that the Declaration and the Constitution had instilled in the hearts of racists and slavers. If the Founding had enabled slavery, as BLM, the 1619 Project, and others insist, that wouldn't have been the case.

By extending the scourge of slavery to the new states and territories that were being added to the Union, the Missouri Compromise and the Kansas-Nebraska Act either kicked the can down the road or amounted to a regression from the Confederation Congress's passage of the Northwest Ordinance in 1787. This oft-ignored key Founding document ordered that "There shall be neither slavery nor involuntary servitude in the said territory" northwest of the Ohio River.[42] On the philosophical genesis of the Northwest Ordinance, we have no less an authority than Calhoun himself, who stated in his Oregon speech that it sprang from the same source as all the other threats to slavery that were so rankling him in 1848. To him, the proposition that "all men are born free and equal"—which he called "the most false and dangerous of all political errors"—was the origin of all the trouble. "To this error, this proposition to exclude slavery from the territory northwest of the Ohio may be traced, and to that the ordinance of '87, and through it the deep and dangerous agitation which now threatens to ingulf, and will certainly ingulf, if not speedily settled, our political institutions, and involve the country in countless woes."[43]

WHY IT MATTERS TODAY

Calhoun was correct that the ideals of the Revolution had inspired the Northwest Ordinance, Frederick Douglass, and the abolitionists whose tireless efforts were about to bring Calhoun's world crashing down. If your purpose in the twenty-first century is, however, to destroy America's institutions and its very view of itself, in order to introduce a new "narrative," and a new way to constitute America, then the Founding must be indicted as being intricately tied to slavery, not as the fountainhead of the arguments and principles that finally led America out of it, and then on to civil rights in the 1960s. So you set out to describe all of American history as a trail of tears, and insist that the country starts in 1619, when the monolith of slavery supposedly begins. This argument is not history, nor even a different interpretation of it, however. This pushes aside established facts and introduces a revisionism based not on fact but on a political purpose. As Peter Wood, the president of the National Association of Scholars, explains in his 2020 book, *1620*, "The larger aim of the 1619 Project is to change America's understanding of itself."[44] This provides the tinder for the conflagration that follows the spark of a death under police custody, provided that the fire is widely spread by activists.

Knowing the facts surrounding slavery and the racism it spawned for centuries helps us understand its barbarity, how it commenced, and how it ended. "The Southern system of plantation slavery did not spring into existence all at once fully formed. It evolved over time in different contexts, according to a host of variable conditions," writes Wood. "We know, for example, that men and women released from bondage acquired considerable property and married, often to white settlers."[45] Virginia did not start prohibiting such marriages until 1691.[46] Such prohibitions were to last two and a half centuries. The American Revolution, far from being waged to protect slavery, as the 1619 Project mendaciously declared, introduced a period of hope, which was extinguished for reasons discussed in this chapter. Grasping these facts, grappling with them—not casting them aside to replace them with an alternative "narrative," as if no truth existed, but just many different versions according to someone's point of view—is what will lead us to racial progress.

The writers of the 1619 Project, and, I would add, their BLM acolytes, do not seem to seek such progress. They "are advocates for a thesis, and it is a thesis that puts racial grievances at the center of America's story," adds Wood.[47]

AFTER THE WAR

By the time secessionist South Carolinian batteries fired on Fort Sumter outside Charleston on April 12, 1861, less than twenty years after Douglass had squared off with Covey on a Maryland field, the contradictions between America's ideals and slavery were too many to be contained. The harrowing Civil War that ensued took the lives of more than 600,000—360,222 of them white Northerners who fought on the anti-slavery side. The Thirteenth Amendment ending slavery, the Fourteenth giving all Americans "equal protection," and the Fifteenth prohibiting disenfranchising voters no matter their "race, color or previous condition of servitude"—the so-called Reconstruction Amendments passed during the five years after the war's end—further perfected the work of the initial ten.

After that came a ray of hope, but the opportunity was missed. After Reconstruction was abandoned in the 1870s, the era of *Plessy v. Ferguson* began. With the introduction of Jim Crow, blacks became a separate caste—exactly what Justice John Harlan tried to prevent when he stood as the single dissenter in the *Plessy* decision and wrote, "in view of the constitution, in the eye of the law, there is in this country no superior, dominant, ruling class of citizens. There is no caste here. Our constitution is color-blind, and neither knows nor tolerates classes among citizens. In respect of civil rights, all citizens are equal before the law"[48]

Southerners who shared Taney's and Calhoun's views on the black race persisted after the Emancipation Proclamation and the Civil War had freed the slaves, and soon enough they found loopholes to deny their compatriots the right to vote. After the failure of Reconstruction to heal racial divides, the country went through eighty years or so of the Jim Crow era introduced by the *Plessy v. Ferguson* Supreme Court decision that legalized "separate but equal." The 1954 *Brown v. Board of Education* decision desegregating public schools and the Civil Rights Act of 1964 brought that era to a screeching halt. Curiously, however, within a few years, we betrayed the promise of color-free law, just as the turning points of the nineteenth century betrayed the liberating spirit of '76, and many of the wokest Americans today are demanding a new version of separate but equal.[49] Justice Harlan's famous words in his *Plessy* dissent—seem to be a direct rebuke of the very foundations of today's identity politics.

The inhumanity of segregation and the grotesquery of lynch-ings (there were nearly 3,500 lynchings of blacks between 1882 and 1968, according to the Tuskegee Institute) produced among some black Americans, especially intellectuals, the same desire for social revolution, and the adoption of socialism, that we see among the BLM leaders today.[50] We will see in the next chapter how many of our enemies, foreign and domestic, attempted to use the period in between *Plessy* and the civil rights era to recruit black Americans to the socialist cause that Douglass fought so hard.

CHAPTER 2

THE SOVIETS' FAILED INFILTRATION

The communist who so vexed Frederick Douglass at the Rhode Island gathering in 1848 was fairly typical of American Marxists of that time. As Carl Guarneri writes, "many antebellum labor leaders were hostile or at least indifferent to the abolitionist appeal because they believed that it diverted attention from the serious problems facing northern workers with the onset of industrial capitalism."[1] Guarneri, a left-wing historian, attributes good intentions to this hostility, explaining that broadening the abolitionist platform to include what he and other socialists term "wage slavery"—capitalism—would attract Northern workers to the abolitionist cause. Socialists who spoke of wage slavery were, of course, relying on the authority of none other than Karl Marx himself, who railed against wages in the *Communist Manifesto*, also published in 1848, and argued in 1863 that, with paid labor, "Slavery has therefore been perpetuated on the earth, but under a sweeter name."[2] In other words, to make abolitionism successful, activists would have to drop abolitionism and just rail against men working for other men, whether for wages or for free.

I highlight this confusion not to make fun of Marxists then or now, but merely to show the contradictory lengths their pathological fixation with wages and private property can take them. It also casts in a clear light the anti-capitalist positions that BLM leaders and critical race theorists in general take today. The goal of the socialist speaker in 1848 wasn't so much to help blacks, but to convert all of America, North and South, to socialism. Freeing the slaves was to be a byproduct of this effort, but not its central interest. Over and over, down to the present day, we see this Marxist attempt to put the demands of world revolution and the destruction of capitalism ahead of the individual self-interests of black Americans, a push that naturally has always met resistance among black Americans. The chapters ahead will tell that story.

In the 1920s, Marcus Garvey, the founder of the largest mass-based African American movement before BLM, warned that smashing capitalism would rob blacks of their escalator to self-reliance and success. In the 1940s and 50s, the NAACP warned that the Soviet Union was infiltrating black communities in order to take over the United States. Today, we see courageous opposition from the likes of professors John McWhorter and Glenn Loury, as well as Shelby and Eli Steele, to the arguments made by the BLM leaders and "anti-racism" trainers that capitalism must be destroyed because it is itself "racist." What we see in Douglass's impatience with the socialist speaker in 1848 was just the tip of the spear. The interests of black Americans and those of Marxists part ways the moment the latter try to recruit the former to their cause of world revolution.

The pattern began early, almost right after the creation of the Soviet Union in 1917. From the Harlem Renaissance in the 1920s to the end of the Cold War in 1990, first the Soviets, and then their fellow travelers in the West, saw an opportunity to exploit the black struggle. This chapter will deal with the Soviet-led efforts, and the next with the campaign by domestic communists to revolutionize America in the 1960s. Fortunately for the sake of freedom, their efforts have tended to be so ham-fisted, so nakedly ideological, that communists have often hurt their own cause. With the Harlem Renaissance, for example, Moscow's insistence on economic dogma, pushing aside the cultural Marxism then nascent among Western Marxists from Frankfurt to Turin to New York's West Village (which has grown to full bloom today in America and Europe with identity politics), completely backfired.

HARLEM ROOTS IN THE 1920S

That the Harlem Renaissance occurred at all is a wondrous thing. The slave population had been liberated only sixty years earlier— not quite two generations—and here were blacks generating a flourishing of intellectual and artistic creativity. As Brown University economics professor Glenn Loury puts it:

> The slaves who were emancipated in 1863 were largely illiterate. They owned almost no land. They had virtually nothing. By the time you get to 1910, we see one of the historically most impressive transformations of literacy in a population that have been observed in the modern world. Go to south-eastern Europe and find some population of poor white people and you can't find anything comparable to that. We actually made ourselves—this is Booker T. Washington's language, but it's actually accurate— "fit for citizenship." The newly emancipated slaves were a very disadvantaged and underdeveloped population. By the time you get to 1910, you've got a wholly different profile of the African American population.[3]

By the mid-1920s, this explosion in literacy led to an outpouring of art and intellectualism in New York's Harlem, whose poets, writers, and activists started to interact with the denizens of a similar phenomenon at the other end of Manhattan, in Greenwich Village, this one led by white writers, journalists, and socialist activists such as John Reed, his wife Louise Bryant, and her sometime paramour, the playwright Eugene O'Neill. James Weldon Johnson, one of the elder statesmen of the Harlem Renaissance, remarked in his 1930 book *Black Harlem* that

> through his artistic efforts, the Negro is smashing [an] immemorial stereotype faster than he has ever done....He is impressing upon the national mind the conviction that he is an active and important force in American life;...that he is a contributor to the nation's common cultural store; in fine, he is helping to form American civilization.[4]

The fact that jazz, blues, ragtime, Louis Armstrong, Duke Ellington, the writings of Johnson, Langston Hughes, Claude McKay, and so on became major contributions to the American identity, right up there with the cowboy of Tex-Mex culture, the New England Puritan, the California gold miner, James Fenimore Cooper, Ernest Hemingway, Aaron Copland, and the Gershwin brothers, is a historical feat.

One obvious problem with these movements is that they were led by intellectuals—and sometimes a handful of them at that—who were distanced from the troubles of average individuals. Intellectuals become enamored of ideas, sometimes good and sometimes bad, and unlike the more practical professions, pay no price when the ideas turn out to be bad. In his piercing 1967 book on the history of black American ideas, *The Crisis of the Negro Intellectual*, Harold Cruse cites the groundbreaking sociologist and assimilation scholar Milton Gordon as observing that, when men and women come together because of a common interest in ideas, they inexorably detach themselves from the population whence they came. "While the Negro intellectual is not fully integrated into the intellectual class stratum, he is, in the main, socially detached from his own Negro ethnic world," writes Cruse.[5] He quotes Gordon as writing in his 1964 best seller, *Assimilation in American Life,* that there is evidence that the "outflow of intellectuals from the religio-ethnic groups in America, their subsequent estrangement from the life of these groups, and the resultant block in communication between the ethnic subsociety and the intellectual, [might] have dysfunctional consequences." Cruse then asks, "how do Negro intellectuals measure up to the complex problem of being spokesmen on behalf of their ethnic group, the Negro masses? . . . to what extent do their analyses of the Negro situation get to the bottom of things?"[6] This raises questions for Cruse as to what degree we should expect intellectuals and activists to have the proper answer on the course black Americans should follow in their quest for racial equality.

A related problem with any movement led by thinkers, poets, artists, journalists, and activists is that they can easily succumb to what Raymond Aron called the opium of the intellectual: Marxism. Being removed from the welfare of ordinary men and women, intellectuals are vulnerable to an abstract theory that purports to care for the people but in fact creates conditions that impede individual improvement and always ends in tyranny. The Harlem Renaissance emerged just as the Soviet Union was being formed and as it began trying to export communist revolution through proxy parties overseas. The communist historian Theodore Draper says, "Sometime in 1921, evidently in response to pressure from Moscow, American communists made the first serious attempt to attract Negro members."[7] Thus we see Harlem Renaissance figures as different as Langston Hughes, W. E. B. Du Bois, and Claude McKay gravitate toward Marxism, either the softer socialist version or outright Bolshevism, both on their own or as a response to Moscow's recruitment. The radical path that BLM's leaders undertook in this century had been trod much earlier.

EARLY MOSCOW PILGRIMAGES

Langston Hughes, a totemic figure in American letters in his own right, had a long history of association with the Soviet Union, though later in life he tried to distance himself from Moscow. Hughes was only fifteen when the October Revolution took place, and right away he fell for Soviet disinformation. In 1932, he was one of twenty-two black Americans to go to Moscow to help make a Soviet propaganda film about race and labor struggles in the American South. The artists had been recruited by Louise Thompson, the African American founder of the Harlem branch of the Friends of the Soviet Union. This front organization had been created in the 1927 meeting of the Communist International (the Comintern) in Moscow to help the Soviet leaders coordinate their efforts to introduce communism around the world. In his 1934 autobiography, *I Wonder as I Wander*, Hughes describes his time in Moscow in flowery terms, even waxing poetic about his experience in packed Soviet buses: "On a crowded bus, nine times out of ten, some Russian would say, '*Negrochanski tovarish*— Negro comrade—take my seat!' ... On the streets queuing up for newspapers, for cigarettes, or soft drinks, often folks in the line would say, 'Let the Negro comrade go forward.' If you demurred, they would insist, 'Please! Visitor to the front'."[8] Hughes wrote these paeans to Soviet life for people back at home, including in the NAACP's journal, *The Crisis*.

The film Hughes and the other black artists traveled to Moscow to make, *Black and White*, was never produced, but Hughes stayed behind and traveled to Soviet Central Asia, majority Muslim regions where religious practices were harshly repressed in Soviet times. Hughes, however, sees only liberation from what he surmised had been discrimination in tsarist times. He swallows wholesale what a young Soviet apparatchik named Kurbanov tells him: "He was a mine of information about the liberation of Central Asia and the vast changes that have come there after the revolution," Hughes gushes, describing Uzbekistan as

> Truly a Land of Before and After—as we listen to him talk. Before the Revolution, emirs and khans, mullahs and beys. After the Revolution, the workers in power. Before, one half of one percent of the people literate. Now 50 percent read and write. Before, education solely for the rich, mostly in religious schools. Now, free schools everywhere. Before, the land was robbed of its raw materials for the factories of the Russian capitalists. Now, there are factories in Asia itself.

On and on, Hughes writes embarrassingly in *A Negro Looks at Soviet Central Asia*; this work was published in Moscow by the Cooperative Publishing Society of Foreign Workers in 1934, which means that this pro-Soviet paean was read by many Americans of all colors in the midst of Stalin's terror.[9]

Hughes was not the first nor the only influential denizen of the Harlem Renaissance to do heavy lifting for the Soviets. Claude McKay, whose poems are sometimes credited with launching the movement, took himself to Moscow in 1922 to attend the Fourth Congress of the Communist International, a trip he called "A Magical Pilgrimage." He was not officially a member of the Communist Party USA, but wrote in his 1937 memoir, *A Long Way from Home*, that he had "the dominant urge to go, and that discovered the way. Millions of ordinary human beings and thousands of writers were stirred by the Russian thunder rolling around the world."[10] McKay also wrote for the NAACP's journal *Crisis* and understood clearly what his role was. "The label of propaganda will be affixed to what I say here. I shall not mind; propaganda has now come into its respectable rights," McKay wrote. "There was nothing unpleasant about being swept into the surge of revolutionary Russia.... No one but a soulless body can live there without being stirred.... Russia is prepared and waiting to receive couriers and heralds of good will and interracial understanding from the Negro race."[11] As University of Louisville African Studies professor Joy Gleason Carew puts it, "it is through McKay's eyes that this new 'Soviet' Russia came into view for Blacks in the US."[12] *Pravda* translated McKay's speech to the Comintern, censoring the parts where McKay spoke about racism inside the Communist Party USA. He stayed in the Soviet Union for six months, leaving in 1923.

The initial invitation to McKay had come from none other than John Reed, the American fellow traveler and member of the Village salon movement in the 1920s—who was made popular in America again in the 1980s when Warren Beatty played him in the movie *Reds*. Vladimir Lenin had asked Reed to speak at the first Comintern Congress in 1920, but Reed, who was white, thought it would have a bigger impact if a black man addressed the Congress. Reed then invited McKay to do it, but McKay demurred, not sure he was up to the task of becoming a spokesman for all U.S. blacks. McKay then went to London, where he teamed up with the British socialist Sylvia Pankhurst and cooperated with her in her socialist journal. Having summoned his confidence, he accepted an invitation to the 1922 meeting of the Comintern. By then, however, Reed had died, and McKay had to raise his own funds.

To Carew, the pioneer roles played by McKay, Hughes, and later the singer Paul Robeson in softening the ground for the coming attempt by the Soviets to subvert American democracy cannot be overestimated.

Not only would they help mold the Russian people's view of the plight of Blacks and build internal solidarity, but also, they would be instrumental in shaping the impression of the Soviet Experiment for Blacks the world over. From McKay's 1922 visit, through Hughes' 1932 sojourn, and Robeson's last visits in the late 1950s, both the Soviets and these Black luminaries took active roles in linking the liberation desires of oppressed Blacks to the political objectives of the Soviets.[13]

McKay's 1922 address added wind to the sails of the Comintern's then burgeoning push to infiltrate black society in order to revolutionize America, an effort that came under the banner label, the "Negro Question." In 1928, the Comintern put in place a plan to advocate for black self-determination in the "Black Belt"—the U.S. South. Within two years that had turned into a fully fledged plan to help blacks set up "a separate Negro state" there, in order for the Soviets to gain a foothold from which, with the aid of northern proletarians, they would launch a revolution in all of the United States.

The Soviet Union's direct involvement in the effort to break the United States in two, as it later did with Korea and Germany, followed failed attempts by the Communist Party USA to grab hold of a mass movement. From the 1920s on, communist infiltration would follow and encounter resistance along two paths created by a split dating back to the mid-1800s. These two orientations can be summed up as the integrationist, or assimilationist, one, and the separatist, pan-Africanist one. The split "has its origins in the historical arguments between personalities such as Frederick Douglass and Martin R. Delany," cofounders of the abolitionist magazine *The North Star,* according to Cruse.[14] We see it play out again later in the mutual hostility between Martin Luther King and Malcolm X. Moscow would promote either the integrationist approach or the separatist, as events suited its purposes, since both assimilationists and separatists could be equally vulnerable to Marxist influence and manipulation. McKay, born in Jamaica, was a pan-Africanist. Du Bois, a believer in racial integration, joined the Communist Party USA in 1961, two years before the end of a long life. By the same token, Marcus Garvey, like McKay a pan-Africanist and anti-imperialist (and also born in Jamaica), was staunchly anti-communist. Indeed, it was Garvey's fight to stop the Communist Party USA from taking over the movement he had built that propelled Moscow to take a more direct hand in creating a separate homeland for blacks on U.S. soil.

GARVEYISM

Marcus Garvey may not have as many schools, avenues, and community centers named after him as Martin Luther King, Jr., Booker T. Washington, Malcom X, W. E. B. Du Bois, or Justice Thurgood Marshall, but his influence rivals that of these better-known black leaders. His Universal Negro Improvement Association (UNIA), which he founded in Jamaica in 1914, two years before emigrating to the United States, reached two million members in 1919, after he established several chapters in northern American cities. It was dedicated "to racial pride, economic self-sufficiency, and the formation of an independent Black nation in Africa."[15] Jacksonville State University professor Shawn Carter puts UNIA's approach in the proper light when he says that its "business entrepreneurial approach to economic self-sufficiency mirrored Booker T. Washington's endeavors."[16] UNIA established several commercial ventures throughout the United States. In the words of Garvey himself, the association sought to "unite, into one solid body, the four hundred million Negroes in the world."

> To link up the fifty million Negroes in the United States of America, with the twenty million Negroes of the West Indies, the forty

million Negroes of South and Central America, with the two hundred and eighty million Negroes of Africa, for the purpose of bettering our industrial, commercial, educational, social, and political conditions.[17]

Among those who claimed Garvey as an important mentor were Malcolm X; Jomo Kenyatta, the founder of Kenya; South Africa's Nelson Mandela; Congo's communist firebrand Patrice Lumumba; and the South African journalist Steve Biko. Martin Luther King, Jr., called Garvey "the first man on a mass scale and level to give millions of Negroes a sense of dignity and destiny."[18] That his influence in the twenty-first century continues unabated can be gleaned from the fact that the writers of the hit television series *The Wire* threw in a reference to Garvey in season four, where Maryland state delegate Odell Watkins berates Baltimore Mayor Clarence Royce for selling out and trying to save his electoral campaign with pan-Africanism: "Just look at you," Watkins yells at the mayor in episode five, which aired in 2006. "You've forgotten your agenda. You've forgotten your base! You think a shave and some Marcus Garvey posters are gonna get you over? Do you think that's gonna make up for jumping in bed with every damn developer?"[19] This was by no means the only mention of Garvey in popular entertainment in this century, showing at least that he's being taught in the universities attended by today's scriptwriters. He is also popular with rappers and hip-hop artists.

Garvey's separatism, anti-colonialism, and plans to create a black homeland in Africa for all blacks led him into many unsavory positions and situations, such as meeting with a Grand Wizard of the Ku Klux Klan in 1922, because they both shared the goal of racial separation, and initial praise for Mussolini and Hitler, because he admired their nationalism. He appeared in public in military regalia and called himself "the Provisional

King of Africa." All of this put him in the sights of a young J. Edgar Hoover, who was then working for the precursor of the FBI. In 1919, Hoover wrote that "unfortunately, however, [Garvey] has not yet violated any federal law whereby he could be proceeded against on the grounds of being an undesirable alien, from the point of view of deportation."[20] By 1924, the U.S. government was able to prosecute Garvey for fraud and put in him prison. President Calvin Coolidge commuted his sentence in 1927 but deported Garvey back to his birth island as an undesirable alien.

On the question of which was a better system, capitalism or communism, however, Garvey was clear-eyed and echoed Douglass's frustration with socialists back in the 1840s. More importantly, Garvey's opposition to Soviet machinations frustrated communist efforts to use black Americans as pawns.

To Garvey, "the only convenient friend the Negro worker or laborer has in America at the present time is the white capitalist. The capitalist, being selfish, is seeking only the largest profit out of labor—is willing and glad to use Negro labor wherever possible on a scale 'reasonably' below the standard white union wage."[21] Thus only capitalism was flexible enough to help black workers get on the ladder of success; it was the system that rewarded, and therefore encouraged, hard work. Communism was the opposite, thought Garvey. Citing Garvey, Carter writes, "He believed that the Communist Party wanted to use the African-American to 'smash and overthrow' the capitalistic white majority, to 'put their majority group or race still in power, not only as communists but as white men.'"[22] To Garvey, communism "was never intended for the economic or political emancipation of African Americans," added Carter. Garvey himself wrote that communism "is a dangerous theory of economic and political reformation because it seeks to put government in the hands of an ignorant white mass who have not been able to destroy their natural prejudices toward Negroes."[23]

One must observe in passing that the one example of a biracial country where communism has been installed, Cuba, wholly substantiates Garvey's warnings. In more than sixty-two years of rule by the Communist Party, Cuba has been led strictly by white men descended from Spaniards, even though the island's population by now must be well over 50 percent black or mixed race (official Cuban statistics say the population of Cuba is over 70 percent white, but that, like all other official Cuban data, does not pass the laugh test). Despite this, the Castro brothers have never ceased to win accolades from radical black leaders. Malcolm X praised Fidel Castro as "the only white person I ever liked."[24] The Black Lives Matter Global Network, the most important organization in the BLM system, had this to say after Castro's death in 2016: "As Fidel ascends to the realm of ancestors, we summon his guidance, strength and power, as we recommit ourselves to the struggle for universal freedom. Fidel Vive."[25]

Despite Garvey's outspoken hostility, the Communist Party USA tried again and again to infiltrate the ranks of the UNIA in order to capture the movement. The push came to a head at the UNIA's 1921 convention. Garvey, to extend an olive branch to communists, especially the African Blood Brotherhood (ABB), invited its founder, the journalist Cyril Briggs, and other ABB members. The ABB was a black liberation organization established in 1919 and run mostly by blacks of West Indian origin that quickly became an arm of the Communist Party USA, itself a branch of the party in Moscow, which was also established in 1919. (The fact that the American party was a mere branch of the Soviet Union was determined early on by Moscow. The statutes adopted by the Second Congress of the Comintern in 1920 stated that "The Communist International must, in fact and in deed, be a single communist party of the entire world. The parties working in the various countries are but its separate sections."[26]) Garvey even let an ally of Briggs, the white communist Rose Pastor Stokes, speak at the convention, which was held at Madison Square Garden and not in Harlem where the UNIA was headquartered, in a sign of how large the movement had grown. "In her speech Stokes pleaded with Garvey and the U.N.I.A. to ally with the Soviets as a means to free Africa from enslavement," wrote Harvard's Ryan Miniot in his 2016 dissertation. "Garvey downplayed the significance of Stokes' speech by reminding the audience that the mere presence of Stokes as a speaker did not indicate that the U.N.I.A. had embraced Bolshevism, asserting instead that she was only one of many invited speakers presenting a wide array of views."[27]

Things got worse, however, as the convention wore on, and Briggs and other ABB members distributed pamphlets criticizing the turn the UNIA was taking. Garvey saw no choice but to expel them from the convention. After this, it was open war between the ABB and Garvey and his UNIA. The Communist Party USA, however, did not desist and kept infiltrating UNIA chapters in the early 1920s, even sending delegates to future conventions. In the end, this effort failed; the Communist Party was not able to take over the mass movement but remained a fringe organization among blacks (at its height, the ABB reached a membership of 3,000, or 0.15 percent of the UNIA's membership), important only because of its sway with elites. Draper writes:

> Garveyism tempted and eluded the communists. They could not find a way to make use of the discontent that Garveyism fed on. By 1925, when the American party went through the Bolshevization process, its Negro work clearly stood in need of general overhauling. The African Blood Brotherhood could not make headway against the Garvey movement, which blocked the Communists off from access to the most rebellious Negro masses.[28]

At that point Moscow decided to take a more direct hand. In 1925, "instructions came from Moscow to replace the African Blood Brotherhood with an American Negro Labor Congress," writes Draper, who, as a former correspondent for the *Daily Worker* and TASS, often had a front seat at these events.[29] The ANLC ended up being a failure, too. For the five years it lasted, the ANLC remained isolated from working-class blacks—exactly the people on whose behalf communists purported to speak. Even after the UNIA collapsed after Garvey's arrest and deportation, the great mass of American blacks refused to gravitate toward communism.

The failure stung. One of the founders of the ANLC, Lovett Fort-Whiteman—the first African American to join the party and a delegate to the Comintern—was removed from leadership in 1927 and later accused of "counter-revolutionary activities" by Joseph Stalin, the new Soviet leader. Once dubbed by *Time* as "the reddest of the blacks," Fort-Whiteman was shipped to a Siberian gulag, where he died in 1939. "The ANLC could not pick up the pieces of the Garvey movement. This failure made inevitable another reconsideration of the Negro Question in Moscow," was Draper's summation.[30] Sure enough, sometime in 1925, Stalin told Otto Hall, a black American communist studying in Moscow, in words that would resonate for decades: "The whole approach by the American party to the Negro Question is wrong. You are a national minority with some of the characteristics of a nation." Stalin asked Hall and others to write him a memo on the Negro Question according to those lights. The separate-state idea was sown.

In *Message to the People*, Garvey provided his own summation when he wrote, "the scheme coming from the white communists is to make the Negroes communists. It is a vile and wicked scheme."[31]

A SEPARATE NEGRO STATE

Stalin wasn't the first to envision a separate black state. Briggs, who, like Garvey, was also of West Indian origin (having been born in Nevis), had advocated for a separate homeland for blacks even before the October Revolution. Draper writes that, in a two-part editorial that appeared in the *Amsterdam News* in September 1917, titled "Security of Life for Poles and Serbs—Why Not For Colored Americans?," Briggs echoes Garvey's call for a black homeland, only departing from the idea that it should be on African soil. The editorial read,

> As one-tenth of the population, backed with many generations of unrequited toil and half a century of contribution, as free men, to American prosperity, we can with reason and justice demand our portion for purposes of self-government and the pursuit of happiness, one-tenth of the territory of [the] continental United States.[32]

The states Briggs envisioned as forming this new homeland were not in the South, but in the then sparsely populated West, parts of Nevada, California, Washington, Oregon, or Idaho. In 1921, another editorial again called for "salvation for all Negroes through the establishment of a strong, independent Negro state," this time "in Africa and elsewhere."[33] Stalin's words to Hall in 1925, however, set the course.

At its Sixth Congress in 1928, the Comintern took the first step by calling for "self-determination in the Black Belt," by which it meant Southern states.[34] This idea called for a "national revolutionary movement among the Negroes" in the South.[35] An editorial in the *Daily Worker* in 1929 made the party's position clear: "The Party must come out openly and unreservedly for the right of Negroes to national self-determination in the southern states, where the Negroes form a majority of the population."[36] An FBI report, later declassified, explained that "by 'self-determination' the party maintained that the Negroes, as a separate race in the Southern States constituted a majority of the population and had the right, if they so desired, to secede from the United States and form their own government and nation."[37] But even this wasn't sufficient. Soon enough, however, the Soviet plan became much more ambitious and included an entire separate country.

In 1930, a new resolution called for demonstrations, tax boycotts and even an uprising that would lead to a separation of the Southern states if the United States remained capitalist. Moscow also continued during this time to try to attract black support by, for example, offering free legal help to the Scottsboro Boys. These were nine young African American teenagers, one as young as thirteen, who were accused of rape by two white women after an altercation with white men on a train in 1931. They had been held in prison in Scottsboro, Alabama. A court found them guilty, sentencing eight of them to death. The International Labor Defense, the Communist Party's legal arm, took up their defense in a clear attempt to make inroads among black Americans (one of their recruits was the mother of Angela Davis, the Herbert Marcuse disciple who has had so much influence on the BLM movement, as we will see later). "The Scottsboro Boys became a full-fledged, intense communist campaign," writes Paul Kengor in *The Communist*, but one that "compounded an already tragic situation, undermining public support for a legitimate civil rights cause."[38] The Soviet Union also tried with all its might to infiltrate black organizations and to recruit individual blacks as spies and saboteurs.

The Soviet Union failed with this strategy, just as it had failed to woo the masses that responded to Garvey. In 1958, Soviet leaders threw in the towel as far as a separate black homeland was concerned, announcing that American blacks no longer constituted a nation and therefore had no need to attain self-determination. The Communist Party "decided that the American Negro people were no longer a 'stable community'; that the Negro national question was no longer 'essentially a peasant question'; that the

Negroes did not possess any distinctively 'common psychological makeup' [and] that the American Negro people did not constitute a nation," wrote Draper.[39]

One organization that at times covered itself in glory in the endeavor to fight back Soviet interventionism was the National Association for the Advancement of Color People (NAACP). An earlier FBI report that surveyed the period from 1919 to 1953 quoted the NAACP as noting:

> Communist justification for this policy of a separate Negro republic ... is inapplicable to the American Negro. On the contrary, Negroes are and have been for many centuries thoroughly American in every sense of this word, and the history of the Negro in America is warp and woof of the history of the United States. Though millions of American Negroes are subjected to every conceivable variety of economic, political, and social discrimination, these injustices of themselves have not and cannot make them a separate nation. The fundamental social compulsion of the Negro in America is toward integration and assimilation into all aspects of American life on the basis of complete equality. The history of the Negro in the United States proves this.... To preach separation for the Negro is really to become an advocate of a more vicious form of segregation.[40]

The NAACP then added, "for the Negro this is the most dangerous aspect of the Communist drive to corral Negroes and to infiltrate their organizations. If Communists gained influence among Negroes they would not hesitate for a moment to foment racial strife and dissension, and all in the interests of the Soviet Union." It will be one of the themes of this book that the NAACP was clairvoyant and that this is exactly what we're seeing today with the Marxist BLM organizations, all in the cause of world revolution, though not on behalf of the Soviet state, of course.

In its 1956 report, the FBI concluded:

The Communist Party, USA, despite its concentrated efforts, has failed to attract even a significant minority of the Negroes in the United States....It strives to promote its aims through Negro communist front organizations and by infiltrating and controlling legitimate Negro groups....At the present time, it can be stated that along with the decline in the national membership of the Communist Party, USA, the Party has experienced an increasingly greater decline, percentage wise, in its Negro membership.[41]

The words of the NAACP and of the FBI report must be remembered today and taught in our schools. Black Americans are warp and woof of the history of this country. This has been the story all along, from Douglass in the 1840s, through the thousands of Americans who belonged to Garvey's UNIA. Indeed, the Soviets were far more successful in infiltrating and influencing white liberals and their organizations, such as the various peace groups working toward a nuclear freeze or for unilateral disarmament, from the 1950s until the Soviet Union's collapse in 1991. And, of course, the Soviet Union was able to penetrate the administration of Franklin Delano Roosevelt and subsequent administrations to a much greater extent than it ever penetrated black America. "It's evident from now available records that Communist penetration of our government was—over a span of decades—massive. Hundreds of Soviet agents, Communist Party members and fellow travelers were ensconced in official payrolls, beginning in the New Deal Era," wrote M. Stanton Evans and Herbert Romerstein in 2012. "In sum, as shown by a now substantial mass of data, a powerful and devious enemy had by the middle 1940s succeeded in planting myriad secret agents and sympathizers in offices of the U.S. government (and other posts of influence) where they were able to serve the cause of

Moscow."[42] Not with blacks. Though black intellectuals may have fallen for the siren song of communism, and there is evidence that the Soviets may have placed an agent close to Martin Luther King, Jr., as we will see in a future chapter, rank and file black Americans saw through Moscow's actions and said, no thanks.

Then, after the 1950s, the effort to use the plight of black Americans to subvert the United States came from quite a different source: our own home-grown Marxists.

CHAPTER 3

THEN THE 1960s HAPPENED

Marcus Garvey, for all his many quirks and loony ambitions, was clairvoyant in his early stand against Soviet entreaties. He spoke for millions of black Americans who understood that an economic system based on the right to own private property was the key to black success. As we have seen, even after the break-up of the UNIA, his millions of followers refused to follow Moscow's siren song, even when delivered by black front organizations. Indeed, black Americans have a solid record of rejecting both communism and political violence. Whether they looked toward a black homeland in Africa, as many of Garvey's followers did, or sought assimilation into the American mainstream, on a basis of equality that the NAACP called for in a dignified way in the 1950s, they wanted full freedom. The assimilationists pursued peacefully the square deal that every immigrant group had received for centuries. Their leaders—if not all black intellectuals—reflected these aspirations. Something happened, however, as the "Happy Days" Era of Eisenhower gave way to the times of Vietnam, the Kennedy assassination, the civil rights struggle, hippies, drugs, and the sexual revolution—in other words, the

1960s happened. Martin Luther King, Jr., and the NAACP continued to seek peace, but some black leaders hardened. King harked back to the Founders, but he was gunned down, and violence escalated afterward. Suddenly, the Black Panthers, the Black Liberation Army, and other similar radical groups emerged as a force, turned to violence, and embraced communism. To be sure, Garvey's UNIA and the African Blood Brotherhood had always entertained fringe paramilitary aspirations, but what happened in the 1960s was on a different order of magnitude. Men and women such as Stokely Carmichael, Huey Newton, Bobby Seale, Eldridge Cleaver, Angela Davis, and JoAnne Chesimard embraced both Marx's ideas *and* Lenin's means, with an additional dose of Red Guard Maoism. By the time we got to 1972, we had 1,900 domestic bombings in a single year.[1]

This time, blacks were not alone. Other racial and ethnic groups emerged, sometimes invented by government itself at the instigation of leftist activists, whose leaders posited a false analogy to black suffering and a right to claim compensatory justice through racial privileges.[2] So we see the rise in the 1960s and 70s of the Fuerzas Armadas de Liberación Nacional Puertorriqueña (the Puerto Rican terrorist group known by its Spanish-language acronym, FALN), and radical Chinese American groups such as I Wor Kuen and the Red Guards. In 1964, in *One-Dimensional Man*, the Frankfurt School radical intellectual Herbert Marcuse grasps the revolutionary potential of this "substratum of the outcasts and outsiders, the exploited and persecuted of other races and other colors," as long as they were led by a Marxist intellectual vanguard.[3]

Even whites got in on the act, as rich white university students drew inspiration from Fidel Castro and Che Guevara, university men like them, one a lawyer and the other a medical doctor, and thought they, too, could be the white elites to lead a communist revolution that used black resentment to overthrow the establishment, as Castro and Guevara had successfully done in Cuba in 1959. These spoiled kids who had spent placid childhoods in Eisenhower's suburban America thirsted for a thrilling cause and saw an opportunity in the Vietnam War and the struggle for civil rights.

Inside the cesspool of these hardened 1960s radicals the leaders of Black Lives Matter have found their inspiration, their mentors and, among those still alive, their trainers and funders, as we will see in future chapters. To this day, Alicia Garza showers praise on Angela Davis, who also happened to write the preface to Patrisse Cullors's book *When They Call You a Terrorist*—which itself starts out with a poem by Chesimard. To this day, neighborhood organizing outfits founded by operatives of the Maoist group I Wor Kuen in San Francisco, Boston, and other cities fund or provide foot soldiers for the protests of BLM. For this reason, we turn to the 1960s, to these groups and these activists to gain a better understanding of where the BLM leaders may want to take their movement and our country. The former Weathermen involved in either teaching or funding the BLM leaders all now agree that their violence back in the twentieth century was a "terrible mistake."[4] It is tempting to dismiss such disavowals of violence as "too little, too late," or even as too self-serving to take seriously. But their eleventh-hour understanding that bombings and shootings were counterproductive, and that there are better ways to ignite a revolution, should also fill us with an apprehensive desire to dig deeper.

WHITE GUILT

The 1950s may have seemed stifling to some, but to many they were happy days. In 1957, an astonishing 96 percent of Americans told Gallup that they were very or fairly happy.[5] Then innocence quickly faded. What happened?

Intellectuals such as Shelby Steele and Joshua Mitchell have explored what the loss of the moral high ground represented to the white, Protestant, Eastern establishment in the 1960s (and in the 1960s, the establishment was all those things), and the related toll it took on all American institutions and traditions. The Vietnam War, in the eyes of many, became a bad enough indictment of the inner circle of men who designed our involvement in Indochina: a bright, intellectual set out of Massachusetts that committed the sin of hubris by allowing itself to be called "the best and the brightest" and their surroundings as "Camelot." But the civil rights movement revealed a bigger blemish; it required an outright admission of guilt, one that impeached history. From that moment, the establishment has been on the defensive, seeing institutions, traditions, and mores crater. Fixing slavery had cost more than 600,000 lives. Fixing the problem of segregation meant accepting that white America had looked the other way while segregation, disenfranchisement, and lynchings took place. And that meant owning up to a sin.

As Steele told NPR in a 2006 interview, one of the "unintended consequences of the civil rights victories in the mid-60's was what I call white guilt. By that, specifically, what I mean is that when America had to acknowledge the wrongs of the past—that for four centuries it had, in fact, oppressed black Americans, anytime you acknowledge a wrong, one of the prices you pay for that is a loss of moral authority."[6] Steele added, in a 2019 op-ed for the *Wall Street Journal*, that from the 1960s flowed a conviction that "America's magnificent founding principles were not enough to ensure a free and morally legitimate society."[7] He goes on in his 2015 book *Shame: How America's Past Sins Have Polarized Our Country*: "In the 1960s, America underwent what can only be described as an archetypal 'fall'—a descent from innocence into an excruciating and inescapable self-knowledge."[8] The *Vanity Fair* writer Bryan Burrough puts it this way: "Then, as if overnight, things changed. More than anything else, it was the pictures young Americans began seeing on those televisions in 1960—of stoic Southern blacks dragged away from all-white lunch counters, of black protesters being beaten bloody by red-faced Southern deputies."[9]

The loss of moral authority could have been temporary, and that authority could have been regained by the inception, finally, of color-blind governance; Americans of all colors could have left behind the segregationist past and shared moral authority not as a function of their race but as a function of their deeds and character. Black Americans, now free of legal discrimination, could begin the work of joining mainstream society. In fact, some historians of this period have remarked that, in the South, where blacks did perceive some progress, there was some reconciliation. The riots, looting, and destruction that continued after the Civil Rights Act was signed into law took place almost entirely in the North and West.

Many things thwarted resolution nationwide, however. The racist attitudes of many whites, especially (but not only) in the South, were not snuffed out overnight on June 2, 1964, when Lyndon B. Johnson signed the Civil Rights Act into law. The fact that the abject treatment of blacks by far too many whites continued must understandably have stung many blacks. But the promise was never that change would come overnight in people's hearts; the promise had been that color consciousness would be taken out of public policy decision-making.

That had been the capstone of years, if not decades, of struggle. The core principle of the civil rights era was that discriminating on the basis of race was evil. But this was almost instantly reversed, and the promise of color-blind governance was extinguished just as instantly, when activists who wanted to transform the country in other ways seized the opportunity and began to manipulate the acknowledgment of past wrongs.

Several steps were taken while crossing this Rubicon in the late 1960s, but a significant stride that gave this demand expression came in sociologist Charles V. Hamilton's 1968 essay for the *New York Times*, "An Advocate of Black Power Defines It." Hamilton wrote:

> It must be clear by now that any society which has been color-conscious all its life to the detriment of a particular group cannot simply become color-blind and expect that group to compete on equal terms. Black Power clearly recognizes the need to perpetuate color consciousness, but in a positive way—to improve a group, not to subject it.[10]

This became writ. Soon, the white elite, because of guilt or fear of societal breakdown, or a mixture of both, accepted Hamilton's rejection of color-blind policy making. McGeorge Bundy, the head of the Ford Foundation, wrote in *The Atlantic* in 1977 that "To get past racism, we must here take account of race. There is no other present way." The essay was so impactful that this line was repeated nearly verbatim by Justice Harry Blackmun in his concurring opinion in the landmark 1978 *Regents of the University of California v. Bakke* case, which first authorized the racial preferences of affirmative action. "In order to get beyond racism, we must first take account of race," wrote Blackmun.[11]

Sixties activists did something else audacious and succeeded again because of the manipulation of white guilt: they expanded the groups to which the law would now show favor, the new minorities. They did this by drawing a false analogy between blacks and all the other categories. The activists pushing this new view pretended that the members of the newly invented categories, such as Hispanics or Asian Americans, or all thirty-two genders that were to come decades later in New York, had suffered as much as blacks in the South. People who wanted to draw the analogy to white women spoke of "Jane Crow."

It was all false, but it worked. The white establishment bought it either because they panicked when they saw the riots, or out of white guilt. Either way, they gave in to the activists' demands. The activists who promoted the identity categories and the feelings of victimization then purposely alienated people in these groups from America, whose history, institutions, traditions, and Founders were to be held in contempt.

The 1960s thus opened wounds that festered, and the infection spread to the whole national body. The patient is in intensive care half a century later, as the white guilt born in the 1960s has metastasized in the 2020s into a self-flagellating "allyship" that has whites ritualistically denouncing their country, its history, and its institutions, which they blame for a supposedly continued racism that lives no longer in the statutes but now in the unacknowledged subconscious of the nation.

To Mitchell, the guilt came forth on both sides of the Atlantic, as citizens of the 1960s were "haunted by the historical wounds their nations have authored—in America, the wound of slavery; and in Europe, the wounds of colonialism."[12] In an email to the author, Mitchell expands:

Guilt is no small part of the answer. Christianity no longer brought atonement, just happy talk. So, the left offered a deal: renounce your nations, your churches, and your heternormative [*sic*] families, and we will set you free of your guilt. That's where we are today. In the early years of the civil rights movements, black students wanted to have the right to read Shakespeare in college along with white students. Today, identity politics wants to erase Shakespeare.

The admission of guilt extracted from the American body

in the 1960s not only helped pave the way for the betrayal of the civil rights movement's color-blind premises, but also gave justification for violence in the United States and in Europe and her colonies. Many of our 1960s radicals fed off the anti-colonial movement occurring at the time, taking inspiration from the work of many writers and revolutionaries, but especially that of the Martinican intellectual Frantz Fanon. His slogan "by any means necessary" would become a meme repeated again and again by men such Malcolm X, Stokely Carmichael, and Noel Ignatiev. The individuals and movements that were formed toward this end have had a direct impact on Black Lives Matter.

Again, all of this was the inverse of the truth. The American individuals and institutions that admitted to past sins did so because they aspired to live by the nation's loftiest founding values, demonstrating the vacuity of the charges that all of America is rotten. The promise of "all men are created equal" sustained men from Jefferson to Lincoln to King. But if we need to understand why we have BLM in the early twenty-first century, the 1960s and the manipulation of guilt is the right place to start looking.

MALCOLM, STOKELY, HUEY, ANGELA, AND ASSATA

If we look for an early departure from the peaceful demands to be accepted into the American mainstream preached by Martin Luther King, Jr., we must start with Malcolm Little, who later changed his name to Malcolm X. His father, Earl, was a Baptist minister, and he and his Grenadian-born wife, Louise, were proud and long-standing members of Garvey's UNIA; Earl was at one time the president of the UNIA's Omaha, Nebraska, division, and Louise was its secretary. As often happens with activism, the children were involved. In his autobiography, Malcolm X recalled of his father that "the image of him that made me proudest was his crusading and militant campaigning with the words of Marcus

Garvey. . . . It was only me that he sometimes took with him to the Garvey U.N.I.A. meetings which he held quietly in different people's homes."[13] Malcolm and many historians conclude that Earl was murdered by white supremacists because of his work with the UNIA, and that they threw his body over tram tracks to make it look like suicide. Whatever the truth—and the chances are very good that this is what happened, given the harrowing degree of discrimination the Little family received wherever they lived—the police classified it as a suicide, and Louise never collected insurance payments. She was declared mentally unstable and institutionalized in a few years, and Malcolm and most of his ten siblings or half-siblings were distributed to foster homes. Eventually, Malcolm Little fell into a life of petty criminality and ended up in prison. There he found the Nation of Islam, or this politico/religious movement found him. Thus was Malcolm X born.

Malcolm X was more Muslim—a preacher for the Nation of Islam—than Marxist, but he was both. He foreshadows what we hear today from writers such as Robin DiAngelo and Ibram X. Kendi as he excoriates capitalism. He once told a rally in Harlem, for example, "You can't have capitalism without racism." At another time, he said, "You can't operate a capitalistic system unless you are vulturistic. . . . You show me a capitalist, I'll show you a bloodsucker."[14] Above all, however, he was a separatist, an enemy of everything represented by Martin Luther King, Jr., whom Malcolm dismissed as a "20th century or modern Uncle Tom."[15] Malcolm in fact scorned King's entire assimilationist approach, an approach we will see repeated. "Whoever heard of a revolution where they lock arms . . . singing 'We Shall Overcome'? You don't do that in a revolution. You don't do any singing, you're too busy swinging," he said.[16] Malcolm X even dismissed the valiant Jackie Robinson as an Uncle Tom, because by breaking the color line in baseball he joined the system, rather than breaking it.

We can say, then, that Malcolm inherited Garvey's African separatism but none of his healthy suspicion of communism or understanding of capitalism's value to a group of people who want to rise. Malcolm X did somewhat redeem himself after a 1964 pilgrimage to Mecca, pulling back after his return from his condemnation of the entire white race. But it was too late. His earlier outbursts, and above all his high profile in the media, had alienated him from the Nation of Islam leadership. Elijah Muhammad, the group's top leader, and Louis Farrakhan, one of Muhammad's mentees and the Nation's leader today, started to spread the word that Malcolm X should be assassinated, and, unsurprisingly, he was gunned down on February 21, 1965, by men associated with the Nation of Islam. Two months before Malcom X's death, Farrakhan had called him a "traitor" and written that "such a man is worthy of death." Decades later, Farrakhan told *60 Minutes* that "As I may have been complicit in words that I spoke, I acknowledge that and regret that any word that I have said caused the loss of life of a human being."[17]

Perhaps because of their association with Louis Farrakhan, whom they won't denounce despite his overt anti-Semitism, BLM's leaders don't quote Malcolm often. But when they do, they predictably hark back to the early Malcolm, not to the post-Hajj, kinder one who rejected race hatred. In the middle of 2020, as the nation burned, Patrisse Cullors chose to video herself reading these words from an April 3, 1964, speech that Malcolm X delivered in Cleveland, just days before he flew off to Mecca:

No, I am not an American. I am one of the 22 million black people who are the victims of Americanism. One of the 22 million black people who are the victims of democracy, nothing but disguised hypocrisy. So I am not standing here speaking to you as an American, or a patriot, or a flag waver or a flag saluter. No, not I. I am speaking as a victim of this American system, and I see America through the eyes of the victim.[18]

To be fair to Malcolm X, he does have fans who appreciate him not for his calls to victimhood, but for the opposite, his defense of black self-help. "Malcolm X is my great heroic leader of all time, and his message of self-help still stands," Shelby Steele said in the exchange cited in the preceding chapter.[19]

After Malcolm X, there followed men and women willing to operationalize his call for revolution. Bryan Burrough, a historian of the era on the staff at *Vanity Fair*, writes that "After Malcolm, the mantle of militancy was passed to a newcomer on the national scene, a tall, slender twenty-four-year-old named Stokely Carmichael."[20] One year after Malcolm's assassination, the Trinidadian-born Carmichael wrested the leadership of the Student Nonviolent Coordinating Committee (SNCC, pronounced "snick," a voter-registration group) from the nonviolent John Lewis, who went on to become a civil rights lion and a long-serving member of the U.S. House of Representatives before passing in 2020. One of Lewis's supposed sins was that he had encouraged SNCC members to vote for the Democratic Party in an election, rather than set up an independent party as the radicals wanted. "What does it say if the chairman is that far out of touch with his organization?" Carmichael remarked.[21]

The transfer of power to Carmichael was a harbinger: Lewis was a disciple of Martin Luther King, marching alongside him in Selma and other places; Carmichael was heavily influenced by Malcolm X. Years later, when he was touring Havana to confer with his hero Fidel, Carmichael explained to Mexican journalists why he kept the name of SNCC even though he didn't mean to practice the principles embedded in it. He said,

We used the name "nonviolent" because at that time Martin Luther King was the central figure of the black struggle and he was still preaching nonviolence, and anyone who talked about violence at that time was considered treasonable—amounting—to treason, so we decided that we would use the name nonviolent, but in the meantime we knew our struggle was not about to be nonviolent.[22]

We saw a very loud echo of this half a century later in 2020, when Alicia Garza dismissed John Lewis, who was then dying of late-stage pancreatic cancer, because he pled with rioters to go home in late May. Not two months before his death, Lewis said,

To the rioters here in Atlanta and across the country: I see you, and I hear you. I know your pain, your rage, your sense of despair and hopelessness. Justice has, indeed, been denied for far too long. Rioting, looting, and burning is not the way. Organize. Demonstrate. Sit-in. Stand-up. Vote.

To which Garza had a very Carmichael reply: "It's a familiar pattern: to call for peace and calm but direct it in the wrong places," she told the *New Yorker*'s David Remnick. "Why are we having this conversation about protest and property when a man's life was extinguished before our eyes?"[23]

Strains soon arose between King's nonviolent push for a biracial civil rights movement, one where black and white marchers, arms locked, faced down Southern racists, and the now violence-prone, Carmichael-led, SNCC. At a march in 1966 in Mississippi where the forces of both men converged, Carmichael argued that whites should not take part in the demonstrations and, to King's chagrin, he won the day. Soon, the "We Shall Overcome" chants by King's followers were themselves overcome by the mock chants of "We Shall Overrun" led by Carmichael's SNCC's militants.

The new party that SNCC formed under his leadership, the Lowndes County Freedom Organization, in Alabama, sported a black panther as its symbol, and sure enough in due time several black groups around the country began to style themselves as Black Panther parties.

An important breaking point finally arrived on June 16, 1966, in Greenwood, Mississippi, a moment Burrough describes as "the moment that changed everything, when the civil rights movement began to morph into something new and frightening to many Americans."[24] Upon release from his twenty-seventh arrest, Carmichael told a crowd of supporters that "the only way we gonna stop them white men from whuppin' us is to take over. We've been saying freedom for six years and we got nothing. What we gonna start sayin' now is black power."[25] The crowd chanted the slogan back approvingly, and it stuck for all eternity. The moment is often compared to the point in 2013, after the acquittal of the man who killed Trayvon Martin, when Alicia Garza first used the phrase "Black Lives Matter," which became a social media hashtag and later a movement.

The Black Power movement was to have reverberations that are felt to this day. In *Reassessing the Sixties*, Harvard's Randall Kennedy argues that Black Power "established the premises, tone, rhetoric, and style that many of the most prominent black activists of the past thirty years have embraced and adopted."[26] In a 2019 paper for The Heritage Foundation, Hillsdale's David Azerrad writes that today's identity politics is a direct outgrowth of the Black Power movement, because in it one can find

the core components of what we now call identity politics: the indictment of America as a fundamentally and irredeemably racist country; the hostility, bleeding into hatred, toward whites; the rejection of assimilation and integration in favor of cultural separatism; and the demands for color-conscious recognition, preferential treatment, and positive rights rather than equal rights under color-blind law.[27]

A year after the "moment that changed everything" in Greensboro, Mississippi, Carmichael authored a landmark book with Charles V. Hamilton that put in stark terms how Black Power was just that, a play for power, not for justice. "In the end, we cannot and shall not offer guarantees that Black Power, if achieved, would be non-racist," they wrote. "The final truth is that the white society is not entitled to reassurances, even if it were possible to offer them."[28] It is in this book that we first find the term "institutional racism."

Carmichael in time chafed under the administrative responsibility of running SNCC, and in 1967 bowed out of the leadership position from which he had unceremoniously ousted Lewis. He was now an international star and embarked on a global journey that took him to Africa and Europe. In London, he referred to the experience of blacks in the United States as that of "internal colonies." That caught the ear of the Cuban Embassy, which issued him an invitation to attend the upcoming conference of the Organization of Latin American Solidarity. Castro had formed this front group to counter the pro-American Organization of American States (OAS). SNCC, too, was invited, and Carmichael, who kept close contacts with SNCC, was made an "honorary delegate."

Carmichael toured the island with the communist dictator, during which time they discussed political theory and race relations. In a speech in the far eastern city of Santiago, in Castro's native province of Oriente, the man who was in the midst of repressing his compatriots, black and white alike, throwing them into dungeons when not marching them in front of a firing squad, praised Carmichael as "One of the most prestigious leaders for civil rights in the United States....It is a signal honor that those who represent the highest revolutionary values, the highest intellectual values, the ones who in all parts of the world defend the most just things, are present here this afternoon."[29] American audiences were appalled when they learned that Carmichael had said in one of his speeches in Havana that "We are preparing groups of urban guerrillas for our defense in the cities...it is going to be a fight to the death."[30]

BLM leaders don't quote Carmichael often—he's not mentioned, for example, in books by Garza and Cullors. Perhaps this absence stems from his view that the only role black women should play in the Black Power movement was as sexual partners. The leadership of BLM is all women, while the leadership of the Black Power movement was mostly men. Academics who study the movement, then and now, do draw strong links between the two, and some have even speculated that BLM's all-female cast makes today's movement more successful in achieving the transformation it seeks, as it is perceived as less threatening.[31] There are some similarities. Opal Tometi, known for touring Caracas and praising Nicolás Maduro's dictatorship in exchange for his support, is hardly the first radical black leader to tour the Caribbean in search of like-minded dictators. In 2016, sixty-seven former members of SNCC issued a letter supporting BLM, with the message "Y'all take it from here."[32]

Upon his return to the United States, Carmichael began to realize that the violent movement he had kickstarted had finally started to morph into an urban guerrilla movement, but it was to be led by another entity, the Black Panther Party. While many parties had ensued from his Lowndes party, the one that finally claimed the mantle of leadership was the party formed in Oakland, California, by Huey Newton and Bobby Seale, the Black Panther Party for Self-Defense. Its militants were easily identifiable by the boots, turtlenecks, and black berets they wore to honor Castro's aide-de-camp Che Guevara—and of course by the guns they carried everywhere. Their idol, again, was Malcolm X, but they also read Che Guevara and Frantz Fanon's *The Wretched of the Earth*, a work on anti-colonialism that remains widely influential to this day. Soon, word of their increasingly tense standoffs with police in the Bay Area spread to the rest of America, and the group gained prominence. Seale and Newton were joined by the even more mercurial Eldridge Cleaver, who advocated for the rape of white women. "Rape was an insurrectionary act. It delighted me that I was defying and trampling on the white man's law...and that I was defiling his women," he wrote in an essay.[33]

The April 4 assassination of Martin Luther King, Jr., sparked riots in 120 U.S. cities, and the Panthers tried to use the occasion to start a revolt. "It was King's death and the image of brave Panthers seeking to avenge it that cemented the party's national reputation," wrote Burrough.[34] But it was also the peak of their power. After that, the impact of the Panthers waned. All three—Seale, Newton, and Cleaver—went in and out of prison, Seale for his participation in the demonstrations at the Democratic National Convention in August 1968 (which is why he's known today as one of the "Chicago Eight" tried for the mayhem). J. Edgar Hoover's ubiquitous FBI had kept tabs on the Panthers, and soon after becoming president in 1969, Richard Nixon proceeded to arrest many of them. By 1971, the Black Panthers started to break into a New York–based East Coast branch, and a Bay Area, West Coast branch.

From this split came a splinter group that took violence to another level, the Black Liberation Army. "The BLA was ultimately a by-product of tensions between the smooth, cliquish Panthers of the West Coast, and the angry, Afro-centric, dashiki-wearing Panthers of New York," writes Burrough. It was also the result of a split between Newton and Cleaver, who, from exile in Algiers, became one of the group's spokesmen. The

BLA, a Marxist, revolutionary, violent faction, may have been disorganized and leaderless, but it "was a credible group of violent urban guerrillas, the first and only black underground of its kind in U.S. history."[35]

The group's stated purpose was to "take up arms for the liberation and self-determination of black people in the United States."[36] The BLA's own statement to the "black movement" started by observing that "Capitalism and imperialism as an economical system is in a deep crisis at home and abroad." The first two of its three enumerated principles read:

1. That we are anti-capitalist, anti-imperialist, anti-racist and anti-sexist.
2. That we must of necessity strive for the abolishment of these systems and for the institution of Socialistic relationships in which Black people have total and absolute control over their own destiny as a people.[37]

Before the movement petered out in 1981, it had killed at least ten policemen nationwide, wounded many more, and had been involved in several bank robberies.[38]

The BLA was the lethal, underground branch of something larger called the Black Liberation Movement. That BLM's initials are the same as those of the Black Liberation Movement has not escaped leaders like Alicia Garza, and she likes to gamely repeat "BLM, BLM." It is noteworthy that Garza, Cullors, and Tometi draw inspiration from these toxic splinters of the Black Panther Party. Two of them, Angela Davis and JoAnne Chesimard, deserve further attention for this reason.

Davis was born in Birmingham, Alabama, in 1944, at the height of segregation, Jim Crow, and violent attacks against peaceful African Americans by the likes of the Ku Klux Klan. Though she first joined the Communist Party when Martin Luther King, Jr., was assassinated in 1968, her mother, Sallye Bell Davis, was a member of the Southern Negro Youth Congress, affiliated with the party, and involved with the Soviet defense of the Scottsboro Boys discussed in the preceding chapter.[39] Communists visited often. "As a child I had the opportunity to spend time with black communists who had come to Birmingham to help organize, to organize the Southern Negro Youth Congress," she told Julian Bond in a 2009 C-SPAN interview. Angela Davis was, thus, the very definition of a red diaper baby.[40] In 1959 she was given a scholarship to attend high school by the Soviet-leaning American Friends Service Committee and moved in with a family whose father was also pro-Soviet. As the *New York Times* put it, she "went off to live in Brooklyn with the family of a white, Episcopal minister who had lost his church during the McCarthy period."[41] Angela's high school in Greenwich Village, Elisabeth Irwin High School, where communists blacklisted during the McCarthy era taught, was dubbed the "Little Red School House."

Davis later received another scholarship, this time to attend Brandeis University in Boston, where she graduated magna cum laude. It was at Brandeis that Davis first met the Frankfurt School's Herbert Marcuse—at a demonstration during the Cuban Missile Crisis—and started studying under this purveyor-par-excellence of critical theory (which aims at demolishing Western institutions to introduce communism; it will be discussed in chapter 7). While she was at Brandeis, the Klan firebombed a church in Birmingham, gruesomely murdering four girls whom Davis had known, an event that Davis says marked her life. She studied French and German and left to study in Paris and Frankfurt. While she was overseas, the Black Liberation Movement began to explode: "I ended up studying in Germany when these new developments in the Black Movement happened. The emergence of the Black Panther Party. And my feeling was, 'I want to be there. This is earthshaking. This is change. I want to be part of that.'"[42] She returned to the United States to study philosophy once again under Marcuse at the University of California, San Diego, before earning a doctorate from Humboldt University in Berlin, which also counts among its alumni G. W. F. Hegel, Karl Marx and W. E. B. Du Bois.

Humboldt was inside East Berlin, the capital of one of the harshest Soviet satellites. Though she is often associated with the Black Panthers, Davis was in fact a member for only six months, predictably finding them too sexist. The women, she once complained, were expected to "sit, literally, at the feet of the men."[43] Davis's more lasting and deeper attachment has always been to world communism. In 1980 and 1984 she ran as a candidate for vice president under the Moscow-controlled Communist Party USA, even though she has complained that the party wasn't radical enough for her tastes. "When I joined the party, it was a difficult decision, because I always considered the Communist Party to be so conservative. They were my parents' friends," she told Julian Bond in her 2009 interview on C-SPAN.[44] As a member of the party, she gravitated toward the wing that identified the struggle of black Americans with Third World revolutionary causes, spending most of her time with the party's all-black Che-Lumumba Club, named after the Argentine and Congolese revolutionaries.

An early gig was as a philosophy professor at UCLA in 1969, but when word leaked out of her revolutionary connections, Governor Ronald Reagan had the Board of Regents fire her (the move was contested by courts and other critics). She then put Marcuse's philosophies of radical change into street praxis. She joined the cause of the Soledad Brothers, a group of black prisoners at the prison by that name who received support from leftist celebrities from Jane Fonda to Linus Pauling and Lawrence Ferlinghetti. One August day in 1970, Jonathan Jackson, the seventeen-year-old brother of one of the inmates, George, broke into the prison in a botched attempt to free the prisoners. Jackson ended up killing Judge Harold Haley with a shotgun with a sawed-off barrel that had been purchased two days earlier by Angela Davis. She immediately went into hiding (and onto the FBI's Most Wanted list) but was arrested two months later and charged with murder, kidnapping, conspiracy, and helping to plot the raid.[45]

Davis became an instant cause célèbre, championed not only by liberals in Los Angeles and the Upper East Side of Manhattan but also by communist dictators from Havana to East Berlin and Moscow. John Lennon and the Rolling Stones wrote ballads about her. She was acquitted of all charges in 1972, in part because of her own actions as her cocounsel. She said the state's case was based on "male chauvinism," because the prosecution had presented her "passionate love" of George Jackson as her motive. The jurors later admitted that the cause of "women's liberation" had been one of their primary causes for selecting a woman as foreman. She signed the verdict "Ms. Timothy, fore-person."[46]

After this, Davis embarked on a world tour that took her to Havana and East Berlin, where she was lionized by Castro and Erich Honecker (from whom she received the Lenin Peace Prize in 1979). She has always defended both men, derided Soviet dissidents languishing in the gulag as nothing more than "common criminals," and has never renounced violence. Today a "professor emerita" at the University of California, Santa Cruz, she tours college campuses around the country, where her lectures fill within minutes. She proclaims "I have always been a communist," to rousing ovations from students, and is very clear that ethnic studies and other critical theory–inspired disciplines are to be used as "the intellectual arm of the revolution," and that multiculturalism should be a weapon to dismantle "racist, sexist, homophobic, economically exploitative institutions."[47] "I still imagine the possibility of moving beyond the democratic-socialist arrangement," she told Bond, who himself decried the fact that America's anti-communism had prevented the civil rights movement from being the communist paragon it might have been. ("The exclusion of actual communists, the civil rights movement went through, resulted in creating a movement that looked to the Sermon on the Mount, and Gandhi, instead of Marx, for a critique of American society, and we suffered tremendously because of that," Bond responded to Davis). Davis came out as a lesbian in 1997. More importantly, she has had a deep impact on the thinking of today's BLM leaders, as we will see in the next chapter.

Davis is hardly the only communist, African American woman to serve as the lodestar of BLM leaders. An even more violent member of the Most Wanted list, JoAnne Chesimard, plays a larger role in BLM lore. Now on the lam in Havana and known as Assata Shakur, Chesimard is not able to influence young college minds directly, as Davis is, but Garza, Cullors, and Tometi are all infatuated with her.

Unlike Davis, Chesimard was convicted of involvement in the 1973 shooting murder of New Jersey State trooper Werner Foerster on the New Jersey Turnpike near Newark. She was arrested some miles away after she and her accomplices tried to make a run for it. After a series of court cases and declared mistrials, during which she was often "shouting at judges and frequently being dragged from courtrooms," she was convicted of murder in 1977 and given a life sentence.[48]

Chesimard's life had many parallels with Davis's. She spent time in New York City, in her case Queens, and also lived for a time in the South, with her grandparents in Wilmington, North Carolina. She enrolled in the Borough of Manhattan Community College in the mid-1960s, when she was first arrested at a demonstration in 1967, and later transferred to City College, where she also pursued radical politics. Afterward she, too, joined the

Panthers. Burrough says that during the violence that accompanied a Panther split in 1971, "she was shot in the stomach during some kind of robbery at a Midtown Manhattan hotel, probably an early BLA drug ripoff."[49] It was with the BLA that she made her mark and became known by the New York police as the "heart and soul of the BLA." Burrough describes her as a "ferocious, machine-gun-toting, grenade-tossing, spitting mad Bonnie Parker of the 1970s."[50] Her daring escape from the Clinton Correctional Facility for Women on November 2, 1979 sealed her name in legend. She hid for a time in a safe house in the Pittsburgh area before mysteriously making her way to Castro's loving arms in 1980, either through the Bahamas or Mexico. President Obama did not even try to press for her extradition during the 2015 negotiations that led to the normalization of relations with Havana. We will see in the next chapter to what degree she seems to have influenced BLM.

One Susan Rosenberg was suspected of involvement in Chesimard's daring escape, for which she, too, was put on the FBI's Most Wanted list. Rosenberg went into hiding for three years but was never tried for her alleged help in the Chesimard escape, nor for a 1981 Brinks robbery that left two policemen and a security guard dead. She was arrested in 1984 after she was "found storing 12 assorted guns, nearly 200 sticks of dynamite, more than 100 sticks of the highly explosive DuPont Trovex, and hundreds of false identification documents." The then–U.S. Attorney for the Southern District of New York, one Rudy Giuliani, decided that charges of conspiracy, possession of firearms and false documents would suffice to convict her, and he was right. In 1985, a federal grand jury sentenced Rosenberg to fifty-eight years at a maximum-security prison. She served sixteen of those before President Clinton commuted her sentence on January 20, 2001, on his last day in office.[51]

Rosenberg is important to our story not just because of her connection to Chesimard but also because of her role as a funder of BLM, a subject we will treat in chapter 5. In addition, she was a member of several violent groups attempting to overthrow the elected government of the United States, including the Weather Underground. It is to this group, also influential among BLM leaders, that we now turn.

Just as the BLA was an urban, terrorist spin-off of the Black Panther Party, itself somewhat of a violent spin-off of the once-peaceful SNCC, the Weather Underground splintered from the peaceful Students for a Democratic Society (SDS). SDS was the new name given in 1960 to the old Student League for Industrial Democracy, a branch of the Intercollegiate Socialist Society, which was founded in 1905 by old-style socialists such as Jack London and Upton Sinclair. From 1960 on, SDS attracted white students who were growing enraged by pictures of blacks being beaten for nonviolently fighting segregation, and by America's growing involvement in the war in Vietnam. In 1962, the leaders met in Lake Huron, Michigan, and issued a manifesto called "the Port Huron Statement." It starts out with these words: "We are the people of this generation, bred in at least modest comfort, housed now in universities, looking uncomfortably at the world we inherit."[52] The overall document deals more with how to build a bridge between traditional liberals and socialists than with the black struggle, however. The original draft of the statement did not mention the word "Negro" until page 33 of the fifty-page document, after long passages on communism, the war, the welfare state, and the policy of deterrence with the Soviet Union. The words "Negro" or "Negroes" are used thirty times, and "civil rights" thirteen times, while combinations of communist/communism are used forty-five times (though the final edited version had more earlier mentions of the plight of blacks).[53] A call for "accepting more or less authoritarian kinds of socialism" was taken out in editing.

SDS meandered through most of the 1960s, its high point (or

low point) being the gathering of some 10,000 protesters at Chicago's Grant Park to disrupt the Democratic National Convention in August 1968. Mayor Richard J. Daley sent "Chicago's finest" to charge the demonstrators, and the ensuing melee, now the stuff of hippie legend, only helped Richard Nixon win the election that November on a law-and-order platform. SDS's undoing followed a by now familiar pattern. Just as men such as Malcolm X, Carmichael, and Cleaver began to disdain King's nonviolence, rich boys and girls at our top universities began to despair that anything short of street violence could achieve revolution in the United States. Burrough quotes a member of SDS, Dotson Rader, as saying "The meaninglessness of 'democratic' methods was becoming clear to us in the spring of 1967. The Civil Rights Movement was dead. Pacifism was dead."[54] Soon a well-heeled but at times viciously sadistic SDS core, led by people such as William Ayers, his now wife Bernardine Dohrn, Mark Rudd, and John Jacobs, took over the movement. The Cuban Revolution was their model, and they studied the writing of the *soixante-huitard* French intellectual Régis Debray, then teaching in Havana. Debray had written that "small, fast-moving guerrilla groups...could inspire a grassroots rebellion, even in the United States."[55] The trick was for them to be guided by an intellectual revolutionary vanguard, as Marcuse had prescribed.

The split finally came at the SDS convention in Chicago in 1969, when eleven of the putschists signed a new manifesto, much less gentle and kind than the Port Huron Statement, which they titled "You Don't Need a Weatherman to Know Which Way the Wind Blows."[56] The statement declared that they were dedicated to the "destruction of U.S. imperialism and the achievement of a classless world: world communism." The statement did not use the word "Negro" as the Port Huron Statement had, but the word "black." Black Americans were an internal colony of the United States, no matter where they lived, not just in the "black belt nation in the South" that the Soviets had given up on a decade earlier, the Weathermen wrote. Blacks had, therefore, to organize separately (something with which, as we have seen, Carmichael agreed). Meanwhile, the white Weathermen pledged to set up a clandestine, revolutionary movement, akin to the Red Guard in China, "with the full willingness to participate in the violent and illegal struggle." Again, as in the Port Huron Statement, the struggle of blacks for civil rights and acceptance in mainstream America seemed to matter little to the Weathermen except as a prop to achieve world revolution.

Completely taken over by this virulent strain, SDS finally closed its headquarters in 1970. The Weathermen did become a violent underground group that staged bombings throughout the United States, leading the FBI to declare them a terrorist group. They "declared war" on the United States, but by the late 1970s were a completely spent force, their members living clandestinely until they were found by the police and arrested. Though they did make many statements about killing cops, soldiers, and even innocent people, they were mostly inept, managing to kill three of their own during a bomb-making exercise. The three individuals killed in the Brinks job may have been their only victims.

Former Weathermen are extremely relevant today, however. After giving up a life of political violence, Ayers got a teaching degree at Columbia Teachers College and in the 2000s introduced a young up-and-coming politician by the strange name of Barack Obama to all the right leftists in Chicago. He is also a major backer of the BLM cause. Indeed, the relevance of the Weathermen today has a lot to do with the fact that some of its former members have trained BLM leaders and are involved in Antifa, or, as in the case of Rosenberg, in the funding of the organization. We will delve into this in the following two chapters.

The "Message to the Black Movement" by the BLA leadership quoted earlier had a phrase that encapsulates how all the individuals and organizations treated in this chapter felt. "Reform of the oppressive system can never benefit its victims, in the final analysis the system of oppression was created to insure the rule of particular racist classes and sanctify their capital. To seek reform therefore inevitably leads to, or begins with, the recognition of the laws of our oppressor as being valid."[57] It is a sentiment with which both Douglass and Dr. King disagreed, as they worked all their lives for equality for all under the American system promised by the Founders. This BLA statement does speak for today's BLM, however, as we will see in the following chapter.

CHAPTER 4

BLM

The stage was the broadcast studios of the far-left show that runs on PBS stations, *Democracy Now!*, and the date January 27, 2017. Donald Trump had been inaugurated president a week earlier, yet the leftists onstage seemed strangely triumphant. On one side of the set sat the show's host, Amy Goodman, and on the other Alicia Garza, BLM's primus inter pares, and next to her Angela Davis. George Floyd was still alive, and the riots and looting of 2020 were three years into the future. Davis, however, took note of how much BLM had achieved compared to all previous attempts to bring the revolution home. She also praised her companion for finally elbowing black men out of leadership. Garza, for her part, could not have been more effusive in her recognition of what Davis represented to BLM as a mentor. Goodman clearly understood she was attending a passing of the historic torch.[1]

"Thank you so much, Alicia, thank you so much," Davis said, before hugging and kissing her ideological protégée. "I see myself as witnessing [the BLM movement] on behalf of those who didn't make it this far, who are no longer with us," said wistfully the now stately matron of American communism, half a century removed from the philosophy classes with Marcuse, the shootings, the prison breakouts, and the FBI's Most Wanted list. Carmichael, Cleaver, and Malcolm had not been able to witness the Promised Land, but Angela was still there to see Garza change America. "The work that you, and Patrisse, and Opal, and the entire Black Lives Matter, and the entire movement for Black Lives, have accomplished over this period is phenomenal. As a matter of fact, before this period, you never saw official acknowledgments of racism. Even Obama did not talk about the problems of police violence and racism. And now it's on the agenda." She added for good measure that Trump had been elected because voters did not see in Hillary Clinton (whom Davis referred to only as "the opposing candidate") "the person they needed to give expression to this new consciousness."

Garza for her part could only gush about the totemic figure next to her. Using the strange new terms with which the woke express themselves, Garza said, "I have to say, Angela, one of the things I appreciate so much about you is that you're not waxing poetic about things that happened. You're still very much in relationship to all of us. You're still teaching us and still learning from us and still pushing us to get sharper, to get stronger, and to keep fighting. And that is really rare, so I want to say thank you. Thank you for being a constant presence for us. You are always 100 percent available, and paying attention, and it means a lot to all of us."

Davis's impact on BLM was clear when Garza added, "I also want to say, you are one of my greatest teachers. I have a bookshelf full of your writings." Davis had made them understand, said Garza, how to fight against the state. "The work you have done to inform not just us, but this nation and this world, about the carceral state, and how it operates, to make it plain, so that we can enter into it to dismantle it, is phenomenal, you are not just a professor or a theorist, you are an organizer!"

In Angela Davis, the BLM revolutionaries had a link not just to the Panthers and to such harsh practitioners of communism as the East German state, but to earlier dark forces. Cullors, Garza, and the others had learned from Davis personally, and she had been taught by Marcuse. He himself had been a disciple of the German philosopher Martin Heidegger at the University of Freiburg in the 1920s. Heidegger, the director of the Friedrich Nietzsche Archive, later became a member of the Nazi Party. He was a close friend of Nietzsche's sister Elisabeth, a virulent anti-Semite. And Nietzsche was well known not only for his nihilism and relativism but also for proclaiming to the world that "God is dead." Objective reality did not exist for Nietzsche; the "good" was only what the masterclass (who to Nietzsche had the right to rule) thought was beautiful, just as the "bad" was what the masterclass thought flawed and ugly. The idea that history is not composed of a set of facts, but is the narrative of the all-encompassing "white supremacy" that must be torn down, has a long pedigree for BLM. Aristotle's dictum that "for this alone is lacking even to God, to make undone the things that have once been done" is meaningless to those who see revamping history as a way to change the future.[2]

A BRAND-NEW DAY

Angela Davis's words on that January morning were prophetic. Fast forward four years, almost to the date (when these lines were being written), and BLM's demands were indeed on the agenda. Her harsh indictment of Hillary Clinton allows us to comprehend the alacrity with which Obama's vice president, now sworn in as the forty-sixth president, obediently executes the dictates of BLM. On his first day in office, Joseph R. Biden signed his "Executive

Order on Advancing Racial Equity and Support for Underserved Communities Through the Federal Government," which included several of the BLM demands. All federal departments and agencies were enjoined to do an inventory and ferret out "systemic racism." Government data not already disaggregated by identity categories would now be put through the meat grinder. Identity affinity groups (for example, UnidosUS, which used to be known as La Raza) would be given a seat at the table again, or, more properly, the trough. The executive order revoked a Trump-era federal ban on using critical race theory to harass employees in so-called anti-racism trainings. It then tackled history itself, also revoking the 1776 Commission, whose remit had been to return America to an objective teaching of history. The reason the new administration gave was that the Commission and its report "sought to erase America's history of racial injustice."[3] Biden later called it "offensive and counterfactual." Removing the commission and ending the ban on CRT trainings had been, it is important to note, BLM demands.

That accusation was baseless, as were the media articles that called the report "racist" without bothering to offer a scintilla of evidence. But that wasn't the point. It is highly doubtful that Biden was watching *Democracy Now!* on January 27, 2017, but he had internalized that BLM's host of complaints had to be "on the agenda" now—or at least someone very close to him was advising him that this was the case. To lead a leftist party that had chosen a working-class Irish Catholic from Scranton only because he was the safe bet to beat Trump—Lunch Pail Joe, and not the open socialist from Vermont—he had to heed Davis's words and "give expression to this new consciousness." And Biden would not be allowed to forget this. On election night, across the country in Portland, an Antifa mob of some 150 terrorized city residents in a night of riots before marching on to Democratic Party headquarters, which they attempted to torch and ended up by breaking its windows and covering it with graffiti. One protester held a sign that read, "We don't want Biden. We want revenge for police murders, imperialist wars and fascist massacres." Other slogans are best not repeated.[4] Riots and demonstrations broke out in Denver and Seattle, too.

THE REVOLUTION AT HOME

The year 2020 had changed everything in the America Joe Biden inherited, a change that, whatever Antifa's vicious antics, was really orchestrated by BLM's leaders. The year 2020 only cemented what Davis had already declared three years earlier. The killing of George Floyd, a forty-six-year-old black man, by a Minneapolis cop on May 25, in a manner that appeared to most Americans to be a clear case of police brutality, gave the BLM leaders an opening to instigate months of sustained protests, riots, and lootings that shook to the core an American society already deeply traumatized by several months of the COVID-19 pandemic. The organizations quickly disseminated the videos of Floyd's agonizing death and used social media to plan protests from coast to coast, protests that could turn violent. Every aspect of society was put on edge, from the office (where the trainings described above proliferated further, prompting Trump to act) to sports, whose arenas became pantheons to Black Lives Matter. The mayhem left more than two dozen people killed and between one and two billion dollars in damage.

The historic (an overused word that fits this time) impact of the BLM-organized mayhem can be gleaned from the glowing press reports that were written as city buildings burned. A *New York Times* profile in early July, properly titled "Black Lives Matter May Be the Largest Movement in U.S. History," quoted a professor emeritus at Stanford, Douglas McAdams, as saying:

It looks, for all the world, like these protests are achieving what very few do: setting in motion a period of significant, sustained, and widespread social, political change. We appear to be experiencing a social change tipping point—that is as rare in society as it is potentially consequential.[5]

This consequential change was organized by the BLM organizations, a fact that the press didn't quite want to tell the American people, because everything had to look spontaneous. It could still be gleaned from a rigorous reading of reports. The *Times*, for example, explained that "One of the reasons there have been protests in so many places in the United States is the backing of organizations like Black Lives Matter. While the group isn't necessarily directing each protest, it provides materials, guidance and a framework for new activists." How this was done was explained to the *Times* by Deva Woodly, a professor at the New School: "those activists are taking to social media to quickly share protest details to a wide audience. . . . These figures would make the recent protests the largest movement in the country's history."

That BLM was deeply involved in driving people to the protests and riots after Floyd's death can be seen in BLM's own 2020 Impact Report, released in March 2021. "The average open rate for nonprofit emails is about 25%. In early June, our email providing event and safety resources to people wanting to mobilize saw a 63% open rate," it boasted, using "event and safety" clearly as a euphemism for mobilizing protesters. In addition,

BLMGNF was again looked to as a resource during the summer's protest. In this second half of 2020, the BLMGNF website was visited by over 24 million people. The single most active day was June 2, 2020, with 1.9 million visitors. This is an almost 5,000% increase compared to our most trafficked day in March 2020. . . . Over the course of 2020, we sent 127,042,508 emails. From these emails, 1,213,992 actions were taken.[6]

BLM's deep involvement in the protests and the riots can also be seen from figures gathered by the Armed Conflict Location and Event Data Project (ACLED) and the Bridging Divides Initiative (BDI), which are supported by Princeton University. Their U.S. Crisis Monitor is actually pretty sympathetic to BLM and its causes. It nonetheless reported last September that by that point we had had a lot of protests, more than 10,000 (that number later grew to more than 12,000 for 2020). Most of them were "peaceful" said the report, but around 5 percent turned into riots. Five percent of that number is a lot of riots, or 633. Buried inside the ACLED report—because its authors plainly buried the story—journalist Joy Pullman of *The Federalist* discovered that BLM activists were involved in 95 percent of the 633 incidents that ACLED coded as "riots" for which the identification of the participants was known. (The report opened with the ominous words: "The United States is at a heightened risk of political violence and instability going into the 2020 election.")[7]

A *New York Times Magazine* article further explained how BLM leaders had gained even more power from the time it was founded: "while much of the nation's attention drifted away from Black Lives Matter, organizers and activists weren't dormant." Garza told the *Magazine* writer that "the movement's first generation of organizers has been working steadily to become savvier and even more strategic over the past seven years."[8] The *Los Angeles Times* meanwhile wrote that "The unprecedented size and scope of recent rallies speaks to how Black Lives Matter has transformed from a small but passionate movement into a cultural and political phenomenon." What BLM had done was to channel outrage over the killing of George Floyd "into a sustained mass campaign for profound social change. The group has political sway that would have seemed unimaginable just a few months ago."[9]

The transformation they have prompted is rolling through all levels of society. It's evident from the seemingly banal, such as fraternities, sororities, and marching bands disappearing from colleges, to the surge in CRT trainings at work and the firing of long-standing newspaper editors for running material that runs counter to the dictates of Black Lives Matter.[10] If your daughter's AP Spanish language class devoted the entire 2020–2021 academic year to probing systems of oppression in Latin America, it was because of the BLM year. If your son is reading Ibram X. Kendi, it is because of BLM. If your town or city has formed an "Anti-Racism Ad Hoc Committee" that will undertake witch hunts for any civic activity, no matter how innocent, that some intrusive neighborhood martinet can denounce as racist, that is because of BLM. If your priest, minister, or rabbi ruins your weekend by lecturing you on social justice and white privilege, that is because of BLM. Biden's obeisance is due to BLM. BLM changed our lives in 2020, and it will continue to do so into the future. It now has a Political Action Committee to influence whom we elect to write our policies, and a school curriculum to make sure future generations are brainwashed in their ideology. The media ubiquitously calls what is happening a "racial reckoning." It is, however, a well-planned and well-executed political blueprint.

The history of BLM founders Garza, Cullors, and Tometi would give context to these sweeping changes, if only the media would tell it. Even before they created the hashtag expression #BlackLivesMatter in 2013 that later became an empire of revolutionary organizations around the world, they belonged or associated with an interlacing web of socialist groups that have been trying to overthrow the American system for decades. The social media power of this network made the hashtag go viral in the first place. That, too, was not spontaneous. Journalists running interference for the BLM leaders blithely dismiss Cullors's own admission that she and Garza were "trained Marxists." PolitiFact even ran a so-called fact check based on the supposed vagueness of that remark.[11]

It is imperative, therefore, to understand who these leaders are. To sum it up, Garza, Cullors, Tometi, and other important leaders, such the head of the Los Angeles chapter, Melina Abdullah, are every bit as communist as Angela Davis. They just haven't joined the party, because it is male dominated, because it is now even stuffier than when Angela Davis derided it as a club for old people, and because they don't have to.

WHO'S WHO

We have already seen the ideological debt the BLM leaders owe Angela Davis. JoAnne Chesimard also figures very high in the pantheon of heroes. Patrisse Cullors's memoir, written with asha bandele, *When They Call You a Terrorist*, opens up—before Angela Davis's foreword—with a little ditty by Chesimard that repeats the most famous line in the *Communist Manifesto*:

> It is our duty to fight for our freedom.
> It is our duty to win.
> We must love each other and support each other.
> We have nothing to lose but our chains.[12]

It is known as the "Assata chant" and it is repeated constantly by the three leaders and thousands of demonstrators coast to coast. "'This is how we close out every meeting, every event, every action, every freeway we've shut down, every mall we've shut down, you'll hear this chant reverberated throughout this country, and you'll hear this chant in other countries, now too," Cullors, with Tometi alongside, told a crowd in 2015. "This is from our beloved Assata Shakur, who is on the Number One on the FBI's Most Wanted List, and she is a powerful leader who many of us are inspired by. Many of us have 'Assata Taught Me' sweaters. So, three times, and you're going to start off with a whisper and you're going to just repeat it."[13] Indeed, "Assata Taught Me" T-shirts are also all the rage among BLM protests.

Another constant intellectual influence on the BLM leaders has been Frantz Fanon, a mid-twentieth-century pan-Africanist writer born in Martinique, who praised the use of violence and preached that truth is not absolute, but whatever helps the revolutionary overthrow the system. There are many others, the vast majority being black Marxists who mix the experience of U.S. blacks with the colonial experience around the globe.

Because the media that informs the vast majority of Americans never gives a full rundown of who the BLM leaders are, including their associations and ideological attachments, it is important here to give a fuller view of the four main personalities.

Opal Tometi

Probably owing to a fallout she had with Garza in 2015, Opal Tometi is the least known of the BLM leaders. She was born in Phoenix, Arizona, in 1984 to immigrants from Nigeria, and fully embraces pan-Africanism. Tometi's biography says she is "a student of liberation theology and her practice is in the tradition of Ella Baker, informed by Stuart Hall, bell hooks, and black feminist thinkers," which nicely sums up Tometi's portfolio of activities.[14] Liberation theology is Marxism applied to Christianity in the Third World, and Tometi is the most internationally attuned of the three BLM leaders. Stuart Hall is a Jamaican-born Marxist academic and founder of the so-called school of British Cultural Studies, which again demonstrates Tometi's international interests. Ella Baker sympathized with socialism and, as a longtime member of SNCC, pushed the organization not to engage in anti-communist activities, whereas hooks is a Kentucky-born activist more in the anarcho-socialist tradition.

In a 2019 interview with Dazed, Tometi said her Nigerian family had faced constant harassment in the United States (which somewhat jars with the history of success by Nigerians in America). She also made the point that the movement had much bigger ambitions than just police brutality and incarceration: "it's great to see that people now understand that when we say 'Black Lives Matter,' we're not just talking about police brutality—although that is a key catalyzing moment." One of the goals was reparations, she added. "Reparations are about repairing the damage, right? We can't have fairness if the damage hasn't been reconciled," she said, which would strike some people as a strange thing for the daughter of immigrants with no history of slavery in her ancestry to say.[15]

It is Tometi who can be seen hanging out with the global hard left, including one time when she visited Nicolás Maduro in Caracas in 2015. Soon after, she issued something akin to a manifesto titled "Black North American Solidarity Statement with the Venezuelan People." It was a fiery diatribe that praised the Venezuelan dictatorship as "direct democracy," and, in the style of Angela Davis excoriating Soviet dissidents in her day, derided the Venezuelan opposition. It said, in parts:

> In these last 17 years, we have witnessed the Bolivarian Revolution champion participatory democracy and construct a fair, transparent election system recognized as among the best in the world—a democratic process that has advocated the rights of Afrodescendants and other oppressed people within Venezuela and across the globe.... *We reject the hypocrisy of the Venezuelan elite—who like settlers everywhere—cling to their white privilege to the point of even lynching Afrodescendants.* (Italics in the original.)[16]

Nicolás Maduro is not the only communist with whom Tometi has associated. She has also had meetings with the Rosa Luxemburg Foundation, which was set up by former operatives of the former East German government, the most draconian communist state among the Soviet satellites.[17] At the time of this writing, she was the executive director of the far-left Black Alliance for Just Immigration (BAJI).

Patrisse Cullors

Patrisse Cullors is more oriented around U.S. politics and even more doctrinaire than Tometi. She was born in Los Angeles in 1983 to a lower-middle-class family. Her father, Alton, left the family when she was six, after his dismissal from his job at GM caused friction with his wife. At one point, Cullors's mother informed her that not Alton, but another man named Gabriel was her father. Patrisse reached out to him and liked him, especially the fact that he's a rehabilitated former drug user. But then Gabriel relapsed and got sent to prison on drug charges, at the same time that one of Patrisse's brothers, and Patrisse herself, started getting in trouble with the law because of drug use. All this turmoil began what turned out to be a lifelong animosity toward what she and her comrades call the "school-to-prison pipeline" and "the carceral state." While all of this was going on, Patrisse was being further radicalized by another source, the magnet high school to which her intellect had gained her entry, Cleveland High in the San Fernando Valley. In her memoir she gives a rundown of her initiation as a militant.

"Cleveland's humanities program is rooted in social justice, and we study apartheid and communism in China. We study Emma Goldman and read bell hooks," she writes, adding that the program exposed her to alternative religions, and she began to question her strict Jehovah's Witness upbringing. "We are encouraged to challenge racism, sexism, classism and heteronormativity."[18] After graduation, a history teacher told her about a radical seven-day camp, the Brotherhood-Sisterhood social justice camp, and Cullors enrolled in it. She studied more about "systems of oppression" and was encouraged to celebrate her lesbianism.

An organization called the Strategy Center came to the camp to make a presentation. "After the camp ends, I join the Strategy Center and for a year they train me to be an organizer," Cullors writes, explaining how she mixed learning how to organize for something called "the Bus Riders Union" with ideological training. "I read, I study, adding Mao, Marx, and Lenin to my knowledge of hooks, Lorde and Walker."[19]

The Labor/Community Strategy Center is the brainchild of none other than Eric Mann, a former Weatherman who spent eighteen months in prison for assault and battery. Mann has not given up on the Weather Underground's goal of spreading a communist revolution around the world and trains his young charges on exactly how to do that. Mann calls his Center the "Harvard of Revolutionary graduate schools," or "the University of Caracas Revolutionary Graduate School." He told University of California, San Diego students in 2008 that the center's purpose is "to build an anti-racist, anti-imperialist, anti-fascist united front."[20]

"People think they can join an organization, and go out, and change the most dictatorial country in the world by just showing up. We don't think so. Organizing is a skill, is a vocation," Mann said. The Center's "six-month, intensive training program" offers a mix of theory—Mann's wife teaches "problems of imperialism, women's studies, strategies and tactics"—and activism. Students are pushed to produce numbers—"How many people did you organize? How did it go?"—or they are eventually weaned out. There are to be no slouches in the revolutionary vanguard. "I spend my time organizing mainly young people who want to be revolutionaries," Mann said. If you're not in organizing, "your life is meaningless," and you risk becoming a "bourgeois pig."

Mann explained how he was always on the lookout for recruits. University students must constantly ask themselves, "Am I making decisions to change the system? Am I being tied to the masses?" The university, said Mann, is the place where Mao Zedong was radicalized, where Lenin and Fidel were radicalized, where Che was radicalized. The concept of the radical middle class of the colonized people, or in my case the radical middle class of the privileged people, is a model of a certain type of revolutionary.

The goal was to "Take this country away from the white settler state, take this country away from imperialism and have an anti-racist, anti-imperialist and anti-fascist revolution."

In her memoir, Cullors describes how Mann took her "under his wing. Eric is older and wiser, and fearlessly anti-racist." Cullors writes that she found "a home at the Strategy Center, a place that will raise me and hold me for more than a decade." Soon her mother and her biological father Gabriel started attending sessions at the Center, and when they both came to graduation, Cullors experienced something that had always been denied her: "for the first time in the whole of my life I will be in a public space with both my parents—the way I had always seen my white friends in public spaces with both their parents." And it all happened at a school where former Weathermen train recruits to overthrow the American system and revolutionize the world.

From this radical cauldron emerged the Patrisse Cullors who is now at the center not just of BLM organizations but also of many others that share their aims. She founded and now directs Dignity and Power Now. At a 2015 meeting of Netroots, she interrupted the proceedings by leading chants of "If I die in police custody, burn everything down!"[21]

Unsurprisingly, Cullors also finds a North Star in Angela Davis. She wrote in the *Harvard Law Review* in 2019 that Davis, a

philosopher, Marxist, and former Black Panther whose work on prisons, abolition, and Black struggle has proven relevant over time—has informed our movements and communities for decades.

Her political theories and reflections on anticapitalist movements around the world have sought not only to transform U.S. society by challenging white supremacy in U.S. laws, institutions, and relationships, but also to act as a catalyst toward building a broader antiracist and antiwar movement internationally.[22]

Alicia Garza

Alicia Garza, who grew up as Alicia Schwartz, the surname of her stepfather, can be said to be the most important of the three. She has received the most media attention, does the highest number of high-profile conferences, and is at the center of the BLM global revolutionary network. All three BLM cofounders express their loathing of capitalism, but Garza may be said to be the most outspoken. "It's not possible for a world to emerge where black lives matter if it's under capitalism, and it's not possible to abolish capitalism without a struggle against national oppression," she told a forum that brings Marxists from around the world together, Left Forum, in 2015.[23]

Garza was born in 1981 in Los Angeles and was raised in middle-class San Rafael in the Bay Area, and in even tonier nearby Tiburon. There she attended a mostly white middle school and began to radicalize, according to a feature in *SF Weekly*. Her parents, who were antique dealers, were "solid liberals," according to Garza.[24] Her mother, particularly, encouraged her activism against abstinence-only sex education in both middle school where, according to Garza, "everyone" was having sex, and later in high school. After that we see the same pattern we saw with Cullors repeated: high school activism followed by recruitment into organizing camps. Thus, after studying politics in college, Garza joined a Marxist preparatory, the School of Unity and Liberation (SOUL), as an intern.

It was there that Garza commenced her official Marxist education. The *SF Weekly* profile on Garza quotes her as saying:

When I trained in sociology, we would read Marx, and we would read de Tocqueville, and we would read all these economic theorists, but in a void. It never got mentioned in those classes that social movements all over the world have used Marx and Lenin as a foundation to interrupt these systems that are really negatively impacting the majority of people.

SOUL, according to another *SF Weekly* profile, is a Bay Area outfit that

> promotes anti-capitalist ideas....Year-round, SOUL goes on the road to high schools, colleges, and community organizations with a series of educational programs that deconstruct the world system of capitalism in accord with a *Political Education Workshop Manual* that lays out detailed lesson plans on topics ranging from racism to homophobia to "why the rich get richer." The loose-leaf, bound manual comes complete with icebreakers to use at the beginning of class, fact sheets quantifying levels of poverty and social inequity under capitalism, and Socratic questions intended to guide the school's young students toward a SOUL worldview.[25]

SOUL was founded in 1996 by Rona Fernandez and Harmony Goldberg to get young "people of color" to "get out the vote." Goldberg, a self-described devotee of Antonio Gramsci, has also been heavily influenced by the experiences of communist revolutionaries in Cuba, China, Chile, and so on.

James Simpson, a budget analyst and economist at the White House Office of Management and Budget between 1987 and 1993 who has intensively studied BLM and communist groups, says SOUL is a front for the Freedom Road Socialist Organization (FRSO), one of the biggest communist groups in the country. Indeed, the two organizations do often work together.[26] SOUL sits astride a multiplicity of other Marxist groups of different sizes, all committed one way or another to overthrowing the U.S. system and implanting Marxism, including Seeding Change, Causa Justa/ Just Cause, LeftRoots (another FRSO front), and People United for a Better Life in Oakland (PUEBLO).[27]

It was at PUEBLO—"the people" in Spanish—that Garza found her next home, when she was hired to organize opposition to building a Walmart in Oakland. As Scott Walter of the Capital Research Center put it, "She didn't care that poor black residents actually wanted the Walmart, nor that the local labor council supported the new store, which did open."[28] This is something we find again and again with leftist leaders who say they are fighting for the people but disdain the people's actual choices. Along the way, Garza also teamed up with the Chinese Progressive Association (CPA) of San Francisco, where she worked on a report in 2010 and, in 2012, appeared as a member of the host committee of the CPA's fortieth anniversary. The CPA San Francisco was set up in 1972 by the Maoist group I Wor Kuen to support China's ongoing Cultural Revolution, improve ties between the United States and Mao's People's Republic of China, and drive organizations associated with Taiwan's Kuomintang party out of America's Chinatowns. Garza also went to work for People Organized to Win Employment Rights (POWER) and, after that, the National Domestic Workers Alliance (NDWA), which Simpson also identifies as an FRSO organization. The NDWA sent Garza to Ferguson, Missouri, in October 2014, two months after the killing of Michael Brown, one of the milestones on the way to making BLM what it is today. It is also important to note that FRSO often teams up with Eric Mann's Labor/Community Strategy Center (where Cullors trained) in public discussions on how to bring about "revolution" in the United States.[29]

In other words, Garza (like her two comrades) is deeply enmeshed in Marxism, Inc.; she's a figure far to the left of anybody who has played a major role in America before (let's not forget that Angela Davis never influenced policy or civil society, as she herself recognizes). When the writer of the *SF Weekly* profile, Julia Carrie Wong, asked Garza in 2015 why BLM seemed to target Vermont's socialist Bernie Sanders, interrupting some of his speeches even though he promoted socialism on the presidential campaign trail, Garza shot back sarcastically:

> Has he? It sounds like he's been talking a lot about being a social democrat, which is still left of where the Democratic Party is, but it's not socialism. It's democratic capitalism. There should be more voices saying, "This is not actually socialism, and socialism is actually possible in our lifetime, and this is what that looks like. What you're talking about is a nicer, more gentle capitalism."

Melina Abdullah

To call Melina Abdullah a red-diaper baby does not do justice to her communist pedigree. Raised by activist parents in the streets of Oakland, she is a third-generation Marxist. "I don't remember the first picket line that I was on, but I remember marching around as a little girl in a hard hat, holding a sign," she told an interviewer in 2020, describing herself as a member of "the Panther Cub generation. All of my friends' parents were Panthers."[30] Her father, John Riemann, is a Trotskyite and union organizer whose observations on all things Marxist can be read on a blog called the Oakland Socialist.[31] Abdullah's grandfather, Guenter Reimann, was a member of Germany's Communist Party in the 1920s and 1930s. A *Guardian* obituary for the elder Reimann, who died in 2005 at the age of one hundred, says that "Reimann was born Hans Steinicke into a bourgeois German-Jewish family in Angermuende, north-east of Berlin. As a schoolboy, he joined the Communist party." Like Marcuse and many other German Marxists, Reimann escaped to the West to flee the Nazis, ending up in New York in the 1930s. He became a world-renowned economist who advised governments and international organizations. As the *Guardian* put it, however, "such men, no doubt, would have been surprised to discover that Reimann's understanding of capitalism derived from the position of desiring its overthrow."[32]

The apple did not fall far from the tree. "White capitalism requires racist, violent policing to protect it. In order to eliminate police violence, and the killings of our people at their hands, we must also target the economic systems that built it and rely on it," *The Daily Wire* reports Abdullah as writing.[33] Abdullah, who took her new surname from an ex-husband, may not be in the public eye as much as the three cofounders of BLM, but as the head of the original BLM chapter, the one in Los Angeles, she merits attention. A professor of pan-African studies at California State University, Los Angeles, Abdullah's life has many similarities with Cullors and others in the movement. Her radical studies in high school were important to her. "Being in that classroom planted seeds. It exposed me to the legacy of my people. Black studies saved my life, literally," she told Fernandez. Like Cullors, Abdullah also brings to her activism personal experiences with seeing people close to her perish because they chose to be involved with drugs, or, as Abdullah puts it, because of "drugs being brought into our community." She has spoken and written about how one of her first boyfriends in eighth grade, Curtis Belton, was gunned down as a result of involvement with drugs.

Abdullah does not shy away from calling for violence against property or even against white people. "Property damage should not be the focus of what we're looking at," she told Fernandez at the height of the 2020 looting. On May 31, six days after George Floyd's tragic death, she told Libby Denkmann of LAist that "the violence and pain and hurt that's experienced on a daily basis by black folks at the hands of a repressive system should also be visited upon, to a degree, to those who think that they can just retreat to white affluence."[34] In fact, one of her main themes is that of a supposed liberal inaction against racism, what Abdullah calls "a liberal brand of white supremacy." Echoing Ibram X. Kendi, but without mentioning him, she told Fernandez, "you're either a racist or an anti-racist."

These, then, are the women who founded Black Lives Matter, for whom Maduro is a model to follow in the United States, who trained with Weathermen on how to start a revolution, and who think that the Bernie Sanders who honeymooned in the Soviet Union is far too conservative. As Simpson wrote in 2016, "The Black Lives Matter movement (BLM) casts itself as a spontaneous uprising born of inner city frustration, but is, in fact, the latest and most dangerous face of a web of well-funded communist/ socialist organizations that have been agitating against America for decades." Predicting the results of a Network Contagion Research Institute (NCRI) report and all of 2020, Simpson continues: "Its agitation has provoked police killings and other violence, lawlessness and unrest in minority communities throughout the U.S. If allowed to continue, that agitation could devolve into anarchy and civil war. The BLM crowd appears to be spoiling for just such an outcome."[35] Let's see, lastly, how Tometi, Garza, and Cullors created BLM.

BLM IS BORN

The moment that gave rise to BLM came on July 13, 2013, when neighborhood watchman George Zimmerman was acquitted of killing teenager Trayvon Martin. Martin was black, and Zimmerman was a dark-complexioned son of a Peruvian mother and a man of German descent. Right away, however, this killing became a black-and-white issue (the media referred to Zimmerman as a "white Hispanic," even though he is clearly not of only European descent). Garza, distraught, wrote a Facebook post in which she stated that "black lives matter." Her comrade Cullors then threw a hashtag in front and spread the phrase on social media. Tometi, meanwhile, started thinking of something larger. As she told Dazed,

> I reached out to Alicia Garza early on, and said, "I've seen this emerging hashtag that Patrisse and you put online a day or two ago. I think we need to build a website and I think we need to elevate it and make sure that we're using it across our network and beyond." And so I built blacklivesmatter.com, out of a Tumblr page. I chose the colors black and yellow because those are my favorite. We shared the page, and people began to amplify the hashtag and take the message to the streets. It became a movement in Atlanta, New York and LA.[36]

Given the great assortment of small and large Marxist associations that the three women could call on, we can quickly figure out how the hashtagged message was amplified and by whom.

The police killing of Michael Brown, another black teenager, in Ferguson, Missouri, in August 2014 gave BLM new impetus. Riots broke out, which the left called the "Ferguson insurrection." Soon Freedom Road was on the scene in the mostly black St. Louis suburb, as were activists from the Communist Party USA, the International Socialist Organization, Socialist Alternative, LeftRoots, and other militants such as Lisa Fithian, the then fifty-three-year-old organizer of the Seattle World Trade Organization riots in 1999 (the event that sparked the new violent left) and the Occupy Wall Street movement. Fithian, who likes to explain her leading roles in riots by always telling people, "I create crisis, because crisis is that edge where change is possible," was particularly significant in the Ferguson riots.[37] A 2003 *New York Times* feature described Fithian in this manner: "You don't go to Fithian when you want to carry a placard. You go to her when you want to make sure there are enough bolt cutters to go around."[38]

BLM's emerging leaders put the crisis created in Ferguson in 2014 to good use. *In These Times*, the socialist monthly magazine started in 1976 by Julian Bond, Herbert Marcuse, and Noam Chomsky, gives a good real-time description of Garza's role in an October 2014 feature:

> The Black Lives Matter team organized a Freedom Ride that Garza says "mobilized more than 500 black people from all over the country to come to Ferguson, to not only stand in solidarity but to lend concrete and material support to organizers who work on the front lines of the Ferguson rebellion."

The article quotes Garza, whom it identifies as not just a cocreator of #BlackLivesMatter but also as a member of the Marxist group LeftRoots, as saying that she wanted to "make sure the organizations and activists on the ground had the capacity to really hold this moment and extend it into a movement."[39] Freedom Road helpfully amplified what was taking place, videoing the event and creating a BLM button.[40]

Garza told *In These Times* that her movement had learned how to triumph from Third World liberation movements. Her work with BLM in 2014, still only a movement, she said,

> is really similar to my work with Left Roots, which is about building a strong, vibrant left that's rooted in communities of color and women and queer folks and others who have traditionally been on the margins, and really developing the strategies we need to build effective, long-term, sustained social transformation.

Ferguson transformed BLM from a hashtag and a movement into a set of organizations, which grew into what is today a sort of global revolutionary empire. In the history section (called "herstory") of the most important BLM outfit, the significance of Ferguson as a turning point is underlined. "We understood Ferguson was not an aberration, but in fact, a clear point of reference," it reads. "When it was time for us to leave, inspired by our friends in Ferguson, organizers from 18 different cities went back home and developed Black Lives Matter chapters in their communities and towns."[41] In 2020, this network was activated to create mayhem in dozens of cities in the United States and in places as far away as Bristol, London, and Paris.

What Scott Walter rightly calls "the first organizational structure" of the movement, the Movement for Black Lives (M4BL), was conceptualized in the midst of the Ferguson mayhem in December 2014 as an umbrella coalition of one hundred nationwide groups (the left has always relied on loose umbrella groups).[42] M4BL took on a more official form at a huge rally for more than 1,500 black Americans who came from coast to coast in July 2015 to the campus of Cleveland State University. Among its dozens of member groups figure Color of Change,[43] a group founded by former Obama official (and former communist) Van Jones, which boasts of getting Pat Buchanan and Bill O'Reilly fired by MSNBC and Fox, respectively; Southerners on New Ground, a self-avowed "queer liberation" group in the South; and the UndocuBlack Network, which says it "blackifies" the illegal immigrant issue by focusing on those who are of African ancestry. "The Movement for Black Lives is ... at the heart of the uprising," wrote Julia Travers in an important July 2020 piece in Inside Philanthropy.[44]

The other important umbrella entity, the Black Lives Matter Global Network Foundation, was loosely formed by thirty activists in Los Angeles in 2013 but not officially incorporated in Delaware until late 2016.[45] BLM GNF is in many ways the official umbrella network, the one you are directed to on the Internet if you type Blacklivesmatter.com. At the time of this writing, in mid-2021, the leadership was in a bit of disarray. For ten months, it had been officially headed by Cullors, who in July 2020 had been named its executive director. But then, suddenly in late May 2021, Cullors announced in a YouTube video that she was resigning.[46] Cullors gave no reason for stepping down, other than to say she wanted to spend more time with her five-year-old son, but she left amid accusations of financial self-dealing and a house-buying spree.[47] She had also recently gone even further to the left, calling in a February 2021 YouTube video for "getting rid of police, prisons and jails, surveillance, and courts."[48] In it she praised both Melina Abdullah and Angela Davis as fellow abolitionists (a Marxist term that is not related to ending slavery), but, interestingly, did not mention Alicia Garza.

Whatever her many shortcomings, Cullors left BLM GNF in solid shape. The foundation appears to have scrubbed the page that listed its officially recognized chapters, but a screenshot of the previous page in my possession reveals sixteen chapters in the United States and Canada (Boston, Chicago, Denver, Detroit, Lansing, Long Beach, Los Angeles, Memphis, Nashville, New York, Philadelphia, South Bend, Washington, DC, Toronto, Vancouver, and Waterloo). In its 2020 Impact Report published in March 2021, BLM GNF said it had given money to all these chapters except for Los Angeles, Long Beach, and New York, for reasons that were not explained, and it named "Canada" as a single chapter.[49] In that report, Cullors said that BLM GNF now had three entities: BLM GNF itself, a new BLM Grassroots—notably led by Melina Abdullah—which is a "chapter-driven advisement and decision-making structure that would work hand in hand with the BLM Global Network Foundation, while remaining focused on local, grassroots level work," and the BLM Political Action Committee. In 2020, Politico reported that BLM GNF "coordinates with more than 150 organizations," while Abdullah's GoFundMe page claims there are thirty-eight chapters around the world.[50]

Purged, too, from the BLM GNF website is one of its most outlandish demands: "We disrupt the Western-prescribed nuclear-family-structure requirement by supporting each other as extended families and 'villages' that collectively care for one another." That disappeared after my Heritage Foundation colleague Andrew Olivastro and I wrote about it in the *New York Post* (an article that has been read by more than a million people); the Global Network scrubbed its website of its most offensive material in September 2020.[51]

The two large partner umbrella networks work closely. "We do a lot of work with the Movement for Black Lives and a number of organizations and individuals and different leaders who are part of that formation," Tometi told E! Online in June 2020.[52] Garza describes the relationship in this manner: "We helped to also pull together an ecosystem that was much broader than the organization that we founded, and that ecosystem is called the Movement for Black Lives and it is taking the world by storm."[53] Travers said of M4BL that "the Black Lives Matter Global Network helped craft its agenda and is among its member partners." It quotes Kailee Scales, managing director of BLM GNF, as saying that M4BL is "a space for Black organizations to debate and discuss current political conditions, develop political interventions." It "convenes leadership around shared movement strategy," Travers added. Along the way, M4BL had to add more feminist positions and emphasize LGBTQ issues in order to fit better with BLM GNF's orientation.

These are both radical, anti-capitalist organizations that seek a root-and-branch change of the way the United States is constituted. The Global Network seems slightly more concerned with keeping up appearances (hence the September scrubbing after polls showed a decline in popularity). M4BL, however, appears to feel no such compunction, openly proclaiming on its website at the time of this writing that "We believe in transformation and a radical realignment of power.... The current systems we live inside of need to be radically transformed, which includes a realignment of global power."[54] No matter how much scrubbing is done, nobody should be under any illusion about there being any difference between the aims of these two umbrella groups. As Alicia Garza told a gathering of Maine liberals in 2019, "We're talking about changing how we've organized this country.... I believe we all have work to do to keep dismantling the organizing principle of this society."[55]

These organizations that aim to dismantle the very principles that support our way of life became powerful in 2020. They are pushing Congress to pass legislation such as the BREATHE Act, which seeks to cut off funding for police and has sponsors in Congress. In October 2020 the BLM Political Action Committee (PAC) was founded, which will allow BLM to spend money on politicians and to lobby for more legislation. "We want to be able to not just speak in 'get out the vote' language," Cullors told Politico in an interview. "Black Lives Matter is launching our PAC so we can talk directly to voters about who we think that they should be voting for and what we think they should be voting on."[56] The PAC went to work right away in the presidential election and in the Georgia runoff elections in January 2021. "Really, the world [is] in their hands right now. That power lies here in Georgia[,] and specifically among Black Georgians," Angela Angel of the Black Lives Matter PAC told Georgia journalists at the height of that election. The PAC produced TV ads that were designed to attract black voters in support of the Democrats Jon Ossoff and Raphael Warnock, both of whom ended up winning by razor-thin margins, handing the Democrats all the levers of elected power in Washington.[57]

In the 2020 Impact Report it released in March 2021, BLM GNF described its work on the BREATHE Act this way:

> During the uprising last summer, our organization came together with Movement For Black Lives (M4BL) to introduce the BREATHE Act. It is a modern-day civil rights bill and a legislative love letter to Black people. BREATHE reimagines public safety, community care, and how we spend money as a society. It invests in new, non-punitive, and non-carceral approaches to community safety that would incentivize states to shrink their criminal-legal systems and center the protection of Black lives—including Black mothers, Black trans people, and Black womxn.[58]

The Impact Report gave this ominous rationale for creating the BLM PAC:

> Now, we know that more politicians, more bills and more laws are not the answer in its entirety. But we do believe in one thing: white supremacy is currently sanctioned by our systems and even some of our elected officials. By engaging directly with our different political systems—by directly challenging them— we want to communicate and affirm that white supremacy has no space in the ways we govern, cooperate, and live. Remember: this is only one piece of our movement tactics.[59]

This is important, especially in the context that, to BML, "white supremacy" is something much more holistic about American society than what average people think when they hear "white supremacy."

The report highlighted how the BLM PAC went after former presidential candidate Pete Buttigieg, whom it offered as a cautionary tale for those who don't follow BLM dictates. Buttigieg, it said, "took the Black vote for granted when he began his presidential campaign. His grave miscalculation cost him the nomination and provided a platform for BLM-South Bend to educate the public about how he perpetuated and was complicit in structural injustices against Black people."[60]

BLM even has a foreign policy, supporting the BDS (Boycott, Divestment, Sanctions) movement against Israel, which Cullors refers to as "the new South Africa."[61] As we will see in chapter 7, an entire arm of BLM is now devoted to pushing curriculum for our children. BLM, lastly, also has an unmatched cultural cachet. The Impact Report said that

> BLM partnered with Hamilton's rapid-response and action team, composed of cast members across the country. They created instructional videos on mail-in ballots for a collection of states. These videos were shared on social media and lived on our Election Center/What Matters 2020 webpage, which was visited by 5 million people.

In addition, "BLM partnered with Sprite to create and launch the Create Your Future campaign. This campaign encouraged young voters to participate in the 2020 election."[62]

A curious thing about all these powerful entities is that both M4BL and the BLM GNF, as well as their multifarious skeins of chapters and affiliates, are officially sponsored projects of other organizations. This arrangement allows these two empires—which are succeeding beyond Angela Davis's wildest dreams at radically changing our way of life by dismantling the organizing principles of this society—to escape scrutiny, assuming anyone in mass media ever dared contemplate mere objective reporting about them. The relationship between BLM and its sponsors is the subject of the next chapter.

CHAPTER 5

FOLLOW THE MONEY

The intricate and shadowy network of revolutionary outfits and individuals described in the previous chapter, along with the ideologically driven mayhem they cause, draws its financial oxygen from the unsuspecting and the suspect alike. These organizations are funded by individual Americans who seek freedom and equality; corporations that depend on capitalism to survive; and deep-pocketed philanthropic foundations that receive their funding from such corporations, from individual capitalists, or from inherited endowments left by capitalists long dead. The irony of people and entities handing gobs of money to organizations that seek to dismantle their way of life, including their freedom to make such money, has been noted often. The *SF Weekly* profile cited earlier put it succinctly in describing how foundations continued to support Alicia Garza's socialist organization SOUL, which is headquartered in an Oakland warehouse known as Mandela Village.

> A score of gold-plated, capitalist foundations regularly pump large sums of money into Mandela Village, even though SOUL

promotes anti-capitalist ideas—including redistribution of the world's wealth to the poor—that, if made real, would mean the end of private property, not to mention philanthropic foundations.[1]

But some of these foundations and big-pocketed donors behind BLM would not mind that; some of the foundations are led by deeply committed Marxists with past or present associations with regimes in Beijing, Caracas, Havana, and Managua, as this chapter will show.

As we have seen, the individual Americans who fund BLM, especially those who did so out of an outpouring of grief over the death of George Floyd in 2020 and not on a regular basis, have not been told by the mass media that there is a political project at hand. Many of the sources for this book, for those who will bother to look at the footnotes, come from recondite Marxist publications and websites. They are there for *New York Times* and *Washington Post* reporters to quote, but they refuse to do so, leaving ordinary Americans, who are too busy to spend their day researching the FRSO, in the dark. That they fund BLM is understandable, if regrettable.

The story of why the men and women who run the philanthropic foundations or corporations give gobs of money to BLM is more complicated. That American companies are increasingly becoming woke is by now an evident fact, but outside the remit of this book. Suffice it to say here that the C-suite is inhabited by Ivy League graduates who have been force-fed critical race theory. As Yuval Levin put it in his 2020 book, *A Time to Build*, "Talk to anyone in management in an elite, white collar company and you'll hear stories of the younger employees expecting the company to enforce a code of political correctness utterly unfamiliar to any world of work until the last few years."[2] The left has also been very good at co-opting the human resources professional organizations, and HR has become a corporate beachhead for radical causes.

As for the foundations, many of them—perhaps most—fall into the hands of leftist administrators after a time, even when they were founded by such capitalists as Henry Ford, Andrew Carnegie, and John D. Rockefeller. This is known as "O'Sullivan's Law," after Margaret Thatcher's aide John O'Sullivan, who famously stated that any organization that is not explicitly conservative will eventually drift into the arms of the left. In other instances, as is the case with the Tides Foundation, NoVo Foundation (a social justice foundation set up by Peter Buffett, the son of Warren Buffett), and George Soros's Open Society Foundations, they were founded from the start by individuals with a deep ideological commitment to the breakup of the system that permitted them to flourish. Why this is the case is also well outside the remit of this book, and more in the field of psychology, if not psychiatry.

It remains important, however, to understand to the best of our ability who gives what to whom, even if we can't always explain why. We should be clear that even the "who" and the "how much" can remain elusive, given the "fiscally sponsored" relationships that the BLM entities have worked out for themselves, which allow them to hide their financial situations and the uses to which they put their money. BLM GNF is a nonprofit, for example, but it does not enjoy its own tax-exempt status with the IRS. Its fiscal sponsors do, because they are 501(c)(3) organizations. Donors seeking to fund BLM GNF or M4BL give that money to ActBlue, a technology company with 501(c)(3) tax-exempt status that makes its fundraising platform available only to "Democratic candidates and committees, progressive organizations, and nonprofits that share our values."[3] As Robert Stilson of the indispensable Capital Research Center explains, "Technically there are three ActBlue nonprofits: 1) ActBlue; 2) ActBlue Civics; and 3) ActBlue Charities. Each one handles donations for a different type of tax status. M4BL and BLM GNF use ActBlue Charities, which is the 501(c)(3)."[4] ActBlue then gives the money to a fiscal sponsor that also has a 501(c)(3) status, minus a 3.95 percent processing fee. The sponsor then doles out the cash to the BLM entities.

Shining a light on what we can thus allows us, at the very least, to hold accountable those who, knowingly or not, are funding entities that seek to destroy a system based on free people, free minds, and free markets.

INDIVIDUALS

Individual donations remained the most opaque until BLM GNF published its 2020 Impact Report in March 2021. The first concrete figure we have appeared in an Associated Press story from June 17, 2020, which said that the "Foundation told AP" (meaning BLM GNF) that in the twenty-three days since the death of George Floyd it had already received 1.1 million individual gifts averaging $33, so more than $36 million.[5] This amounted to almost ten times the $3.4 million in net assets that BLM GNF's then-financial sponsor, Thousand Currents, reported on its 2019 financial statements that it had reserved for BLM.[6] In the 2020 Impact Report published in March 2021, BLM GNF revealed that 2020 had indeed produced a boom. The organization claimed that "across our entities and partners, we have raised just over $90 million in one year, 2020. Of these donations, the average donation via our main fundraising platform was $30.64 and more than 10% of donations were recurring."[7]

Cullors said that, of the $90 million, BLM GNF had given $21.7 million to thirty organizations, twenty-three of which are "led by Black LGBTQIA folks and/or directly serve these communities." These were the Okra Project; TGI Justice Project; T.A.K.E. Birmingham; Trans United; Audre Lorde Project—TransJustice; BreakOUT; Black Trans Circles; BLMP; Solutions Not Punishment Coalition; Marsha P. Johnson Institute; The Transgender

District; Black Trans Travel Fund; For The Gworls; House of GG; Highlander Center; BOLD; Eat Chicago; PANA; Africans Rising; Haitian Bridge Alliance; Trans Justice Funding Project; Trans Housing Coalition—Homeless Black Trans Women Fund; Black Trans Media; House of Pentacles; House of TULIP; Black Trans Femmes in the Arts; Brave Space Alliance; Black Visions Collective; Brooklyn Boihood; and BYP100.

CORPORATIONS

Big business can reveal to the world that it is sufficiently woke in many ways. In January 2021, for example, Coca-Cola stated that its diversity efforts were not working, so it decided to double down. Henceforth, announced the soft-drink giant, new law firms working with Coca-Cola would have to meet stringent new diversity guidelines by providing diversity data and supplying the names of two "diverse" attorneys ready to work on Coca-Cola–related business. For their part, in 2020, Amazon and Microsoft announced they would stop selling facial recognition technology to law enforcement. As 2020 was ending, Nasdaq announced it would ask the Securities and Exchange Commission to approve a corporate governance rule that would require companies listed on the exchange to appoint directors from marginalized communities to their boards. My Heritage colleague David Burton and I denounced the rule as "discriminatory and immoral."[8] Even TikTok, based in the world's biggest repressive state, China, issued a statement on June 1 saying it would make attempts to become more inclusive to black users.

Or, corporations can deviate part of their profits away from owners and donate it to racial causes. Many corporations have done this, and in this case it is best to capture a part of the money that has gone directly to BLM GNF. The long list includes some of the best-known names in big business. One list compiled by Fred Lucas of *The Daily Signal* includes Amazon, Gatorade, Microsoft, Glossier, Airbnb, 23andMe, Unilever, Bungie, Nabisco, Dropbox, Fitbit, Devolver Digital, and Tinder.[9] A full list will not be known unless the Tides Center, BLM GNF's new fiscal sponsor since July 2020, makes its financial statements available. But corporate giving is sure to make up a good amount of the $1.6 billion in funds that BLM organizations reported in December as received since the death of George Floyd. Other lists reveal donations to "BLM," or to some of its partner organizations such as Color of Change, from Silicon Valley companies such as Cisco Systems, Intel, Intuit, Lending Tree, Bravado, DoorDash, Patreon, Skillshare, Loopio, Ubisoft, HelloFresh, Hinge, Guru, InVision, and Carta.[10]

In reality, the majority of the reports of corporate donations going directly to BLM or various members of its octopus-like network come from before the time that I and others started to write about the Marxist nature of the BLM organizations and leaders in July and August. Despite the best efforts by the media to cover *for*, rather than just cover, BLM, the truth about the nature of BLM and the chaos they were engendering seemed to be getting through. By August, companies from Pepsi to Bank of America to Walmart were telling the press that they were *not* donating to BLM organizations.[11] Polling companies, including Pew and Politico/Morning Consult, reported in early September a double-digit drop among Americans, led by those who identified as white or Hispanic.[12] My colleague Andrew Olivastro did a little sleuthing around the website of the Business Roundtable, and on September 23 we wrote,

> Travel across the more than 80 links on the page and you see that these major employers are spreading their shareholders' wealth around—and purposefully funneling it far away from the BLM organizations. The list of programs include Apple and

PepsiCo's hiring efforts, AT&T's direct spending with U.S.-owned black suppliers, and Boeing's investment in long-held community partnerships.[13]

Something had to be done. In September 2020, BLM GNF scrubbed from its page its anti-family language, as well as references to the communist term "comrade." The bad publicity BLM was generating also propelled Patrisse Cullors to the helm of the BLM GNF, as the organization began shedding its previous decentralized "we have no leaders" chic. Ironically, as we have seen, Cullors's own bad publicity may have precipitated her departure from leadership as well, in just ten months. The changes of September 2020 led to a change in the relationship between the BLM organizations and their financial sponsors in the philanthropic world.

PHILANTHROPIC FOUNDATIONS

Cullors's announcement came on September 11, when she let the world know that, back in July, she had become the executive director of BLM GNF, which she referred to as "the umbrella organization for our global movement." Cullors admitted that she had faced internal opposition, and indeed outlets such as *The Economist* reported that some in the network thought the move had been undemocratic. "Many close friends and colleagues affirmed that no one was better-prepared for the job," wrote Cullors, adding, however, "but when I stepped forward in response to the call of my community and family, there were other voices to overcome." The statement had all the opaqueness of a Kremlin announcement of a change in leadership, as did the announcement of her downfall in late May 2021.[14]

Oddly, in September 2020, Cullors had made it clear between the lines that the responsibility was henceforth hers:

These voices caused me trepidation initially, as I took up the mantle of our necessary evolution. Even as I reminded myself that Black women in leadership have always faced disproportionate scrutiny, taking on the onus of our successes and failures was a great deal to bear. And while I anticipated much of the pushback and conflict I have faced, I have still had to come to terms, in my own way, with the weight and implications of accepting this amount of responsibility.

Under her, she said, BLM GNF would remain "a fund-raising body, amplifier and action-oriented think tank for black-led organizations." On-the-ground organizing would be left to BLM Grassroots, led by Abdullah, as we have seen.

The September 2020 leadership change put into context something else of import that had happened in July: BLM GNF had gone from being a fiscally sponsored project of Thousand Currents to enjoying the same relationship with the Tides Center, which is affiliated with the Tides Foundation. Both are deep-pocketed funders of the hardest of the hard left, but Tides had a PR advantage: a convicted domestic terrorist and former member of the Weather Underground did not sit on its board of directors as vice chairman.

Susan Rosenberg joined the board of Thousand Currents in 2015, when it was still known as the International Development Exchange, or IDEX. In 2018, by now under its new name, she became vice chairman. As we saw in chapter 3, Rosenberg had been put on the FBI's Most Wanted list for her alleged involvement in JoAnne Chesimard's 1979 daring prison escape, went on the lam, and was eventually arrested in 1984 when she was caught with a great deal of explosives and other armaments. She was sentenced to fifty-eight years in prison, but Bill Clinton cut that short after sixteen years on his last day in office. In her memoir, Rosenberg has excused her behavior variously as "wanting to be loved," or the realization that "political violence" was the only solution, given that legal protests were not changing America. Despite her alleged involvement in a Brinks robbery that left three people dead, she insists that nothing she did was terrorism and has never apologized. In a 1989 interview from prison, Rosenberg said, "one of the things that's clear is that the government is trying to get us to reassess, to apologize, to get us to say we won't ever do anything again—and, for all of us, certainly for myself, I'm not going to say that to the greatest terrorist state in the world."[15]

It is difficult to see what in that resume cries out "philanthropy," unless, that is, it is for a nonprofit that seeks to fund society-upending insurgencies and groom groups such as BLM. This is what IDEX seemed to want to do in 2013, just as BLM was getting off the ground after George Zimmerman's acquittal for the killing of Trayvon Martin. In that year IDEX received a whopping donation of $150,000, and $300,000 was approved for future years, from one single source, the NoVo Foundation, a social-justice philanthropic entity created in 2006 by none other than Warren Buffett's son Peter and his wife, Jennifer. That single donation amounted to three quarters of all the money IDEX had raised in 2012.

According to groundbreaking research by Sean Cooper of Tablet Magazine, in that same year the NoVo Foundation also approved $750,000 for future payments to Garza's National Domestic Workers Alliance (NDWA), which as we know from the previous chapter is identified as an FRSO front group and was the organization that sent Garza to Ferguson in the fateful year of 2014, as sundry communist groups gathered there after Michael Brown's police killing to put organizational and revolutionary meat on the protest movement.[16] NoVo Foundation gifted or approved for future payments the same amount to NDWA in 2014, when it also approved a further $300,000 in gifts or future gifts to IDEX. In 2015—the year Rosenberg joined IDEX's board of directors—NoVo Foundation stopped messing around: it approved gifts and future gifts of $3.72 million to IDEX, $700,000 of which was specifically earmarked for BLM. NDWA meanwhile received $4.5 million in 2015. By September 2016, BLM GNF had formalized its relationship with IDEX, becoming its fiscally sponsored project. IDEX said in a joint statement that it would provide "fiduciary oversight, financial management, and other administrative services to BLM."[17] IDEX would receive grants, tax-deductible donations and gifts on behalf of BLM and, as a 501(c)(3) organization, does not have to reveal the sources. Garza for her part was quoted as saying that BLM was working to end injustice against black people around the world, and "we need to partner with an organization that can support us as we build these connections on a global scale." In 2016, IDEX changed its name to Thousand Currents. That year the NoVo Foundation approved $3.08 million in grants or future grants to Thousand Currents, a further $4.9 million for NDWA, and $300,000 to Tometi's Black Alliance for Just Immigration (BAJI), also in donations or future donations. Between 2017 and 2018, NoVo Foundation approved 12.9 million in present or future gifts for Thousand Currents, which had installed Rosenberg as vice chair of the board.

Will the transfer of the fiscal sponsorship to Tides weaken the link between BLM GNF and the Buffett family? On the contrary. Tablet revealed an incredible relationship between Tides and NoVo. It turns out that, according to NoVo's 2018 990 forms, the NoVo Foundation gave Tides more than one hundred separate donations worth the whopping amount of $121 million in gifts or future gifts.[18]

As Tablet Magazine's Cooper wrote,

> Shuttling Black Lives Matter over to the Tides Network does more than shield Thousand Currents from intense inquiry. It allows BLM to join a massive repository of projects that can be administered

behind extra layers of protection in the form of donor-advised funds, which allow donors to anonymously fund projects while still reaping tax benefits, and multiple organizational shells which include the Tides Network, Tides Center, Tides Foundation, and a slew of other incorporated nonprofit shell organizations which are housed within a single institutional silo. There, they are overseen by a small band of executives who operate with virtually no outside scrutiny—and can coordinate and leverage the political, social, and financial opportunities that these projects create for whatever forms of gain their donors decide to prioritize.

Tides itself has a long, lefty pedigree. It was founded with money from the R. J. Reynolds Tobacco Company in 1976 by Drummond Pike, a 1960s activist. Today it receives funding from a bevy of leftist funders, including the Annie E. Casey Foundation, the many foundations controlled by billionaire George Soros and his family, the Carnegie Corporation of New York, and a bunch of different Rockefeller foundations. Tides then disburses these funds not just to BLM but also the ACLU, *Democracy Now!*, and so on.[19]

The money from the foundations controlled by the Soros family alone could keep Tides, and others like it, in business for years. In July 2020, George Soros's Open Society Foundations announced a $220 million commitment to what it termed social justice groups. Patrick Gaspard, the president, told an interviewer, "Now is the moment we've been investing in for the last 25 years." Gaspard added that "it's time to double down. And we understood we can place a bet on these activists—Black and white—who see this as a moment of not just incrementalism, but whole-scale reform... we need these moments to be sustained."[20]

The Thousand Currents/Tides Foundation/NoVo axis is hardly the only philanthropic source of funds to all the multifarious outfits that make up BLM. In 2016, the Ford Foundation announced, for example, that it had partnered with Borealis Philanthropy, the Movement Strategy Center, and Benedict Consulting to found the Black-Led Movement Fund (BLMF). The BLMF would "make six-year investments in the organizations and networks that compose the Movement for Black Lives," said Ford in its statement.[21] The number that the Ford Foundation proposed to give to M4BL—which, lest we forget, is so openly committed to ending capitalism that it doesn't bother to scrub its website—was so gargantuan that the Ford Foundation appears to have scrubbed the sum from its own website. It can still be found at such publications as *Fortune*. Here's what the announcement originally said: "The BLMF's strategy is supported by two other components: the first is the Blackprint Strategy, a collaborative process underway to identify movement needs and resource priorities to bring $100 million in new resources to the Movement for Black Lives."[22]

Despite this success with the Ford Foundation, M4BL has had trouble raising money. "For years, many foundations have considered it to be too radical," wrote Julia Travers for Inside Philanthropy. Then in 2020, M4BL nearly doubled the previous year's fundraising levels and began to attract "more attention from institutional grant-makers." Travers writes that on June 8 "a group of leaders from the nonprofit and funding worlds held a call on philanthropy's role.... Close to 700 people participated, including many members of M4BL. The organizers called on philanthropy to provide the racial justice network with $50 million this year. In 2019, M4BL raised $2.7 million."[23] By the time Travers wrote her profile in July 2020, M4BL had already raised $5 million.

Yet some skittishness persisted, so M4BL felt it had to do something. Sometime around Groundhog Day 2021, M4BL suddenly changed fiscal sponsors. Whereas until then M4BL had been sponsored by the far-left Alliance for Global Justice (AfGJ), the new sponsors were the quieter Common Counsel Foundation. The reason for the change was never explained. But just as we can speculate that BLM GNF preferred a sponsorship by Tides, which however far-left it may be, at least did not have a convicted domestic terrorist on its board, we can also assume that AfGJ's association with some of the worst communist regimes on earth may have finally been too much for potential donors. Given AfGJ's support for the Maduro government in Caracas and that AfGJ staff defends the Cuban and North Korean regimes, some philanthropists might have been forgiven for wondering if those were the models that M4BL wanted for the United States.[24]

M4BL'S SPONSORS

The history of M4BL's fiscal sponsors does in fact well illustrate its communist roots and continued proclivities. AfGJ started life as the Nicaragua Network and is the creation of the bevy of severely misguided American youth who flocked to Nicaragua in the 1980s to help the Marxist Sandinista movement that in 1979 overthrew the U.S.-backed dictator Anastasio Somoza. While some of these so-called "Sandalistas" no doubt believed they were helping former peasants build a better life, many others must have understood they were propping up an attempt by Moscow and Havana to take over Central America. When the Nicaraguan people were given the chance to vote in 1990 and threw out their Marxist overlords, the Sandinistas, the staff of the Nicaragua Network remembered the marching orders they had been given. As the AfGJ "Our History" page candidly puts it:

> Sandinistas always told the Nicaragua Network, "What you can do to most help us is to change your own government." We took that instruction to heart in 1990 when the Sandinistas lost an election due to overwhelming US interference and funding as

well as the Nicaraguan peoples' exhaustion from nine years of the US-sponsored Contra terrorist war.[25]

The Sandalistas did exactly that and returned home to begin a campaign to transform the United States itself. In the 1990s, the Nicaragua Network, relocated to Washington DC, became involved in all manner of leftist activism, including the preparation of the 1999 World Trade Organization riots in Seattle that gave so much impetus to today's hard left movements (the ones Lisa Fithian had a hand in organizing, as we saw in the previous chapter). Given its new emphasis, sometime in 1998, the Nicaragua Network officially changed its name to the Alliance for Global Justice. "We incorporated under the new name and when we received IRS designation as a tax-exempt, nonprofit, the Nicaragua Network gave up its own legal existence and transferred its assets to AfGJ, becoming a project of the Alliance," says the alliance.[26]

The AfGJ, too, has tried in 2021 to conceal its intentions. While it used to state plainly on its website that it was "anti-capitalist," it now uses thirteen words to say the same thing: "We stand in favor of community-based development versus corporate globalization and privatization." AfGJ remains open, however, about also opposing America's representative democracy model. "We work for participatory democracy and against false democratic forms that reinforce inequality and undermine communities," says their "Our Mission" page. And despite its newfound work, AfGJ still retains some of its former Sandalista flavor. According to David Hogberg of the Capital Research Center, a Washington DC think tank that closely follows funders in the leftist universe, one of the members of AfGJ's board of directors, Katherine Hoyt, worked for the Sandinista government and has had a long involvement with communist movements in that country and in Chile. "When the Sandinistas advanced against the Somoza government in 1979, she and her husband permitted the Sandinista guerrillas to use her house. At one point, according to Hoyt, the guerillas stockpiled Molotov cocktails in her dining room," writes Hogberg.[27]

AfGJ's sponsorship of M4BL for many years means it remained faithful to the original marching orders it received from the Sandinistas: to transform the United States. And don't expect M4BL to change its stripes. Charles Long, M4BL's resource coordinator since 2016, sounded resolute in an interview he had with Travers. He said M4BL had around forty "deeply intelligent black leaders" who did not make decisions lightly. Many people may want to pick and choose from M4BL's policy platform, "take just a 'pinch,'" he said, but "the only reason you would think that way is because you believe that you have a superior solution, and I can only chalk that up to anti-Blackness and white supremacist thought."[28]

It is not as if the new backers are the Chamber of Commerce. The Common Counsel Foundation is indeed more sedate, explaining that its goal is to "expand philanthropic resources for progressive social movements." It sponsors three other progressive groups and receives funds from the Ford Foundation, the James Irvine Foundation, and the California Endowment. Dig into its website, however, and it soon emerges that on its board sits one Alex Tom, and that among its donations recipients figures the Chinese Progressive Association of San Francisco. This brings us to yet another sponsorship relationship that ties members of the BLM universe to past radical causes.

Alex Tom is a longtime friend and ideological ally of Alicia Garza and has long been associated with the CPA San Francisco, acting as its executive director at one point. In September 2020, I discovered that the CPA San Francisco had become financial sponsors of a BLM-related venture, the Black Futures Lab, a mobilization and advocacy group founded and run by Alicia Garza.

The CPA was founded in San Francisco in 1972 by operatives of the Maoist, pro-Chinese Communist Party militant group I Wor

Kuen. From the start, the CPA San Francisco was doing work on behalf of Maoist China. One of its founders, Fay Wong, explained that "China was an inspiration to us, many of us were from China and those [of] us who were not just found what China was able to accomplish, with the revolution, was very inspiring."[29] China at that time, we should recall, was in the midst of the destructive Cultural Revolution, a time when students mobilized as Red Guards terrorized the population in a campaign to rid society of the "Four Olds"—old ideas, customs, culture, and habits of mind—and submitted individual Chinese to struggle sessions and forced "self-criticisms." It is important to bear this in mind, not just to pause and wonder what exactly about China's revolution could inspire Wong and the other CPA founders, because the comparisons between the Cultural Revolution and our present BLM moment are stark.

A few years after the founding of CPA San Francisco, I Wor Kuen operatives also set up CPAs in Boston and New York. These CPAs are registered separately and are run independently, but interact with each other in a host of other hard-left outfits, such as Seeding Change, Right to the City, and LeftRoots, with which Garza and Cullors are also associated. The three CPAs have also collaborated in publications of the League for Revolutionary Struggle, a Marxist-Leninist organization that I Wor Kuen created by uniting with other communist groups from 1978 to 1990.[30] Lydia Lowe and Pam Tau Lee, cofounders of the Boston and San Francisco groups, respectively, are both identified by the old Soviet term of "cadre" at LeftRoots. They coauthored a paper that later served as the "starting point" for another document that strategized about fomenting revolution.[31]

The CPAs are also tightly knit with FRSO (the communist organization referenced in the last chapter, which remains staunchly Maoist and praises the government of Xi Jinping) and other groups that BLM founders have led. Michelle Foy of CPA

San Francisco is, for example, a member of the FRSO and is on the board of Causa Justa/Just Cause, with which Garza is also associated.[32]

Importantly, the CPAs were on the ground in Ferguson in late 2014 when the then-still fledgling BLM movement gathered with Marxists from around the country to organize itself. In December 2014, days after the Ferguson grand jury declined to charge the killer of Michael Brown on November 24, Cullors and Garza participated in a "national call" with Seeding Change, the far-left group created by CPA San Francisco and of which both the San Francisco and Boston CPA are members. Following that, Seeding Change posted messages calling for solidarity with BLM action. "From San Francisco/Bay Area, Los Angeles to Madison, New York, Philadelphia, Boston, Providence and DC, Asian Americans have been showing up and busting up the 'model minority,' which is used to maintain white supremacy, anti-blackness and capitalism," it said.[33] Another statement urged all Asian Americans to submit to BLM's orders: "It is important for Asian American communities to show up for Black Lives and take the lead from Black communities."[34]

And again in 2020, the CPAs were there to call on their members to support BLM and protest. Not four days after George Floyd's death, the San Francisco, Boston, and New York CPAs were among the signatories of a call for support for BLM, warning Chinese Americans to reject "assimilation into whiteness." It added that "In this painful moment, we ask our Asian communities to choose our shared liberation. Let us also commit to the ongoing work of addressing the anti-Blackness in our own communities and choose to fight for Black lives the way we would our own."[35]

In those heady days of Ferguson, the Common Counsel Foundation, the new fiscal sponsor of M4BL, went through a major reorganization and brought Alex Tom onto its board. It identified him in 2015 as executive director of the CPA San Francisco and was effusive about his ability to organize members of the "Asian American and Pacific Islanders" category. "Alex has played a leadership role in building CPA's service, organizing, and civic engagement programs. In this role, Alex helped launch CPA's new project, Seeding Change, a center for Asian American Movement Building that is building a national pipeline for the next generation of AAPI organizers," it said.[36]

In fact, it was while he was executive director of CPA San Francisco in 2012 that Tom founded the China Education and Exposure Program (CEEP), which was used to deepen ties between American leftists and China. "We built relationships with people in the Party," Tom said in 2020.[37]

(As an incidental aside, for exposing all this in late 2020, I came under a slew of criticism in the media, including the *New York Times* and *Axios*, because I had failed to mention in my original op-ed that the CPA San Francisco and the CPA Boston were independently chartered and run. All of my explanations about their common roots in I Wor Kuen and their joint efforts, and my correction of the record by amending the original post, went for naught. All of which again proves the point not only that the media refuse to report the evident and deep associations of the BLM leaders with Maoism, Marxism, Leninism, Sandinistas, and Castroism, but also that journalists will hound anyone who does. In fact, the *New York Times* report said that "There's no indication that today's Black Lives Matter movement has any formal link to Marxism, or to the Chinese Communist Party.")

CONCLUSION

By 1977, Henry Ford II, the founder's grandson, resigned in disgust as a trustee of the Ford Foundation. He released a letter that read, the foundation is a creature of capitalism—a statement that, I'm sure, would be shocking to many professional staff in the field of philanthropy. It is hard to discern recognition of this fact in anything the foundation does.... I'm just suggesting to the trustees and the staff that the system that makes the foundation possible very probably is worth preserving.[38]

Indeed, this sordid tale of ideological commitment by the fiscal backers of the BLM universe to all the communist "isms" under the sun—and even past instances of domestic terrorism in the name of socialist revolution—should prompt at least some soul-searching by individuals, corporations, and foundations that give to BLM because they want societal fairness. After the months of mayhem the country experienced in 2020, the year of "racial reckoning" so celebrated by the press, the forces described in this chapter have found a vehicle to carry out the Sandinistas' orders to change American society.

Few dare to push against BLM. Even the Trump administration, for all its bluster, refrained. It is easy to see why. The slew of "fact checks" and questions, "do black lives not matter to you, Mr. President?," would be daunting to face. When Vice President Mike Pence did try, Travers wrote, for example,

The movement is still regularly attacked by some on the right. In late June, Vice President Mike Pence said its leaders have a "radical-left agenda" and falsely claimed they support calls to violence. This was the same day Trump tweeted a video wherein a supporter chanted "white power," which he deleted a few hours later.[39]

There were other additional obstacles to surveying BLM, and so most conservative leaders instead focused their fire on Antifa—criticizing it became their "safe space." The following chapter will thus focus on one of these obstacles, erected by the Congressional Black Caucus, and why Antifa (also funded by former Weathermen) became the easier target, even though its societal-changing prowess pales in comparison to that of BLM.

CHAPTER 6

HOW ANTIFA BECAME THE SAFE SPACE

The reflexive view of many progressives that the threat to society from right-wing extremists is much greater than the left-wing version was weaponized this past decade to prevent a feeble attempt by the FBI to keep track of militants who were using the plight of blacks to wreak havoc on the American way of life. The Congressional Black Caucus, officially nonpartisan but in effect a branch of the Democratic Party and which includes former Black Panther Bobby Rush, went to war with the FBI to thwart the effort. Leading the fight was the Brennan Center for Justice, a liberal judicial activist organization. They both received the support of a compliant media. It would not take long for FBI Director Christopher Wray to throw in the towel. The left has been so successful in comparing recent law enforcement attempts to target militants to J. Edgar Hoover's investigations in the 1960s that the bureau now mechanically acknowledges that it shies away from probing "constitutionally protected" activities even if they could reasonably be expected to result in violence.

The lesson for political leaders concerned about growing unrest in 2020 was obvious: if you want to rail against violence, concentrate on an easy target that is both nihilistically violent and visibly mostly white, the anarchist group Antifa. This lawless, decentralized entity became the "safe space" for those who did not want to explain that yes, they believed deeply that black lives very much matter, they just did not agree with the political agenda of the organizations that bear that name. Just as with the louts who invaded the Capitol on January 6, 2021, however, Antifa does not have any of the power to change society that BLM enjoys. But even then, when law enforcement did arrest Antifa thugs, rogue prosecutors tossed their cases without filing charges.

THE FBI

The Federal Bureau of Investigation has been used from its start to track potential threats to the American way of life, from the left or the right. As we saw in chapter 1, FBI founder and long-term director J. Edgar Hoover persecuted Marcus Garvey in the 1920s, even when he had no grounds, and eventually had him arrested when he did find them. Later, in the 1960s, the FBI also kept tabs not just on violent leaders such as Malcolm X and Stokely Carmichael but also on the peaceful Martin Luther King, Jr. This history is complex: yes, the bureau did in many ways save America from communist infiltration, but, yes, it also trampled on the First Amendment–protected activity of a leader who was peacefully pursuing the acceptance in society that blacks had been denied for centuries. We must bear in mind, too, that Attorney General Robert Kennedy, a paladin of liberals, signed off on FBI wiretaps in the early 1960s. The FBI later also acted at the direction of President Johnson, the architect of the liberal Great Society programs that in many ways changed the face of America.

There is also the fact that the FBI's extensive electronic surveillance of King, authorized by Attorney General Kennedy in

1962, took place because a close associate of King's, Stanley Levison, had been a member of the Communist Party USA. Levison quit the party in 1957, a year after he met King, raising further suspicions. It was, according to King biographer David Garrow, "without a doubt King's closest friendship with a white person." The FBI suspected that Levison was a Soviet agent, and he did meet in New York with a top KGB operative several times. Both Kennedys asked King to separate himself from Levison, who was twenty years King's senior and had become very influential, but to no avail. That doesn't mean that King was a communist. Garrow also points out what King said to the African American activist (and former communist) Bayard Rustin about wanting to speak his mind about communism in a speech to SNCC in a 1965 speech: "There are things I wanted to say renouncing Communism in theory but they would not go along with it. We wanted to say that it was an alien philosophy contrary to us but they wouldn't go along with it."[1]

Decades later, the Bureau recognized the potential that Michael Brown's killing on August 9, 2014, had for turning the national protest movement violent. Days before the November 24 announcement of the decision not to prosecute the police officer who killed Brown, the FBI circulated a memo to police departments warning of the "Potential Criminal Reactions to Missouri Grand Jury Announcement." As the FBI described it three years later in a report that the media, the Brennan Center, and the Congressional Black Caucus seized upon to attack law enforcement, the November FBI memo "assessed the announcement of the grand jury's decision in the shooting death of Michael Brown in Ferguson would likely be exploited by some individuals to justify threats and attacks against law enforcement and critical infrastructure."[2]

It is important to remember that Ferguson had suffered almost daily riots and looting since Brown's death in August, and that after the November 24 announcement, Brown's stepfather did indeed shout to a crowd of protesters outside a police station, "Burn this Bitch Down!" Protests and riots followed the grand jury's decision, not only in Ferguson but also nationwide. The damage overnight in Ferguson alone was immense. The day after the grand jury's announcement, the *New York Times* reported that, according to Ferguson police, "there had been 21 fires in and around Ferguson, at least 150 gunshots and damage to 10 police cruisers. At times, officials said, firefighters had to retreat from battling fires because of gunfire and objects being thrown all around."[3]

It is hard to overstate, too, the importance of Ferguson for the political transformation that convulses America to this day. Lest we forget, Garza, Cullors, and Marxists from across the country had converged in the mostly black St. Louis suburb on October 10 for a "Weekend of Resistance" to organize a nation-wide movement with revolutionary demands that expanded well beyond police reform. And the FBI was certainly not wrong about the potential for mayhem. Travis Campbell of the University of Massachusetts tracked more than 1,600 BLM protests nationwide between 2014 and 2019 and published the results on May 13, 2021. Campbell found that "civilian homicides increased by 10% following protests."[4] Vox, by no means a conservative outlet, put the impact this way: "That means that, from 2014 to 2019, there were somewhere between 1,000 and 6,000 more homicides than would have been expected if places with protests were on the same trend as places that did not have protests."[5]

Yet nobody was keeping tabs on this. Certainly not the media, and not our government, either. The days of J. Edgar Hoover were well and truly gone, no matter how loudly leftist critics bellowed about FBI investigations. In 2014 the head of the FBI was James Comey, who made a point of keeping a copy of the letter authorizing Martin Luther King's wiretaps on his desk, to remind himself of what he considered to be an inglorious past. The attorney general was Eric Holder, no Bobby Kennedy (who, however liberal he was, approached communism seriously), and the president was Barack Obama, also no LBJ.

It was in November 2014, apparently, that the FBI began to track at least some BLM activists, using open-source information such as social media postings. According to reporting by the progressive site *The Intercept*, an FBI report four days before the grand jury's announcement warned that some one hundred protesters, which the *Intercept* identified as members of Black Lives Matter, were planning to travel from New York to Ferguson to rally at a Monsanto plant. The activists had already raised $10,000 for bond money and $6,000 for "direct action devices (unknown what those are at this time)."[6] Though many publications have been involved in the effort to expose today's FBI as some sort of Hooverian redoubt, the *Intercept* has led the chronicling, and criticism, of the FBI activity, relying sometimes on outfits like Color of Change, the M4BL partner that, as we saw in chapter 4, boasts of getting Pat Buchanan and Bill O'Reilly fired. The FBI's reports quoted by the *Intercept*, for example, had been obtained by Color of Change following a Freedom of Information Act request in 2018.[7] *The Intercept* has also benefited from many FBI leaks throughout the years, and nearly always relied on Michael German of the Brennan Center, a former FBI agent.

Michael German left the FBI in 2004, embittered about how the bureau had dragged its feet investigating his accusations that an agent in a 2002 undercover terrorism investigation, close on the heels of 9/11, had recorded a telephone conversation without following proper procedure. In German's view, that had violated the civil rights of the individual being investigated. After a year and a half of what he considered inaction, German took his complaint outside the FBI, to the Senate Judiciary Committee. He clearly sees himself as a hero and does not hide that he aids those inside who disagree with the bureau's actions. "I resigned. I joined the American Civil Liberties Union in Washington and have since assisted many intelligence community whistleblowers at all stages of the process, from deciding whether to make a complaint, to seeking new employment after being unfairly fired," he wrote in the *Washington Post* in 2019.[8] A fawning media has always given him a platform, either as an op-ed writer or as a source.

Quite understandably, given the violence and other criminal activity the whole country had experienced since August, the FBI felt it had to act after Ferguson sparked nationwide unrest. On November 25, the Bureau kept tabs on a parked car in Ferguson—a city that was still literally burning after the decision not to indict Brown's killer the day before—that a "confidential human source" had identified as suspicious.[9] Another redacted email chain reported by the *Intercept* revealed other surveillance.[10] A month later, the FBI's Joint Terrorism Task Force was deployed to track a BLM protest planned for the Mall of America in Minneapolis, Minnesota, according to *Intercept* reporting by Lee Fang.[11] Following the killing of five police officers by a protester at a Black Lives Matter rally in Dallas in 2016, the bureau justifiably also started warning police and field agents that BLM events could turn violent or even deadly.

It also emerged in 2016 that the FBI had contacted several BLM activists to find out if they planned to attend the political conventions of both parties in the summer of that election year, particularly the GOP convention. Several media reports said agents telephoned Samuel Sinyangwe and Johnetta Elzie, cofounders of Campaign Zero (a BLM outfit that tries to limit police use of force), and had visited the home of a third cofounder, DeRay Mckesson. Mckesson attended a meeting with President Obama at the White House later that year and demanded that he instruct the bureau to stop visiting the homes of activists. Sinyangwe told Britain's *Independent* newspaper that the FBI should be focusing on the threat of terrorism by "white supremacists."[12]

Comey appeared to be genuinely wrestling for how to find the right balance. In a Georgetown University speech back in February 2015, as Ferguson continued to smolder, Comey reflected on the deaths of Brown and Eric Garner, another black man killed by police in July, and two New York City cops killed by a man upset about the perception of police brutality. Comey said that

> with the death of Michael Brown in Ferguson, the death of Eric Garner in Staten Island, the ongoing protests throughout the country, and the assassinations of NYPD Officers Wenjian Liu and Rafael Ramos, we are at a crossroads. As a society, we can choose to live our everyday lives, raising our families and going to work, hoping that someone, somewhere, will do something to ease the tension—to smooth over the conflict.

Comey told his audience that he was trying to figure out how to reform police departments, but also spoke a truth not many dare repeat today:

> Police officers on patrol in our nation's cities often work in environments where a hugely disproportionate percentage of street crime is committed by young men of color. Something happens to people of good will working in that environment. After years of police work, officers often can't help but be influenced by the cynicism they feel.[13]

Throughout this effort, the FBI had been nothing if not fastidious about reminding its agents and police officers that First Amendment–protected speech and activity was not to be interfered with. A July 2016 report reminded agents that

> The FBI assesses that violence may occur at Black Lives Matter protests against participants, bystanders or law enforcement. Black Lives Matter protests are protected First Amendment activity, and the FBI may not collect or monitor the exercise of First Amendment protected activity unless for an authorized law enforcement purpose.... In the event no violent reaction occurs, FBI policy and federal law dictates that no further record be made of the protected activity.[14]

To Al Jazeera, which reported on surveillance actions, this was, however, nothing but proof of how the "FBI may use specific language to justify data collection and monitoring, specifically in the case of Black Lives Matter." The Al Jazeera dispatch gave the standard American media mom-and-apple-pie description. "Black Lives Matter (BLM), which started as a response to US police killings of unarmed black individuals in 2014, has grown into a movement fighting to end systemic violence against black people," it said.[15]

The Al Jazeera article, just as all the *Intercept* stories cited here, quoted the Brennan Center's Michael German, who is either a one-man quote machine or the source or instigator for all these articles. "Clearly it's inappropriate to be using the Joint Terrorism Task Force to monitor activists [and] the use of a CHS [confidential human source] seems extremely inappropriate. The fact that they're spending resources in this manner reflects poor leadership and is something that they should really take a hard look at," German told Lee Fang in 2015. To Al Jazeera's Sweta Vohra in 2017, German said that the warnings of copycat attacks after the Dallas shooting of eleven, resulting in five deaths, constituted the "blending of activities" of protesters and "someone they [the FBI] acknowledge is a lone actor [which] can be misleading in police documents." To Fang's *Intercept* colleagues George

Joseph and Murtaza Hussain, German said in 2018, "This is clearly just tracking First Amendment activity and keeping this activity in an intelligence database. Even if you made the argument that it is about a propensity for violence, why isn't there a discussion of that propensity? Instead, they are discussing bond money, not detailing a criminal predicate or even a possibility of violence."

THE FBI REPORT

In August 2017, the FBI finally issued an intelligence report meant only for official use on the attacks law enforcement could expect. It never mentioned BLM in any form, but had a new term, "Black Identity Extremists." The awkward new label, one clearly meant not to explicitly finger BLM, plus the fact that the FBI unwittingly suffered from incredibly poor timing, allowed critics to pounce on it once the secret report was duly leaked to the press, as it was two months later to the online magazine *Foreign Policy*. The bad timing came from the fact that the report was published on August 3, nine days before a highly publicized right-wing protest in Charlottesville, Virginia, where a white nationalist killed a counterprotester.

The secret report by the FBI's Domestic Terrorism Analysis Unit was straightforward and correctly pointed to Ferguson as a catalyzing moment. The executive summary read:

> The FBI assesses it is very likely Black Identity Extremist (BIE) perceptions of police brutality against African Americans spurred an increase in premeditated, retaliatory lethal violence against law enforcement and will very likely serve as justification for such violence. The FBI assesses it is very likely this increase began following the 9 August 2014 shooting of Michael Brown in Ferguson, Missouri, and the subsequent Grand Jury November

2014 declination to indict the police officers involved. The FBI assesses it is very likely incidents of alleged police abuse against African Americans since then have continued to feed the resurgence in ideologically motivated, violent criminal activity within the BIE movement. The FBI assesses it is very likely some BIEs are influenced by a mix of anti-authoritarian, Moorish sovereign citizen ideology, and BIE ideology. The FBI has high confidence in these assessments.[16]

The leaked report's many references to Ferguson or 2014 as the spark, plus the examples of premeditated acts against police officers it offered, make it clear that BIE was shorthand for BLM, which is not to say that the writers of the report were not spot on. It said, for example, that "BIE perceptions of police brutality against African Americans have become organizing drivers for the BIE movement since 2014." The examples included Micah Johnson's July 7, 2016, shooting of eleven people, five of whom were killed, at a BLM protest in Dallas. BLM leaders quickly said they were not responsible because Johnson was not a member of a BLM chapter or affiliate and had merely participated in the march.[17] Another example was Zale H. Thompson, who attacked four Queens police officers with a hatchet because he was angry about police attacks on blacks. Citing electronic communications, the FBI report made clear how in "In his own writings," Thompson had "advocated for armed struggle against 'the oppressors' and 'mass revolt' against the US social, economic, and political systems, which he perceived to be 'white dominated'"—language that comes straight out the critical race theory mantras that the BLM leaders constantly spew.[18]

The report also included another example of a premeditated attack by a man with links to the New Black Panther Party. The report said that on November 21, three days before the grand jury announcement, a BIE was arrested and eventually convicted for purchasing explosives the subject intended to use in the Ferguson area upon release of the grand jury verdict for the police officer involved in the shooting death of Brown. He previously discussed a desire to kill the white St. Louis County prosecutor and the white Ferguson police chief who were involved in Brown's case, according to FBI information.[19]

That was a reference to Olajuwon Ali Davis, who was arrested in Ferguson along with Brandon Orlando Baldwin, who inexplicably was not mentioned in the report.

A writer for the *Intercept* reported that "According to their nearly identical sentencing plea agreements, Davis and Baldwin, who met during the protests over Brown's killing, discussed acquiring guns and bombs and wanting to organize Ferguson protesters to 'be like an army.' Baldwin told an FBI informant that he wanted to 'build bombs and blow things up'." Baldwin also told the FBI informant, "We are at war, you understand, bro." Baldwin's plea included the allegation that "Davis 'put it out there that he was a terrorist'—a reference that appears to have been scrapped from Davis's own plea. Davis and Baldwin pleaded guilty to explosives and gun charges in June 2015, and in September 2015 they were sentenced to seven-year prison terms."[20] Davis and Baldwin, like many others, were radicalized during the Ferguson BLM protests, in which both participated. Davis soon afterward joined the New Black Panther Party, which the media describes as a peaceful outfit that merely directs traffic during demonstrations, in general "keeping the peace." The Southern Poverty Law Center, a very liberal outfit itself, has other views. It says that "The New Black Panther Party is a virulently racist and antisemitic organization whose leaders have encouraged violence against whites, Jews and law enforcement officers."[21]

The *Intercept* article describing (or rather dismissing) the FBI report and its detailed cases of premeditated violence includes, of course, quotes from Michael German, who was, of course, outraged. "In all of them, there is no connection to any national movement; the cases are not linked in any way. This was literally picking six random events and then imagining a movement around them." The long article where the FBI report was leaked in *Foreign Policy*—not an explicitly liberal publication like the *Intercept* and one that has published my own work—said the FBI's report had come "As white supremacists prepared to descend on Charlottesville, Virginia, in August," and "amid a rancorous debate over whether the Trump administration has downplayed the threat posed by white supremacist groups." It, too, quoted "experts and former government officials" who said "the FBI seemed to be trying to paint disparate groups and individuals as sharing a radical, defined ideology. And in the phrase 'black identity extremist' they hear echoes of the FBI's decades-long targeting of black activists as potential radicals." It, too, quoted Michael German, who said pithily, "it's black people who scare them."[22]

Less than a week after the *Foreign Policy* article appeared, the Congressional Black Caucus fired off a stern letter to the new FBI director, Christopher Wray, reminding him of his bureau's history and demanding that it desist from its work regarding Black Lives Matter. "As you are no doubt aware, the FBI has a troubling history of utilizing its broad investigatory powers to target black citizens. During the 1960s, Director J. Edgar Hoover used the Counter Intelligence Program (COINTELPRO) to surveil and discredit civil rights activists and members of the Black Panther Party," it said.

> The assessment and the analyses upon which it is based are flawed because it conflates black political activists with dangerous domestic terrorist organizations that pose actual threats to law enforce-

ment. It relies on a handful of obviously terrible incidents to paint black Americans who exercise free speech against witnessed police brutality as possible violent extremists. These broad characterizations can only serve to further erode trust between law enforcement officials and many of the black communities they serve.[23]

The Caucus demanded that Wray appear before all forty-nine members to explain himself.

Wray was dragged before the House Judiciary Committee in December, where he faced angry Democrats. California Democrat Karen Bass, a Black Caucus member who supports a regime in Cuba that tramples on all free expression, predictably told Wray, "my big concern is that local law enforcement will misinterpret that and will clamp down on people exercising their First Amendment rights." At first, Wray was resolute, telling the committee he "will not withdraw intelligence assessments based on public outcry." But at another committee meeting in June 2018, Wray started walking things back. He said that the "feedback" had "prompted us to go back and take a very hard look at how we are bucketing the different categories of domestic terrorism....I think it's been a useful learning experience for us, and I expect we will see some changes in how we do things going forward."[24] By the following year, the walk-back was complete. At a hearing of the Senate Judiciary Committee in July 2019, Wray said in an answer to New Jersey Democratic Senator Cory Booker, also a Caucus member, "We don't use the term Black Identity Extremism anymore."[25]

ROGUE PROSECUTORS

Less than a year later, things began to look up again. In June 2020, Attorney General William Barr announced the creation of a Justice Department task force on "anti-government extremists." In

August, Erin Neely Cox, U.S. Attorney for the Northern District of Texas and co-head of the task force, told the Senate Judiciary Committee that the FBI had opened more than three hundred domestic terrorism investigations into the violence that had taken place since George Floyd's death in late May, and arrested more than one hundred protesters in Portland, Oregon, alone, as it was a focus of the violence.[26]

This may sound like success, but something else was happening at the other end of the law enforcement universe to thwart the FBI and the Justice Department again. Woke district attorneys elected across the United States consistently refused throughout 2020 to file charges against rioters and looters and simply released them back on the street to create mayhem once again. The rogue prosecutor movement seeks to replace district and state attorneys with new "progressive prosecutors" whose goal is to end prosecution of a variety of crimes, many of which are often associated with political violence, no matter what the law says, and to end cash bail, as my Heritage Foundation colleagues Charles "Cully" Stimson, Zack Smith, and Lora Ries have demonstrated through a long series of papers and articles. In the words of one of the movement's most enthusiastic supporters, Rachel Barkow, a professor at NYU School of Law, its goal is "to reverse-engineer and dismantle the criminal justice infrastructure."[27] One such rogue prosecutor, Boston District Attorney Rachael Rollins, published her list of fifteen crimes "for which the default is to decline prosecution." They include trespassing; shoplifting; larceny under $250; disorderly conduct; disturbing the peace; receiving stolen property; breaking and entering under some conditions; and wanton or malicious destruction of property.[28] George Gascón, Los Angeles's rogue prosecutor, has a similar list.[29] San Francisco District Attorney Chesa Boudin, another rogue prosecutor, is the son of Kathy Boudin and David Gilbert, Weather Underground members who were involved in the Brinks robbery. Kathy Boudin served two decades in prison as a result, while Gilbert remains behind bars. Chesa was raised by Bill Ayers and Bernardine Dohrn.[30] Both he and Gascón are facing recall petitions.

The movement relies heavily on money from the foundations controlled by George Soros, which, as we saw in the last chapter, made a $220 investment in social justice organizations in 2020. Alexander Soros, son of the billionaire and vice chairman of the Open Society Foundations, told the *New York Times* that "these investments will empower leaders in the black community to reimagine policing [and] end mass incarceration."[31] The Soros family and its foundations were heavily involved in several key district attorney races, where they successfully contributed to the election of rogue prosecutors, including $1.45 million on the DA race in Philadelphia. The movement also now has powerful friends in high places. Vice President Kamala Harris, who for seven years was San Francisco's district attorney, followed by seven years as California's attorney general, asked people to give money to the Minnesota Freedom Fund (MFF), a charity that receives a lot of money from celebrities, to raise bail for 2020 protesters. On June 1, a week after Floyd's death, Harris, not yet on the Biden ticket, tweeted, "If you're able to, chip in now to the @MNFreedomFund to help post bail for those protesting on the ground in Minnesota." MFF ended up raising a gargantuan $35 million during the riots. But, according to an article in the *Washington Examiner*, by early August a Minneapolis TV station "reported that the fund bailed out defendants from Twin Cities jails charged with murder, violent felonies, and sex crimes."[32]

And what happened in Portland itself, the city where the Justice Department boasted of success? The rogue district attorney for Multnomah County, Mike Schmidt, refused to prosecute 543 cases, or more than half of the protest-related cases referred to his office by the police. My colleagues Ries and Smith sifted through a data dashboard of Portland's "protest" cases and found in mid-October that

> From May 29 to Oct. 5, law enforcement referred 974 cases to the DA's office. Many of the cases are of repeat offenders, but, curiously, the dashboard does not indicate how many. The DA rejected 666 cases, or nearly 70%. Of the rejected cases, 543 (over 81%) were dismissed in the "interest of justice." The DA's office does not define this vague term.[33]

If that many violent protesters were released so they could continue to create havoc in one city alone, we can imagine that the number nationwide could well be five figures.

PAPER TRAIL

The FBI assessment of the threat of anti-police hostility was, however, substantiated by academic research. We saw in chapter 4 how the Armed Conflict Location and Event Data report for 2020 linked 95 percent of the riots to BLM activists. In 2020 another paper also appeared, this one from the Network Contagion Research Institute (NCRI) at the Miller Center for Community Protection and Resilience, which is based at Rutgers University (though its principal author also works for the James Madison Program in American Ideals and Institutions, at Princeton).[34]

The NCRI report, which used big data analysis, was straightforward. It said that socialist and anarchist groups have created a growing online structure that supports violence, especially against the police, and supports extremism that is tailor-made for anyone seeking to dismantle the organizing principle of this society. "During opportune moments of vulnerability, these groups take advantage of social unrest over major events such as the COVID lockdowns and George Floyd's killing," the NCRI report said. "The target of much of the recent outrage in these events has been the most visible institutional manifestation of state authority and raw power: the police."

NCRI said that, though its findings were preliminary and should serve as a basis for future research, it could still "draw several conclusions from what we discovered." Among these were that:

- An online structure supporting anarcho-socialist extremism appears to be rapidly growing.
- Many of the features of anarcho-socialist extremism seem to parallel the key tactical structures documented in libertarian-anarchist and Jihadi extremism: Use of memes, cloistering in fringe and private online forums and organizing militias.
- The appearance of posts with anti-police outrage and/or memes and coded language increased over 1,000% on Twitter and 300% on Reddit in recent months during social justice protests.
- Extreme anarcho-socialist fringe online forums on Reddit use memes calling for the death of police and memes for stockpiling munitions to promote violent revolution.
- Extreme anarcho-socialist fringe online forums on Reddit underwent growth in membership and participation during the quarantine and recent social justice protests....
- We find evidence that both militia and anarchist networks play key roles in the recent social justice protests from controlling perimeters at CHAZ [CHOP][35] to coordinating nation-wide anarchist-inspired violent protests online.[36]

As NCRI concluded, "these data hint that insurgent behavior, stochastic terror and even attacks on vital infrastructure may be fomenting, and even indicate the possibility of a mass-casualty event. The need for regular, reliable and responsible reporting with methods such as those used in this briefing with similar computational techniques is now imperative."[37]

None of this appears to matter to those who are sympathetic to the goals of the BLM leaders and who would hate to see the FBI resume any of its former investigation of those who would use the threat of violence or daily disruptions to subvert the American system. Two months before the NCRI report was published, and barely one month after George Floyd's death, Michael German ran a long opinion piece in Britain's *The Guardian* newspaper, which the Brennan Center later republished. In it, he warned the FBI against keeping tabs on what the BLM organizations were doing.

Characteristically, German blamed the violence on the police, and warned that the FBI should "put its investigative authorities to better use by holding those officers accountable, rather than monitoring a new generation of Black activists." The op-ed gave a general overview of all FBI investigations of black Americans, starting, as one might have expected, with Garvey and then bringing up the Martin Luther King example. Exposure of this abuse, he said, had led to reforms by Gerald Ford's Attorney General Edward Levi, who in 1976 issued new guidelines limiting "FBI investigations of political activity by requiring a reasonable indication of criminal activity before intrusive investigations could be launched." However, German charged, George W. Bush's Attorney General Michael Mukasey had weakened these limits in 2008. "Mukasey's guidelines authorized a new type of investigation called an 'assessment,' which required no factual basis for suspecting individualized wrongdoing before agents could employ intrusive investigative techniques," German wrote. He then gave a litany of all the FBI probes of BLM highlighted in this chapter, which German knew about, since he is widely quoted in these media reports.[38]

In reality, post-Mukasey we remain constrained in what we can do in terms of domestic intelligence gathering, as German knows full well, since, as the record shows, he has been involved for years in making sure that these shackles remain in place;

his *Guardian* article was just an instance of "working the ref." The federal government is very limited in its ability to collect any kind of domestic intelligence in any activity that could be deemed protected by the First Amendment, which is the reason Karen Bass, Michael German, and the reporters writing about this issue repeat the incantation. This limitation is wise. Conservatives who may wish it were otherwise, who might long for at least some semblance of a modern J. Edgar Hoover keeping an eye on groups and individuals who want to introduce socialism into our society, should reflect on what would happen to their protected activities when the left is in power. This is not an abstraction. Remember how official Washington went after the Tea Party in the early 2010s? This peaceful group of Americans who started to organize in basements and backyards in 2010 to protest President Obama's plan to introduce Obamacare were unfairly portrayed by the media as white supremacists and then hounded by the IRS. The FBI, however, should be allowed to investigate all violent activity, which is not protected by the Constitution, and all activity that would reasonably lead to violence; in that vein we should remember the large percentage of riots that were linked to BLM. And, obviously, the media should resume its job of reporting on the facts.

ANTIFA

But at least we can now understand why, when our elected officials wanted to show they were doing something about riots, it was to Antifa they turned. Soon after the George Floyd protests were starting to get under way in Minneapolis in late May, President Trump tweeted, "The United States of America will be designating ANTIFA as a Terrorist Organization."[39] In July 2020, Louisiana Senator Bill Cassidy introduced S.Res.279, "A resolution calling for the designation of Antifa as a domestic terrorist organization."[40] Antifa is mostly white, its activities are almost always violent, and it does not have Karen Bass going to bat for it at the federal level. It became the "safe space" for conservative leaders who didn't want to pay the cost of being accused of violating First Amendment rights or, worse, being called "racist" for going after BLM. We can assume that the vast majority of the arrests in Portland were of Antifa hooligans: 77 percent of the tossed cases were white and only 10 percent were black, and BLM activists are much more racially balanced than that.

Antifa is a decentralized, violent, anarchist movement. Most sympathetic media accounts of it (and most media accounts of it are sympathetic) trace its origins to anti-fascist movements in Italy and Germany in the 1920s and 1930s, after the rise of Benito Mussolini and Adolf Hitler, and indeed "Antifa" is a contraction of "anti-fascists." Many on the left dismiss it as a problem, going so far as to deny its existence. "Unlike white supremacists, Antifa is an idea, not an organization, not a militia," candidate Joe Biden said in the September 29, 2020, national debate with President Trump. American Antifa is, however, a home-grown product; it is not an organization like the BLM chapters are, but there are units that gather under the label, and the only thing German about it is its Nietzschean nihilism.

Antifa gathers together both Marxists and anarchists; indeed, its logo has a red and a black flag, to signify both these movements. Militants sometimes espouse causes such as environmentalism, but mostly they care about the violent suppression of conservative speech. Antifa's supporters in the media and the academy justify the violence and the denial of their compatriots' First Amendment rights by saying that fascism and Nazism spread in Europe at first through peaceful speech, and it should have been suppressed at birth. But all this does is, once again, to equate normal conservative speech with racial hatred and racist speech (which in this country is also constitutionally protected, however abhorrent we may find it). The Torch Network, the best-known organized Antifa group, explains its denial of other people's speech rights by stating on its website that "Torch does not use the state to prevent anyone's free speech. The right to free speech restricts the state from censoring ideas, it does not stop the public from opposing hateful ideas. The fact that people dislike what bigots have to say and want to make that known is not prohibited by the concept of free speech."[41]

Though it is hard to pinpoint exactly when and where it was born, experts trace the modern American Antifa's origins to three distinct sources: the punk rock bands and related skinhead movement of the 1980s, the anti–World Trade Organization riots in Seattle in 1999 (which appear again and again in several chapters), and the Occupy Wall Street movement in 2011. It got a lot of its initial media attention following the "Unite the Right" rally of white nationalists in Charlottesville, Virginia, on August 11–12, 2017, when Antifa militants showed up to fight with the yokels who organized the protest.

A week later, the *New York Times* described Antifa as a

> loose affiliation of radical activists who have surfaced in recent months at events around the country and have openly scuffled with white supremacists, right-wing extremists and, in some cases, ordinary supporters of President Trump. Energized in part by Mr. Trump's election, they have sparred with their conservative opponents at political rallies and college campus speaking engagements, arguing that one crucial way to combat the far right is to confront its supporters on the streets.

Members of Antifa, the *Times* said, "have shown no qualms about using their fists, sticks or canisters of pepper spray to meet an array of right-wing antagonists whom they call a fascist threat to American democracy."[42] Andy Ngo, a writer who has covered

Antifa for years, wrote in his book on the group that, after Trump's election, Antifa has "mutated into a unique contemporary breed of violent left-wing extremism."[43]

In a comprehensive paper he did for Real Clear Investigations, the journalist Mark Hemingway agrees that "Antifa is, in fact, hard to pin down. It has no known leaders, no address, not even a Twitter account. A number of specific groups involved in street violence embrace the antifa label. Those groups, in turn, are highly secretive and loosely organized."[44] The Torch Antifa Network, adds Hemingway, however, "today is the closest thing to an Antifa organization." It began as the Anti-Racist Action Network (ARA), created in Minnesota in 1987 by a group of skinheads who sought to prevent right-wing groups from recruiting adherents at punk rock activities, and then renamed itself as Torch in 2013. On its website, the Torch Network names ten chapters, from Sacramento to Atlanta, and says they can name themselves whatever they want and organize however they see fit. The only thing they have to do to be affiliated with Torch is accept the five points of unity, which are:

1. **We disrupt fascist and far right organizing and activity.**
2. **We don't rely on the cops or courts to do our work for us.** This doesn't mean we never go to court, but the cops uphold white supremacy and the status quo. They attack us and everyone who resists oppression. We must rely on ourselves to protect ourselves and stop the fascists.
3. **We oppose all forms of oppression and exploitation.** We intend to do the hard work necessary to build a broad, strong movement of oppressed people centered on the working class against racism, sexism, nativism, anti-Semitism, Islamophobia, homophobia, transphobia, and discrimination against the disabled, the oldest, the youngest, and the most oppressed people. We support abortion rights and reproductive freedom. We want a classless, free society. We intend to win!

4. We hold ourselves accountable personally and collectively to live up to our ideals and values.

5. We not only support each other within the network, but we also support people outside the network who we believe have similar aims or principles. An attack on one is an attack on all.[45]

The website emphasizes the point that Antifa exists mainly to disrupt conservative speech. "Anti-racists and antifascists have an obligation to deny a platform to bigots so that they can't spread their message and recruit," it says.[46]

Hemingway cites testimony that Kyle Shideler, director and senior analyst for Homeland Security and Counterterrorism at the Center for Security Policy, gave in August 2020 to the Senate Judiciary Committee, in which he described Torch as "one of the largest regional networks of Antifa in the United States." Shideler also identified Michael Novick, "the web registrar of the Torch Antifa website," as a singularly important figure. "Novick is a former member of the Weather Underground terrorist group. He is a founding member of the John Brown Anti-Klan Committee and a founding member of Anti-Racist Action–Los Angeles," Shideler told the committee.[47]

Novick spoke at an ARA conference in Chicago alongside better-known former Weathermen Bill Ayers and his wife, Bernardine Dohrn (friends of Barack Obama in his Chicago days).[48] Their topics made it clear that these former Weathermen have not lost their Marxist stripes. Novick spoke about the role of "settler colonialism and white supremacy in forming class consciousness," while Dohrn gave a lecture on "white supremacy and the contours of anti-racist organizing and activism." Novick's affiliation to the John Brown committee, which was also created by Weathermen in 1978, is important in several ways. As Hemingway points out,

three members of the John Brown group were convicted for their roles in a string of bombings in Washington and New York between

1982 and 1985—including an explosion in the U.S. Capitol building in 1983, along with explosions at three military installations in the D.C. area, and four more bombings in New York City. Two of the three served long prison terms, but on his last day in office, President Clinton commuted the 40-year sentence of the third, Linda Evans, after 13 years. Evans had also been involved with both the Weather Underground, as well as the John Brown group.[49]

Hemingway cites author Susan Lang's 1990 book *Extremist Groups in America*, in which she writes that the John Brown committee "is thought to be a front for the May 19th Communist Organization," a group with ties to the Weather Underground and whose best-known former member today is Susan Rosenberg, who as we saw in the last chapter sits on the board of Thousand Currents, the BLM fiscal sponsor.[50] It is worth noting, in this vein, that both Evans and Rosenberg were among seven people whom the FBI charged in 1988 with a bombing of the Capitol that caused $250,000 in damage five years earlier.

In 2019, Novick traveled to Havana to celebrate the anniversary of the founding of the Venceremos Brigade, a group that Castro formed in the 1960s to recruit Americans to the cause of the Revolution. Two other famous members of the Venceremos Brigade were Susan Rosenberg and Karen Bass.

Such cross-fertilization among far-left groups and personalities has always been common, so we shouldn't be surprised to find Antifa, BLM, the John Brown committee, Torch, Novick, Bass, Rosenberg, Ayers, and Dohrn all grouped together. In a radio interview in June 2020, Ayers said that BLM was "the latest iteration" of "a centuries old struggle for freedom" of which the 1960s and the Weather Underground were a part.[51]

Antifa acts together with BLM often, and may have common backers among aging Weathermen who glimpse the promised land of revolution, but does not have one iota of the latter's cultural and political impact. It is also mostly white, and works from the ground up, reversing the top-down Leninist structure of an intellectual vanguard (which is what Garza, Cullors, and Tometi represent) leading a potentially revolutionary base. In many of these ways, Antifa resembles the louts who invaded the Capitol on January 6, 2020. Its membership is violent and is not filled by people with college degrees who write for law review journals. There is no Antifa curriculum, proposed legislation, or signs on people's lawns, just as the Proud Boys, too, cannot claim any of those things. These are among the many reasons why our elected officials can today rail against Antifa, and why police arrest its members in Portland. Antifa, unlike BLM, also does not base itself on a recognized academic discipline, critical race theory. It is to this, and its influence on today's curricula, that we now turn.

CHAPTER 7

SCHOOLING THE REVOLUTION

What gives Black Lives Matter a salience that Antifa and the Proud Boys could never match is that its anti-capitalist rantings and its obsessive analysis of all phenomena through the prism of race is supported by an academic discipline. Hard as it may be for those who have heard their utterings to believe, BLM activism rests on a body of thought that has a certain internal consistency because it works around contradictions, and the thinking behind it takes place at universities. Under these theories, race can be a social construct, but that does not prevent it from having a greater importance than any other trait; also, tolerance requires the repression of some ideas because ideas hurt people. To say that BLM is backed up by an academic theory does not mean that the thinking is based on facts; no, America does not have a "mass incarceration" problem, nor is it "structurally racist," no matter how many university professors say so. Nor does it mean that such theory is based on the four cardinal virtues of prudence, justice, temperance, and fortitude, all of which are opposed in some measure by BLM. Lastly, we should also not fall into the trap of believing that because something is called a "discipline" or a "philosophy," or has several chaired professors at major universities associated with it, it meets the tests of intellectual rigor or academic objectivity and meticulousness.

An academic discipline does, however, provide BLM activists with a way of thinking and explaining the world. It also means that BLM and its supporting universe can then turn this certain *weltanschauung* (and German is the proper language for it, as it is there that it originated) and turn it into curricula that can corrupt the minds of children in K–12 schools (and yes, much of this starts in kindergarten). This philosophy—again, a neutral term that does not connote legitimacy—has a name: critical race theory. The curricula go under different labels: the 1619 Project curriculum of the *New York Times* is the best known, but Black Lives Matter at School is gaining ground. The theories and the curricula cannot be understood without the other. Both CRT and the lessons being taught to our children are Marxist in origin. Leftists seem to have grasped better than conservatives that ideologically indoctrinating children is the key to the future. The reason why 2020 happened, why every facet of our lives has been transformed, and why we can't tell at this point if republican self-government will survive, is that what happens on campus does not stay on campus.

CRITICAL RACE THEORY'S ANTECEDENTS

As its name clearly implies, CRT is closely associated with other disciplines known as critical legal theory, critical pedagogy, and so on. All of these are offshoots, in turn, of critical theory. This approach began in the German city of Frankfurt in the 1920s and 1930s, when the Institute for Social Research was established at the University of Frankfurt in 1923. Colloquially known as "the Frankfurt School," the Institute was one of the first so-called neo-Marxist, or Western Marxist, schools. It was modeled on the Marx-Engels Institute in Moscow, and for far too long the Institute continued to excuse Soviet repression. As late as 1934, Max Horkheimer, the first long-lasting director of the Institute, revealed his true feelings for the Soviet state in an essay collection known as *Dammerung* (in German, both "dawn" and "twilight"). "He who has eyes for the meaningless injustice of the imperialist world, which in no way is to be explained by technical impotence, will regard the events in Russia as the progressive, painful attempt to overcome this injustice," he wrote.[1] Though much of its early work took place during the worst of Joseph Stalin's terror, the school maintained an official silence about the events taking place inside the Soviet Union.

In fact, the Frankfurt School was originally going to be called the *Institut für Marxismus* (Institute for Marxism), but its founders thought the name too provocative. This dissimulation would remain a constant of the school. After the school moved to Columbia University's Teachers College in 1934 to escape the Third Reich, its scholars stopped using terms such as "Marxism" or "communism," using instead "dialectical materialism." The historian Martin Jay, in one of the best and most sympathetic histories of the school, *The Dialectical Imagination*, writes that "Careful editing prevented emphasizing the revolutionary implications of their thought."[2]

Despite assiduously hiding their intentions (or more likely, because of it) the school did valuable service on behalf of international communism. "The Frankfurt School was to become a major force in the revitalization of Western European Marxism in the postwar years," writes Jay. "In addition, through the sudden popularity of Herbert Marcuse in the America of the late 1960s, the Frankfurt School's Critical Theory (*Kritische Theorie*) has also had a significant influence on the New Left in this country."[3]

Critical theory, which emerges in Horkheimer's 1937 essay "Traditional and Critical Theory," married the dialectical approach of philosopher G. W. F. Hegel to Marxism's emphasis on class conflict, Nietzschean nihilism, and Sigmund Freud's work on the subconscious. It simply amounted to a barrage of criticism of all the institutions of America and Europe, in order to bring down the entire edifice. In the postscript to the essay, Horkheimer explains that critical theory is "not just a research hypothesis which shows its value in the ongoing business of men; it is an essential element in the historical effort to create a world which satisfies the needs and powers of men." The individual satisfaction of needs had always been an obstacle to the revolution that Marxists wanted, so a different world had to be created in which this was no longer the case.[4]

Under the watchful care of these committed Marxists, critical theory became a tool, sometimes sharp, sometimes blunt, with which to constantly either bleed or bludgeon *all* the institutions of Western society—the family, the church, the capitalist system, and the concept of a nation-state that beckons patriotism. All had to be destroyed, criticized to death, the better to substitute in their place new institutions that would suit the goals of Marxism: central planning, a command economy, the obliteration of the individual, the death of God. The only problem was the worker: he was too contented. Instead of brutalized proletarians constantly rising up to overthrow the bourgeoisie, capitalism succeeded in turning members of the working class into the middle class. The stubborn individual persisted. In America, the Frankfurt scholars witnessed that the American worker was even wealthier and more aspirational than the European one. His false consciousness was deeper.

Most of the scholars returned despondent to Germany after the war, but Marcuse remained ensconced in American academia. In the 1950s and 1960s he got to witness new phenomena on which he was quick to seize: the sexual-liberation movement and the upheavals associated with the civil rights era and the anti–Vietnam War movement. In the first, Marcuse discovered an irresistible urge with which to smash the institutions. As he writes in *Eros and Civilization*, his 1959 best seller:

> The body in its entirety would become…a thing to be enjoyed—an instrument of pleasure. This change in the value and scope in libidinal relationships would lead to a disintegration of the institutions in which the private interpersonal relations have been organized, particularly the monogamic and patriarchal family.[5]

In this Marcuse was, of course, reinventing the wheel and following the dictates of Karl Marx and Friedrich Engels, who set their sights on the family when they invented communism in 1848. In the *Communist Manifesto* itself, the pair called for the "abolition of the family." Noting that even radicals resisted "this infamous proposal of the Communists," they asked, "On what foundation is the present family, the bourgeois family, based? On capital, on private gain. In its completely developed form, this family exists only among the bourgeoisie."[6]

In the riots of the 1960s, Marcuse happened upon a new revolutionary base: "Underneath the conservative popular base is the substratum of the outcasts and outsiders, the exploited and persecuted of other races and other colors," Marcuse wrote.[7] These minorities required an intellectual vanguard to lead them, as "their opposition is revolutionary even if their consciousness is not." Unless the Marxist vanguard came along and instructed these potential revolutionaries into their victimhood, the revolution would remain postponed. "All liberation depends on the consciousness of servitude, and the emergence of this consciousness is always hampered by the predominance of needs and satisfactions."[8] (Again, as with Horkheimer, we see that to the critical theorists, as to Gramsci, the satisfaction of needs by individuals is the obstacle to consciousness.)

In short order, others discovered that, because black Americans alone would not suffice to overturn the system, the categories of minorities to be filled with grievances would need to be multiplied. The relentless criticism of critical theory would stoke the grievances among the new minorities in a way that had failed among the workers as a class. (Other radical intellectuals later envisioned extracting "whiteness" from the white worker in order to unite the entire working class, as we will see in the next chapter.)

Marcuse was one of the few academics of his time to praise the agitation of Students for a Democratic Society, to whom he spoke at one event, and he influenced members of the Weather Underground. He taught directly not just Angela Davis, but also Weather Underground member Naomi Jaffe and Yippie leader Abbie Hoffman.

By this time, critical theory's destructive machinery was ready to morph into its legal and racial modifications, to more easily transform America.

CRITICAL LEGAL THEORY

Critical theory's first American offspring, the anchor baby that implants it on American shores, was critical legal theory. It takes the approach of CT and applies it to the law, which to the proponents of CLT is just a set of statutes written by the powerful and the wealthy so they can maintain their power and wealth, on the backs of the downtrodden. The Cornell Law School's Legal Information Institute explains critical legal studies in this manner:

> Critical legal studies (CLS) is a theory which states that the law
> is necessarily intertwined with social issues, particularly stating

that the law has inherent social biases. Proponents of CLS believe that the law supports the interests of those who create the law. As such, CLS states that the law supports a power dynamic which favors the historically privileged and disadvantages the historically underprivileged. CLS finds that the wealthy and the powerful use the law as an instrument for oppression in order to maintain their place in hierarchy.[9]

The goal, for those who missed it, was "to overturn the hierarchical structures of modern society." Just as we can trace CT's birth either to the foundation of the Frankfurt School in 1923 or to Horkheimer's essay in 1937, CLT has an official start: the Conference on Critical Legal Studies at the University of Wisconsin at Madison in 1977. CLT also has its pantheon of intellectuals, the most important of whom are Duncan Kennedy, Roberto Mangabeira Unger, and Robert W. Gordon. CLT proponents openly admit in their writings their debt to Horkheimer and the Frankfurt School scholars, but they did not just use CT as a tool to tear down American jurisprudence; they also mixed in an unhealthy dose of postmodernism. Parisian rather than German, postmodernism was also destructive of traditions and norms, but worked by undermining reason and language. Words, to postmodernists such as Jacques Derrida and Michel Foucault, could have any meaning. The text did not depend on the writer's intentions, but was a tabula rasa with which the reader could let his imagination run wild. Postmodernism was just as Hegelian in its dialectical approach and as Nietzschean in its relativism as CT had been, but was even more impenetrable. That made it less practicable, and when academics intent on radically transforming all the institutions came around in the next iteration, critical race theory, the woolly revelries of postmodernism were dropped in the search for real-world action.

CRITICAL RACE THEORY

Like BLM, CRT sees everything through the lens of race, and all societal disparities as a result of racism. CRT practitioners take from CT the criticism of all cultural institutions in order to fundamentally transform society but use race as the target. Indeed, the existence of disparities proves that racism is at play, and to deny this is racist. CRT is therefore the logical endpoint of Marcuse's search for a revolutionary "substratum of society," and its purpose is to "instill the consciousness of servitude" that is required by revolution. That CRT is a descendant of CT should be clear from its name alone, but journalists never mention the link when they write about it, because they would then have to admit that CRT is Marxist. CRT writers themselves are not shy about revealing all these connections, however. "We discovered ourselves to be critical theorists who did race and racial justice advocates who did critical theory," said Kimberlé Crenshaw, the American scholar who first coined the term "critical race theory," in a 2019 panel.[10]

CRT practitioners can sometimes be just as abstruse in their writings as their predecessors, but they are also more American in their determination to turn academic philosophies into street-level activism. For this reason, they also often make use of short vignettes written in simple language, parables that illustrate the daily and constant racism that they say saturates American society. They also internalize the idea that identities cobbled around such immutable characteristics as sex, race, or national origin may be synthetic social constructs, but have the revolutionary potential that Marcuse fingered. Kimberlé Crenshaw, the CRT scholar who came up with the term "intersectionality" (which means that overlapping oppressed identities confer greater victimhood), expressed why postmodernism needed to be jettisoned for this political purpose:

While the descriptive project of postmodernism of questioning the ways in which meaning is socially constructed is generally sound, this critique sometimes misreads the meaning of social construction and distorts its political relevance.... But to say that a category such as race or gender is socially constructed is not to say that that category has no significance in our world. On the contrary, a large and continuing project for subordinated people—and indeed, one of the projects for which postmodern theories have been very helpful in thinking about—is the way power has clustered around certain categories and is exercised against others.[11]

Crenshaw's work on intersectionality, and that of others in the CRT realm, was heavily influenced by the work of the Combahee River Collective, a group of black lesbian socialists in Boston in the 1970s, and the statement its members signed in 1977. The collective was upfront about its Marxism, stating that

We realize that the liberation of all oppressed peoples necessitates the destruction of the political-economic systems of capitalism and imperialism as well as patriarchy. We are socialists because we believe that work must be organized for the collective benefit of those who do the work and create the products, and not for the profit of the bosses. Material resources must be equally distributed among those who create these resources.[12]

The statement foreshowed intersectionality by alluding to "simultaneous factors of oppression." It is also the first time the term "identity politics" is mentioned, and it is tied directly to victimhood: "this focusing upon our own oppression is embodied in the concept of identity politics."

CRT, therefore, is more explicitly devoted to what happens next, after the old institutions have been torn down. The godfather of CRT, Derrick Bell was very clear on the object of CRT. "As I see it, critical race theory recognizes that revolutionizing a culture begins with the radical assessment of it," he writes. But there is a purpose to the torrent of criticism. CRT, he adds, "is often disruptive because its commitment to anti-racism goes well beyond civil rights, integration, affirmative action, and other liberal measures."[13] CRT, he says, calls for a "transformative resistance strategy."[14]

Because insurrection is openly advocated, the abstractions of critical theory and postmodernism are to be avoided. Abstraction "smuggles the privileged choice of the privileged to depersonify [sic] their claims and then pass them off as the universal authority and the universal good," writes Bell.[15] That does not mean that abstract thought is absent in CRT writing; it does mean that CRT emphasizes something real, race, over an abstraction, class.

Exponents of CRT are also openly in opposition to liberal democracy and other Enlightenment values and offer the theory as a radical departure from the civil rights movement. Richard Delgado, a professor at the University of Alabama who is seen, along with Bell, as another leading proponent of CRT, writes that "Unlike traditional civil rights discourse, which stresses incrementalism and step-by-step progress, critical race theory questions the very foundations of the liberal order, including equality theory, legal reasoning, Enlightenment rationalism, and neutral principles of constitutional law."[16]

That does not mean that the dissimulation that we saw the Frankfurt scholars practice in the 1920s and 1930s is not at work. We see it again and again a century later, when those who want the state to direct resources, that is, to implement central planning, and decry how the market does the job under capitalism, still studiously avoid the word "communism." (Though many CRT practitioners, like CRT pioneer Angela Harris, openly praise Marx.) The furthest the BLM leaders will go is to say they are "trained Marxists"—and their mentor Angela Davis is beyond all pretentions—but most often, CRT practitioners will just disparage capitalism. Ibram X. Kendi repeatedly says or writes, gamely, that he is an "anti-capitalist." The noted CRT trainer Robin DiAngelo almost gave the game away in a 2020 interview with the *New York Times Magazine*, but in the meantime did a fairly good job of explaining the problem the woke have with free markets. "I avoid critiquing capitalism—I don't need to give people reasons to dismiss me. But capitalism is dependent on inequality, on an underclass. If the model is profit over everything else, you're not going to look at your policies to see what is most racially equitable." The interviewer, Daniel Bergner, did allow himself an important reflection: "I was asking about whether her thinking is conducive to helping Black people displace white people on high rungs and achieve something much closer to equality," he wrote. DiAngelo's answer, however, revealed that "she was entertaining an alternate and even revolutionary reality."[17]

Kendi and DiAngelo are examples of an improvisation that CRT has managed to pull: so-called anti-racism trainings that blossomed in 2020 following the death of George Floyd. Kendi and DiAngelo may be anti-capitalist, but they charge anywhere from $15,000 to $20,000 for sessions that can be as short as an hour or two. Their clients include corporations, which rob their shareholders to pay for these sham modern-day versions of Red Guard struggle sessions in Mao's Cultural Revolution; Congress, which robs the taxpayer in this instance; and even school districts, which rob this time not only the taxpayer but also the schoolchildren who will have to go without other resources so that Kendi, DiAngelo, and their ilk can get paid. Some of these CRT "trainings" teach young children that traits needed for success, such as punctuality, love of the written word, or hard work—attributes that used to be considered virtues—are functions of something called "whitism," and therefore to be eschewed. The purpose here is not to succeed by joining the system, but by failing and then blaming the system, a grievance to be nurtured so that the aggrieved will then have enough built-in bile to overthrow the system.

That the brainwashing of college students and even school-children must take place in order for the revolution to succeed has long been a staple of Marxism. As Angela Davis put it to students at California State University, Los Angeles in 2016, pan-African studies are "the intellectual arm of the revolution."[18] And let's not forget former Weatherman Bill Ayers's stomach-churning praise for Hugo Chávez's communist indoctrination of Venezuelan children at a 2006 meeting in Caracas, or, as he called it, "the profound educational reforms under way here in Venezuela under the leadership of President Chávez. We share the belief that education is the motor-force of revolution....I look forward to seeing how you continue to overcome the failings of capitalist education as you seek to create something truly new and deeply humane."[19]

An earlier communist who understood the importance of this work, György Lukács, the education and culture commissar during the short-lived Hungarian Soviet Republic of Béla Kun in 1919—and who later was an influence on the Frankfurt School—also instituted a system to instruct young children into sexual perversions, in order to smash that most central of societal institutions, the family. As Lukács's biographer described it,

> special lectures were organized in schools and literature printed and distributed to "instruct" children about free love, about the nature of sexual intercourse, about the archaic nature of bourgeois family codes, about the outdatedness of monogamy, and the irrelevance of religion, which deprives man of all pleasure. Children urged thus to reject and deride paternal authority and the authority of the church, and to ignore precepts of morality,

easily and spontaneously turned into delinquents with whom only the police could cope.[20]

It is not difficult, then, to see why one of BLM's most important new projects is the set of curricula it disseminates among the country's 14,000 school districts, bringing CRT to children pretty much as the 1619 Project of the *New York Times* has done.

BLACK LIVES MATTER AT SCHOOL

Education can be used to liberate and to enslave. In the eighteenth and nineteenth centuries, slaves and freedmen fought a long and valiant battle for the freedom to read and write, and, as we saw in chapter 1, those who wanted to keep black Americans enslaved did everything in their power to stop them from learning. But as we see in the examples of Lukács, Marcuse, and Davis, education can also be used to indoctrinate and destroy. In the case of Black Lives Matter at School, the program is used to spread the BLM ideology to children as early as kindergarten. This ideology, of course, comes with a dose of homosexual, anti-capitalist, and anti-family indoctrination so heavy that it would have made Lukács blush.

The educational branch of BLM is Black Lives Matter at School, which was started in October 2016 in Seattle, when some teachers and students started coming to school wearing T-shirts that read "Black Lives Matter: We Stand Together." From there it spread to Philadelphia, where the practice of devoting an entire week of the school year to BLM began the following year in the first week of Black History Month, which falls in February. After that, it became a nationally organized event. Per their website,

During the 2017–2018 school year, from February 5 to 9, thousands of educators around the U.S. wore Black Lives Matter shirts to school and taught lessons about structural racism, intersectional black identities, black history, and anti-racist movements for a nationally organized week of action: Black Lives Matter at School. Educators in over 20 cities participated in this national uprising to affirm the lives of Black students, teachers, and families including, Seattle, Philadelphia, Los Angeles, Chicago, Detroit, Boston, New York City, Baltimore, Washington, D.C., and beyond.[21]

Organizing the distribution of curriculum recommendations to the nation's unsuspecting educators, and what is now known as the "Week of Action" or the "Black Lives Matter at School Week," is a self-described "national committee of educators" that includes a steering committee.[22] The official name is Black Lives Matter at School. In a statement issued on November 16, 2020, the committee said that "The Black Lives Matter at School National Steering Committee strives to be the village that protects all Black lives from oppressive and racist institutions of learning."[23] And, rest assured, it's not just a week of indoctrination that they offer. As the organization's "About" page tells you, "This work is happening year round across the country."[24] Despite the appearance of diffuseness of power that accompanies all BLM endeavors, BLM at School is concentrated like a laser beam on BLM's agenda. The landing page of BLM at School in fact includes the "Assata chant" that contains Marx's exhortation that workers "have nothing to lose but their chains." BLM at School is also powerful. One of its partners is the National Education Association (NEA), the largest teachers' union and the largest white-collar union in the United States. A "Solidarity Statement" supporting the 2018 Week of Action was signed by a long list of celebrities from the hard-left world: Opal Tometi (the member of the founding triumvirate who seems to be most involved in the educational endeavor); former Weatherman Bill Ayers; Ibram X. Kendi; *Intercept* columnist and all-around provocateur Shaun King; Michael Bennett, a defensive end for the Seattle Seahawks; Adam Sanchez, a curriculum writer for the Zinn Educational Project; as well as a gaggle of professors from universities as prestigious as Princeton and Chicago.[25] What BLM at School does is spread CRT's obsession with race, and Lukács and Marcuse's perversions, to very young minds.

In September 2020, as President Trump and other conservatives started to point out the dangers inherent in these curricula and in CRT trainings, the BLM at School Steering Committee issued a rousing defense. Quoting bell hooks on the need to defeat the "imperialist white supremacist capitalist patriarchy," the committee's statement said that "Conceptual frameworks like critical race theory (CRT), curated syllabi/resource guides like the BLM@School Curriculum Resource Guide, and critical historical analysis like the 1619 Project are indispensable to providing foundations for principled struggle, abolitionist visions, and radical imagination."[26] Members of the steering committee include Tamara Anderson, cofounder and organizer of the Racial Justice Organizing Committee; Awo Okaikor Aryee-Price, a self-described "anti-racist educator, Consultant, and Organizer"; Jesse Hagopian, who teaches ethnic studies at Seattle's Garfield High School; Denisha Jones, director of the Art of Teaching Program at Sarah Lawrence College; and Erika Strauss Chavarria, a high school Spanish teacher in Howard County, Maryland, and a member of the board of directors of the National Education Association. Hagopian and Jones coauthored a 2021 book titled *Black Lives Matter at School*, a collection of essays that demonstrates how the BLM agenda is already being taught across the country. In the foreword, Opal Tometi promises that this new curriculum can "radically transform our learning environment."

Click on the Curriculum Resource Guide that the steering committee was defending and the first two resources you will find are educational material for "Queer Organizing" and a "Trans Day of Resistance." If you keep on clicking on the hundreds of links that BLM at School provides you discover that very little is BLM original material, but you end up connecting with the entire universe of hard-left programming, which BLM has curated for the nation's educators.

There's the recommended curricula and books of the far-left nonprofit Teaching for Change, which includes the writings of Howard Zinn and James Loewen—who wrote *Lies My Teacher Told Me*—both of whom are dedicated to tarnishing America's Founding Fathers.[27] One can also find the "Social Justice Standards" of the organization Learning for Justice, a project of the Southern Law Poverty Center.[28] The Learning for Justice curriculum promises that, in grades 3 to 5, "Students will know that the United States was founded on protecting the economic interests of white, Christian men who owned property. In the process, it protected the institution of slavery." In the framework for students in grades 6 through 12, the children will be taught that "Protections for slavery were embedded in the founding documents; enslavers dominated the federal government, Supreme Court and Senate from 1787 through 1860. Students will demonstrate the ways that the Constitution provided direct and indirect protection to slavery and imbued enslavers and slave states with increased political power."

If an educator perusing the BLM at School recommended curricula wanted to use math, rather than history, to reprogram her young charges, she would use the recommended lesson on probability and statistics. It promises that "In this unit we used probability to explore police stops and searches in Oakland, CA. We made predictions based on the total population and random sampling. We used compound event probability to analyze the likelihood of searches leading to arrests."[29]

The BLM at School starter kit for the Week of Action is very specific about how each of the five days is going to be used. Each day of the week is dedicated to different principles:

Monday: Restorative Justice, Empathy, and Loving Engagement
Tuesday: Diversity and Globalism
Wednesday: Trans-Affirming, Queer Affirming, and Collective
    Value
Thursday: Intergenerational, Black Families, and Black Villages
Friday: Black Women and Unapologetically Black[30]

One learns, moreover, that these principles correspond "to the thirteen guiding principles of Black Lives Matter." Curiously, the webpage of BLM GNF that used to house these thirteen principles has now been scrubbed. But they are easily found elsewhere. On the DC Educators for Social Justice website, we discover that they are:

1. Restorative Justice
2. Empathy
3. Loving Engagement
4. Diversity
5. Globalism
6. Queer Affirming
7. Trans Affirming
8. Collective Value
9. Intergenerational
10. Black Families
11. Black Villages
12. Unapologetically Black
13. Black Women[31]

Some of these are pretty unambiguous, while others are just plain woolly. No. 2 promises "a commitment to practicing empathy." Others are less straightforward. No. 6, for example, say "We are committed to fostering a queer-affirming network. When we gather, we do so with the intention of freeing ourselves from the tight grip of heteronormative thinking or, rather, the belief that all in the world are heterosexual unless s/he or they disclose otherwise." No. 7 states that "We are committed to embracing and making space for trans brothers and sisters to participate and lead. We are committed to being self-reflexive and doing the work required to dismantle cis-gender privilege and uplift Black trans folk, especially Black trans women who continue to be disproportionately impacted by trans-antagonistic violence." Nos. 11 and 12 include, respectively, calls to be "free from patriarchal practices," and for the "disruption of Western nuclear family dynamics and a return to the 'collective village'." This brings us squarely back to Marcuse's desire, mentioned earlier in this chapter, to have the "disintegration of the institutions in which the private interpersonal relations have been organized, particularly the monogamic and patriarchal family."

Restorative justice appears often in BLM at School literature. The explanation given in the BLM guiding principles is vague— "We are committed to collectively, lovingly and courageously working vigorously for freedom and justice for Black people and, by extension all people"—and doesn't quite do justice to what is being attempted. Dig deeper and you realize that what "restorative justice" attempts to do is put the criminal and the victim on the same plane, as people who have been harmed, and then seek conflict resolution—"inclusive" meetings of all parties involved. Punishment is absent. The Colorado Restorative Justice Coordinating Council, which was actually established by the Colorado legislature, describes traditional justice as asking "What laws have been broken? Who did it? What punishment do they deserve?" Restorative justice, on the other hand, asks a complete set of different questions: "Who has been hurt? What are their needs? Whose obligation is it to meet those needs?"[32] The American legal system is therefore dispensed with. Where there is no criminal, there is no "carceral state." There is also, of course, no peace for a community where the criminal continues to prey upon neighbors.

Under the guise of restorative justice, police are rapidly disappearing from schools, where they are needed not just to keep unruly students from harming others, but to save the lives of a potentially larger number in case of a shooter. On June 22, the board of the Minneapolis Public Schools voted unanimously to remove all policemen from its schools, an action that has been replicated across the country.

In an omen of what may yet to come, the BLM at School steering committee on December 10 issued a list of demands in an open letter addressed to then President- and Vice President-elect Joe Biden and Kamala Harris. Topping the list of things that needed to be accomplished within the administration's first one hundred days was a demand that the administration end tracking (as if the federal government could do any such thing), saying that "tracking is the modern-day segregation inherently fuels equity gaps [*sic*] and creates disparate access to resources that are largely stratified along divisions of race and class." Standardized testing, for its part, "is a direct result of racist eugenics policies and beliefs designed to prove Black inferiority." Another demand called for Biden/Harris to "appoint an experienced, Black educator for Secretary of Education who opposes corporate education reforms such as high-stakes testing and school privatization." A third demand called on the administration to "create federal policies to decrease and eliminate law enforcement in schools," again, strangely ignoring the fact that educational policies are left to some 14,000 local boards of education. Other demands included calls to increase outlays for "culturally responsive counselors"; eliminate all student loans; "resume complaints from trans students to the Department of Education which were halted by [former Education Secretary Betsy] Devos in 2018. Reinstate pre-Devos measures on protections for trans students"; and eliminate bans on federal

CRT trainings and revoke the 1776 Commission (of which I was a member).[33] In retrospect, it is chilling to consider that Biden acted on some of these demands in his very first day in office.

That education holds the key to our future is a cliché, but it is nonetheless true. All of which means that we should be very worried about our future. Despair, however, is not an option. What we should do will be covered in the following conclusion.

CHAPTER 8

CONCLUSION

America post-2020 has entered a period of mass hysteria not unlike that which plagued the village of Salem in the Massachusetts Bay Colony in the winter of 1692. The intensely Puritan town had just undergone a smallpox epidemic when girls and young women started to have fits that were then declared to be spells of bewitchment. Generalized panic soon spread throughout Salem and the entire colony. Before it abated the following year, twenty women accused of being witches had been hanged, five others had died in prison, and an elderly man had been executed by being crushed with heavy stones. Overall, close to two hundred people would be accused, and though the sentences were revoked in 1711 by order of a court, which paid compensation to the accused and their descendants, the impact of the witch hunt and the family separations it caused lingered for decades, if not centuries. This episode in American history has been the subject of allegories ever since.

A comparison can certainly be drawn again today, when sizable portions of the country appear to walk around in a trance, repeating axiomatically that the freest, most prosperous society in history is a "systemically, structurally and institutionally racist" hell, one where "people are hurting." Google that last phrase and "black lives matter" and you get nearly 200,000 responses. The trance affects all the races, but whites—particularly if they are liberal and most pointedly if they are also wealthy and highly educated—have perhaps become the most mechanical in their formulaic condemnation of the country, its history, and its institutions.

There is a difference from 1960s-style white guilt, however. What is demanded today, and white liberals freely give, is not just an acceptance of past wrongdoings and laws to put things right, but the wholesale self-denunciation of an entire race, country, and way of living. White guilt has metastasized into paroxysms of self-abasement and ritualistic self-condemnations in our classrooms, offices, places of worship, and government offices. "'Black is beautiful' has now given way to 'White is ugly,'" writes David Azerrad.[1] These performative mortifications come roughly under the label of "allyship."

So emotional can the outpourings of self-condemnation become, however, that the leaders of Black Lives Matter have begun to complain that these expiations can render people unable to follow BLM dictates, or can be used as performative activity with no action behind it. Racial catharsis is not enough; there must be action. "The thing I don't like about the word ally is that it is so wrought with guilt and shame and grief that it prevents people from doing what they ought to do," Alicia Garza told the NoVo Foundation's Jesenia Santana in 2016. Garza prefers "co-conspirators," "accomplices," or the old standby, "comrades," that is, actors who will use their "white privilege" in the cause of BLM. "Co-conspiracy is about what we do in action, not just in language," Garza added.[2]

The academy has supplied theoretical ballast to support this view. The anti-racism research guides at Tufts University's Hirsh

Library explain that the problem with allyship is that it "does not encompass the action of rejecting the benefits one receives from white supremacy." Co-conspirators, however, are "people who are actively fighting against the system of white supremacy and in particular the benefits they receive from it," as Tufts quotes Garza saying.[3] Patrisse Cullors puts it this way: "Some of us think that allyship is not enough. When you're an ally you get to show up when you want to and you get to step back when you want to. That allyship is really just convenient. Many people are asking for folks to be accomplices," she said in a YouTube video.[4] "The need to distinguish between white allies and white accomplices derives from the proliferating number of people identifying as allies who are not working toward disrupting the heteropatriarchy, but are rather cycling through and maintaining systems of privilege and oppression," write academics Jessica Powell and Amber Kelly.[5]

SELF-DENUNCIATIONS AND THEIR PURPOSES

The outbursts of white allyship and BLM demands that they be channeled into political action have a political purpose. Just so we are not mistaken, what the BLM leaders and their academic cheerleaders are really demanding is that rank-and-file Americans now channel their newfound zeal into dismantling capitalism. The equation is straightforward: as we saw in the previous chapter, the white worker of the 1960s was too contented to rise and revolt, and the only ones who might do so were, in Herbert Marcuse's infelicitous phrase, "the substratum of the outcasts and outsiders, the exploited and persecuted of other races and other colors." But what if we took "whiteness" out of the white worker? What if the white worker willingly renounced his "white privilege" and "white supremacy"? Then the entire working class would unite, and finally, really, overthrow the bourgeoisie!

It should surprise nobody who has read up to this point that the intellectual who originated the term "white privilege," gave us the modern usage of "white supremacy," and pioneered the field known as "whiteness studies"—all of which have been so key to BLM's success—was a white, communist professor who was active from the 1960s to his death in 2019. His name was Noel Ignatiev, and he openly advocated an approach he called "race treason"; in 1992 he cofounded a journal called *Race Traitor: Journal of the New Abolitionism*, which called on whites to betray their race and actively work toward its abolition. Ignatiev sought "to abolish the white race by any means necessary," a phrase he used often. His *New York Times* obituary helpfully explained that "Dr. Ignatiev always felt compelled to point out, he was not advocating some sort of mass extermination, just a change in presumptions." The obituary quoted Ignatiev as saying at a 1997 conference at the University of California, Berkeley: "There is youth culture, and drug culture and queer culture; but there is no such thing as white culture. Without the privileges attached to it, the white race would not exist, and white skin would have no more social significance than big feet."[6]

The *Times* obituary left out the fact that Ignatiev was a member of the Communist Party USA, which he left in 1958 to cofound the Provisional Organizing Committee to Reconstitute the Marxist Leninist Communist Party, a Stalinist/Maoist spin-off of the CP-USA. Indeed, Ignatiev's fight against "white privilege" or "white supremacy," another term whose modern usage he invented, and the white race itself was merely a fight against capitalism. This much he made clear in a 1967 letter to the Progressive Labor Party, which was published by the communist group the Sojourner Truth Organization.

Speaking of "white chauvinism," which he called "bourgeois poison aimed primarily at the white workers," Ignatiev wrote that its material base was white supremacy, "which is a crime not merely against non-whites, but against the *entire* proletariat." The elimination of white chauvinism, therefore,

certainly qualifies as one of the class demands of the entire working class. In fact, considering the role that this vile practice has
historically played in holding back the struggle of the American
working class, the fight against white supremacy becomes the
central immediate task of the entire working class.... As soon as
white supremacy is eliminated as a force within the working class,
the decks will be cleared for action by the entire class against its
enemy.[7]

Writing ten years later about the letter, Ignatiev went out of his way
to make sure its class struggle meaning was not misunderstood:
"The article is talking about only one struggle, the proletarian
class struggle, in which the rejection by white workers of white
supremacist ideas and practices is crucial to the emergence of
the proletariat as a revolutionary class."

In a 1996 book, Ignatiev explained further the political reasons
that self-condemnations are necessary: "The existence of the white
race depends on the willingness of those assigned to it to place
their racial interests above class, gender or any other interests they
hold. The defection of enough of its members to make it unreli-
able as a determinant of behavior will set off tremors that will
lead to its collapse."[8] In other words, to defect from whiteism, to
be a traitor to it, means essentially for the individual to cease to
satisfy one's needs, the old bugaboo of critical theorists, which
they blamed for being an obstacle to revolution. "All liberation
depends on the consciousness of servitude, and the emergence
of this consciousness is always hampered by the predominance
of needs and satisfactions," as Marcuse said.

How professors can carry out their accomplice work can be
seen in academic Jessica Powell's description of her own experiences. "I embody my role as an accomplice-scholar through the
deliberate inclusion of social justice education in every course
I teach as well as through my pedagogical work with students
and colleagues outside of the classroom," writes Powell, quoting

Ignatiev, former Weatherman Bill Ayers (who, lest we forget, is now an "education reformer"),⁹ Ta-Nehisi Coates, and "pedagogy of the oppressed" writer Paulo Freire. "As a teacher educator, I challenge my students to engage in critical action as well as... 'reality pedagogy', which in today's schooling environments can only be realized through 'creative insubordination' [a phrase borrowed from Ayers]." Powell says she and her students "explore together in dialogue and action what it means to take the stance that Black lives matter in our classrooms."¹⁰

Ignatiev is more direct. In the last university class he gave, he said,

> If you are a white male, you don't deserve to live. You are a cancer, you're a disease, white males have never contributed anything positive to the world! They only murder, exploit and oppress non-whites! At least a white woman can have sex with a black man and make a brown baby but what can a white male do? He's good for nothing. Slavery, genocides against aboriginal peoples and massive land confiscation, the inquisition, the holocaust, white males are all to blame! You maintain your white male privilege only by oppressing, discriminating against and enslaving others!¹¹

One of the principal differences between 1692 and 2020, thus, is that the Salem witch trials were not politically motivated, but this other stuff surely is. There was no project to transform the newly chartered Massachusetts Bay Colony. People did not instill a fear of witches into unsuspecting teenagers with the ulterior motive of changing society's political and economic model. In 2021, people have been whipped into a frenzy for a political reason. When you Google "people are hurting" and "Black Lives Matter," one of the first pages Google takes you to is a call to action that BLM GNF made only four days after the death of George Floyd. Calling the tragedy "a breaking point," the page uses it as a call for defunding the police and for resources to be diverted to black Americans.

The "people are hurting" mantra is now repeated everywhere, including by teenagers in wealthy suburbs who have known hunger only as a form of dieting and who are much more likely to have spent a night in Venice or Florence than in a troubled neighborhood within an hour's radius of their newly renovated homes. The nature of the exaggerated claim is in fact such a constant of the entire movement, so intense, that it can only emanate from a desire for political change, as a catalyzing call to action to dismantle "the organizing principle of this society," as we saw Garza call for in chapter 4. What they're doing is once again manipulating white guilt (and fear, too), just as their predecessors (who in some cases were their mentors, trainers, and funders) did in the 1960s, as we saw in chapter 3.

The exaggerations are not new. We saw in that same chapter how Eric Mann refers to the United States as "the most dictatorial country in the world" and in chapter 5 how, to Susan Rosenberg, it is "the greatest terrorist state in the world." Both hold this view of the United States while embracing evil regimes that are actually dictatorial and terrorist. The BLM activists who wrote up the call to action on March 30, 2020, have thus learned well from their convicted terrorist mentors. The difference between the two eras is, however, important. Whereas the Weathermen failed spectacularly to change America with their homemade bombs, they have succeeded beyond their wildest expectations with the social activists they have taught, trained, and funded. Weather Underground founder Bill Ayers was up to something when he realized that terrorism was not going to change America; he then got a PhD in Education from Columbia University's Teachers College (yes, the same place that took in the Frankfurt School's academics in 1934). Decades later, he was squiring a young politician by the name of Barack Obama around Chicago, and later still was endorsing the BLM curriculum.

By now, a generation of young Americans have been schooled on Howard Zinn, whose *People's History of the United States* was published in 1980 and continues to be a best seller because teachers continue to use it. They also regularly imbibe Ignatiev's "white supremacy" and "white privilege" concepts, which are now repeated from every lip. And things are now going to get markedly worse, with the 1619 Project's curriculum already being used in at least 4,500 classrooms, and through the efforts of Black Lives Matter at School. As we have seen, after the tumultuous year of 2020, BLM has a curriculum, a political action committee, a bill in Congress, and even a foreign policy. It has managed to change, and not for the better, every facet of American life. So it is reasonable for reasonable Americans to ask themselves, how on earth can we reverse all this?

THE LONG WAY BACK

The first step is to admit to ourselves that it will not be easy. We did not become a nation under a spell overnight; 2020 merely put an ongoing trend into the passing gear. Lasting success may have to wait for a political leader to emerge, from either party, who will say "no, none of these things people repeat today are true, and the practices we accept are damaging to society." The allegory here is to the fable of the child who cried that the emperor had no clothes. That act broke a spell. What we have today is a spell: a minority of the population has bought into the "people are hurting" mantra because of "white supremacy," while the majority knows this is untrue but remains silent because they fear speaking out. Until that political leader emerges, the rest of us must hold the fort.

The way to do that is by speaking the truth, by unmasking as a deceitful political plan the idea that America is uniquely hideous and evil. Milton Friedman was on the money when he said that politicians will not become messiahs on their own until the environment of opinion is created for them to do the right thing. "The important thing is to establish a political climate of opinion which will make it politically profitable for the wrong people to do the right thing. Unless it is politically profitable for the wrong people to do the right thing, the right people will not do the right thing either, or, if they try, they will shortly be out of office," he wrote in 1975.[12]

The way has been opened by President Trump, who dared to go further than his predecessors in the fight against many of the practices that will be discussed in this chapter. This work must now be taken up by someone with the same temerity, but a different disposition. For one thing, there are many potential liberal allies, who care about defending liberal values, to be had, and repelling them would be a waste. Of course, hard leftists will try to use the ghost of the January 6 riot to smear any attempt to break America free of its present stupor. But these tactics, too, must be exposed by all of us. What we must all do, to the degree that we can, is become an army of John the Baptists, preparing the ground so that a leader who takes the current threat to society seriously may emerge.

We start by exposing the exaggerations and the damage that they cause. For that, we must be armed with facts. Since criminality and the rate of incarceration tops the list of BLM grievances—it is in fact the façade behind which these organizations and individuals conceal their goal of upending all of society—we should start with the biggest lie of all, the "carceral state."

CRIME

Any crime level is tragic, in that some innocent victim has had her or his life harmed if not snuffed out, with an impact that then reverberates throughout the family and the community. At the same time, it is also true that the crime rate *and* the incarceration rate have been dropping steadily over the years, the latter most dramatically among African Americans. Data from the FBI's Uniform Crime Reporting Program going back almost thirty years show what Pew Research called "dramatic declines in U.S. violent and property crime rates since the early 1990s."[13] The granular data actually revealed a dramatic implosion of crime since the early 1990s, which was admittedly a time of very high crime in U.S. cities. In November 2020, six months into the BLM mayhem, the Pew Report said,

> Using the FBI data, the violent crime rate fell 49% between 1993 and 2019, with large decreases in the rates of robbery (–68%), murder/non-negligent manslaughter (–47%) and aggravated assault (–43%).... Meanwhile, the property crime rate fell 55%, with big declines in the rates of burglary (–69%), motor vehicle theft (–64%) and larceny/theft (–49%). Using the BJS [Bureau of Justice Statistics] statistics, the declines in the violent and property crime rates are even steeper than those reported by the FBI. Per BJS, the overall violent crime rate fell 74% between 1993 and 2019, while the property crime rate fell 71%.[14]

What the constant disinformation about people hurting produces is the contradiction that, while crime has been dropping very dramatically and for a very long time, Americans believe the opposite. This is why Pew reported that "In 20 of 24 Gallup surveys conducted since 1993, at least 60% of U.S. adults have said there is more crime nationally than there was the year before, despite the generally downward trend in national violent and property crime rates during most of that period."

And what about the prison rate? As one might expect, it has also been plunging. The Department of Justice's Bureau of Justice Statistics revealed in a report in October 2020 (when it could have been read by anyone taking to the streets during that time to protest the incarceration of black Americans) that "The combined state and federal imprisonment rate for 2019 (419 per 100,000 U.S. residents), based on sentenced prisoners (those sentenced to more than one year), decreased 3% from 2018 (432 per 100,000 U.S. residents). This was the lowest imprisonment rate in 24 years, dating back to 1995. Since 2009, the imprisonment rate—the portion of U.S. residents who are in prison—has dropped 17% overall, including 29% among black residents, 24% among Hispanic residents, and 12% among white residents."[15] In other words, in the decade that led to the BLM riots that shook the entire country, the incarceration rate of blacks dropped by close to a third, two and half times the drop for whites, while the drop for those Americans identified as Hispanic dropped by a quarter.

My Heritage colleague Cully Stimson—who along with former Homeland Security deputy director Lora Ries and Zack Smith has performed incredibly by explaining all this throughout 2020— clarified to me in an email why this has happened.

> It is a widely known fact that (until recently in some liberal cities) crime rates have fallen dramatically in the last 20 years. Our point is this: it is precisely BECAUSE of traditional, independent law and order prosecutors and their programs (domestic violence courts; drug courts; family justice centers; teen/peer courts, and thousands of diversionary programs i.e. alternatives to incarceration) that we have a steep decline in incarceration rates and crime rates.

In conclusion, America currently doesn't have a mass incarceration problem but does have a budding "mass crime problem" because the rogue prosecutors described in chapter 6, along with other liberal forces, have been attacking police and even been preventing the enforcement of the law.

As for BLM's claims about police brutality, Brown University professor Glenn Loury gave a lecture in 2021 that put the exaggerations of BLM in perspective. It is important to quote it at length. Loury said:

There are about 1,200 fatal shootings of people by the police in the US each year.... Roughly 300 of those killed are African Americans, about one-fourth, while blacks are about 13 percent of the population. So that's an over-representation, though still far less than a majority of the people who are killed. More whites than blacks are killed by police in the country every year. You wouldn't know that from the activists' rhetoric.

Now, 1,200 may be too many. I am prepared to entertain that idea. I'd be happy to discuss the training of police, the recruitment of them, the rules of engagement that they have with citizens, the accountability that they should face in the event they overstep their authority. These are all legitimate questions. And there *is* a racial disparity although, as I have noted, there is also a disparity in blacks' rate of participation in criminal activity that must be reckoned with as well....

But, in terms of police killings, we are talking about 300 victims per year who are black. Not all of them are unarmed innocents. Some are engaged in violent conflict with police officers that leads to them being killed. Some are instances like George Floyd—problematic in the extreme, without question—that deserve the scrutiny of concerned persons. Still, we need to bear in mind that this is a country of more than 300 million people with scores of concentrated urban areas where police interact with citizens. Tens of thousands of arrests occur daily in the United States. So, these events—which are extremely regrettable and often do not reflect well on the police—are, nevertheless, quite rare.

To put it in perspective, there are about 17,000 homicides in the United States every year, nearly half of which involve black perpetrators. The vast majority of those have other blacks as victims. For every black killed by the police, more than 25 other black people meet their end because of homicides committed by other blacks. This is not to ignore the significance of holding police accountable for how they exercise their power *vis-à-vis* citizens. It is merely to notice how very easy it is to overstate the significance and the extent of this phenomenon, precisely as the Black Lives Matter activists have done.[16]

All Americans can and should know these facts when they encounter those under the BLM trance repeating that America is a "carceral state," whether on social media or at a backyard barbeque with well-intentioned neighbors who are unlikely to have read about these statistics in the *New York Times*. Americans can also point to research that suggests that police officers actually take longer to shoot African American suspects than white or visibly Hispanic suspects. The participants in one experiment "were more likely to shoot unarmed white suspects than unarmed black or Hispanic suspects. Participants were also more likely to fail to fire at armed black suspects than armed white or Hispanic suspects."[17] None of this is to suggest, of course, that many of the 12,000 or so police departments across the United States do not include racists, or that police do not have a real perception problem with the African American community. They do, and they must address it through real reforms—which would have to include reforms that would curb the oversized influence that police unions currently have in management decisions—not through defunding the police.

THE ECONOMY

And what about the economy? Being employed is not just a pipeline to family formation and the American Dream, but the best way to avoid the nightmares of criminality and incarceration. Hard as it may be to remember after so many months of the COVID plague, the news as we unsuspectingly entered the woeful year of 2020 looked very good indeed. Black unemployment in August 2019 had fallen to a record low of 5.5 percent, beating the previous historic low of May 2018, also under President Trump. CNN did have to report this story in September 2019, because you can't not report economic statistics, but the network managed to do so without mentioning the word "Trump" once. CNN also reported that the unemployment rate "among workers who identify themselves as Hispanic or Latino also fell in August to 4.2%, which matched a record low set earlier this year."[18] White unemployment was also low, but it must have stuck in CNN's craw to report also that "this is the smallest gap on record between the respective unemployment rates for blacks and whites."

Again, it is the responsibility of all Americans who want to break the spell we're under to remind their interlocutors of these facts in private or public settings, such as parent-teacher nights and meetings of the local board of education. No, we must all say, "people were not hurting. In fact, the economy was working for all of us before COVID hit, and the racial gap was closing. In fact, the incarceration rate for African Americans was plunging."

The increase in employment opportunities for black Americans had the desired effect of raising median black household income, which in 2018 was above the 2007 pre-recession peak. Alan Berube, a senior fellow at the left-of-center Brookings Institution, found in late 2019, a few months before the country caught on fire, that "black household income is rising across the United States." Berube wrote,

> In the metro areas with the largest increases in Black median household incomes, employment rates for Black adults rose anywhere from 5.6 percentage points (Riverside) to an astonishing

12.7 percentage points (San Francisco) during that period. There was a positive, significant association between the change in Black employment rates and Black median household incomes across metro areas from 2013 to 2018.[19]

This finding substantiated Abigail Thernstrom's observation in her 1995 book, *America in Black and White*, that the racial gap in the median annual income had been closing since 1940. None of this is to deny that worrisome gaps in education, income, wealth, and so on, persist, but it does suggest that the "people are hurting" mantra may be based more on ideology and politics than in actual numbers.

CRT TRAINING

Despite the numbers we have briefly reviewed, we constantly hear an opposite, parallel reality. The exaggerations of BLM and the consequent mass hysteria have led to a whole range of repugnant practices ostensibly meant to purge the country of its racial sin, of its "unconscious bias." They fall under the generic term of "anti-racism" trainings, and we first saw them in the last chapter. They are performative critical race theory struggle sessions and, just like their Maoist antecedents, they aim to reengineer the mind. When they encourage ritualistic white denunciation and white humiliation, as they often do, they are part of the Ignatievan plan to unite the proletariat. The overall purpose is to make Americans accept the root-and-branch societal transformation that BLM and others seek. Indeed, all the top CRT trainers, whether Robin DiAngelo, Ibram X. Kendi, or Glenn E. Singleton, are declared anti-capitalists. The death of George Floyd put them on a meteoric rise. Robin DiAngelo's book *White Fragility* shot to No. 1 on the Amazon Best Seller list. Ten days after Floyd's death, DiAngelo was pulled in to address 184 Democratic members of Congress by conference call, for a "Democratic Caucus family discussion on race." The *New York Times Magazine* quoted her as telling them, "for all the white people listening right now, thinking I am not talking to you, I am looking directly in your eyes and saying, 'It is you.'"[20]

These sessions rely heavily on cultural stereotypes, intimidation if not borderline sadism, and are so obviously racist themselves, that they would have been rejected offhand just a few years ago. Trainers routinely tell little children, for example, that virtues needed in the marketplace, such as punctuality, hard work, and liking to read and write, are products of "whiteism." One of the reasons these sessions spread is that Americans who question this entire approach have become vulnerable to intimidation, if not outright blackmail. If they don't go along and affirm the distasteful postulates of the new ideology, they risk losing their livelihood, being canceled, being shamed, or all the above. The closest thing to it is O'Brien's chilling warning to Winston in George Orwell's *1984*: "Power is inflicting pain and humiliation. Power is in tearing human minds to pieces and putting them together again in new shapes of your own choosing." Exposing the true nature of these practices is key, therefore, in freeing the man on the street to say, "but the emperor has no clothes."

One man who has been crying this from the rooftops is Christopher Rufo, director of the nonprofit Discovery Institute's Center on Wealth and Poverty, and a one-man anti-CRT wrecking crew. Chris is a happy warrior, one who hasn't let the pugnacity required in his work damage his soul. His work against these noxious practices got the attention of President Trump in the fall of 2020 and led to his ban on CRT trainings in the federal workforce and among federal contractors. One of the things Rufo had discovered, and which led to the ban, was that the Treasury Department had "held a training session telling employees that 'virtually all white people contribute to racism' and demanding that white staff members 'struggle to own their racism.'"[21]

Because of his prominence, whistleblowers now routinely come to Rufo. He's so inundated that he sometimes gladly hands these instances of malevolence over to others, like me, to reveal. This was how he was able to discover in October 2020 that public agencies in Seattle were not only giving these training sessions, but were doing so in groups segregated by race, which violates the Constitution and several statutes. One of the agencies was the King County Library System (KCLS), which had hired the diversity training firm Racial Equity Consultants, one of the many companies happy to suck in taxpayer money to implement segregation and the belief that America is institutionally racist. As Rufo reported, at the KCLS trainings "the consultants 'begin with an anti-oppression framework' and use segregated sessions in order to root out 'institutional privileges and systemic inequities embedded in the current socio-political conditions that influence and affect our institutions.'" Another Seattle agency Rufo uncovered was the King County Prosecutor's Office, where "Prosecutor Dan Satterberg and senior staff have recently required employees to sign an 'equity and social justice' pledge and assigned 'continued training for white employees,' who must 'do the work' to 'learn the true history of racism in our country.'"[22] Because of Rufo's work, the agencies exposed were forced to explain their behavior publicly, though unfortunately they did not cease.

Another example came in New York City in 2021, where Mark Federman, the principal at East Side Community School, which teaches students from sixth to twelfth grade, sent parents a letter encouraging them to become "white traitors" so that they could achieve "white abolition." The letter included a graph with the supposed eight stages of whiteness, going from "white supremacist," the most offensive category, all the way to "white abolitionist," which was the optimal stage, going through such in-between categories as "white privilege," "white benefit," and "white critical." We know that Ignatiev was the one who started all this, and we know why. In this particular case, this scheme was invented by Barnor Hesse, an associate professor of African American Studies at Northwestern University.

As Rufo wrote in *City Journal,*

> Federman and Hesse claim to want to abolish "whiteness" as a cultural and social construct, but they also use the term to describe an immutable racial essence. As University of New Mexico professor Geoffrey Miller has observed: "Applied to any other group, this would sound like a monstrous euphemism for mass extermination and cultural annihilation."[23]

Miller is correct, of course; the belief that whites should be exterminated as a group, or even that they are less than human, is receiving a degree of academic support that would get people fired, if not charged with a crime, if it were associated with any other group. Rufo broke the story after one of the school's parents sent him Federman's letter, telling Rufo he found the letter appalling, as did many parents, but no one dared speak out publicly as they feared being called racist. But the exposure of Federman's appalling behavior, which was reported by the *New York Post,* forced him to send another letter to parents, this time insisting that he had done nothing wrong and pleading with them not to speak to journalists.

A related anecdote that shows sunlight acting as a disinfectant came when Representative Keith Ammon introduced the bill HB544 in the New Hampshire House of Representatives; modeled on Rufo's work (and on which I, too, have given advice), it called for a ban on CRT trainings in schools. A young progressive organizer in New Hampshire immediately took to social media to make the oft-repeated claim that merely speaking about these things put people at risk (because "people are hurting"). Testimony by Professor James Lindsay had, moreover, made her fear for her personal safety, she tweeted. "The testimony is bone-chilling. There is so much work to be done here in New Hampshire. Our neighbors of color simply are not safe, and we must be vigilant and protect them," she added in another tweet.[24] Having said that, the Twitter user (whose name is omitted here because the point is not to embarrass her further) then committed the incredibly dishonest act of cropping a picture of Rufo to conceal the fact that his wife is Asian and his children half Asian (Chris himself is of Sicilian origin). Twitter users did not take this deceitful behavior lying down but commented so much on her feed that she made her account private, complaining about "trolls." Similarly, reports by the College Fix and other outlets that pointed out the hypocrisy of Ammon's legislative colleagues, who accused him of racism while defending curricula that elevate race, were shared on social media.

This does not mean that conservatives should ape the left's cancel culture approach. That would just make society culturally poorer. It does mean that conservatives must simply offer fact after fact when the left makes over-the-top claims, such as, for example, that Lindsay's appearance at the New Hampshire hearing made people of color "not safe"—coupled with cropping out actual "people of color" who are related to Rufo. In a tweet thread on February 19, 2021, Lindsay explained what the strategy should be at hearings, which I quote here in full because it brings together many of the different strands that we need as we conceive of a strategy for fighting back, in hearings or day-to-day interactions:

A few reflections after testifying to the legislative committee in New Hampshire regarding HB544 yesterday.

1 Leftists, both clueless and trained as activists, including academics, WILL SHOW UP. So you should too. Get strong personal or expert testimony and show up against CRT.

2 The general public and most elected officials are generally clueless as to what's going on. It is your job to educate them. While the activists say it's not their job to educate YOU, they know who to talk to, and how. They will do a good job of miseducating our leaders. In the NH meeting, so far as I can tell, only the activist member and the bill sponsor have any idea what CRT is (in theory and reality—Maoist cultural revolution tool) and that it's actually being used in trainings and taught in schools. You have to show up and tell them.

3 The activists will also have submitted written testimony and "evidence." In light of the above, you should too. Show, not just tell, them what's happening in your schools and state agencies. Give details, provide receipts. Annotate and explain how it's the divisive teachings.

4 A communist strategy, as this is where CRT gets its plans, is to isolate and swarm. It's therefore a travesty that other states aren't taking up this fight in parallel to NH yesterday. Agitate your state leaders!

5 The activists are small in number but far more organized than you think. If you know how to organize, organize people to show up. Encourage them to give testimony and to sharpen it. Make sure they have links, times, etc. Make it easy for them.

6 In light of the behavior unbecoming her office by a sitting representative in NH, who should now apologize and step down, expect to be smeared during and after on social media. Don't let this daunt you. Stay calm, make your case, and call falsehoods out as false.

7 Be polite and concise. Try to organize your thoughts ahead of time and be forthright and clear while using emotion minimally and appropriately to your testimony, even when smeared and questioned.

8 Don't hedge on the truth. One woman testified that this repro-
duces the Chinese Cultural Revolution. It does. Tell the truth
plainly as it is, unreservedly and without exaggeration. Say
what's really happening in schools to your kids. Tell the truth.

9 Now that at least one example exists, though there are others,
watch some, learn to anticipate their "best" arguments, and, if
you can, give intentional counter-testimony. Organizers should
help facilitate this if possible by finding relevant expertise.

Someone else who has joined the work of exposing these per-
nicious practices is Bari Weiss, a liberal, Jewish, lesbian journalist
who finally left the *New York Times* in 2020 because of workplace
harassment by her colleagues, which the *Times*'s leadership never
bothered to address. What had caused this bullying? The fact that
Weiss refused to go along repeating the baseless incantations. Now
she, like Rufo, receives constant complaints from worried Americans.
"Every day I get phone calls from anxious Americans complaining
about an ideology that wants to pull all of us into the past," she wrote
in early 2021. These Americans are parents worried about the curriculum their children are being taught, or the trainings they must
accept at work, or because they fear the consequences of saying, no,
the emperor has no clothes. "Almost no one who calls me is willing
to go public. And I understand why. To go public with what's happening is to risk their jobs and their reputations."[25]

On February 19, 2021, Weiss wrote about Jodi Shaw, a staffer
at Smith College, who, in October 2020, after filing an internal
complaint over the trainings at the prestigious Massachusetts
college, finally posted a video in which she said,

I ask that Smith College stop reducing my personhood to a racial
category. Stop telling me what I must think and feel about myself.
Stop presuming to know who I am or what my culture is based
upon my skin color. Stop asking me to project stereotypes and
assumptions onto others based on their skin color.

Smith finally offered Shaw a generous settlement in exchange for silence, but Shaw, greatly to her credit, refused the bribe so she could continue to speak out publicly about this scourge plaguing our country. Because she is a single mother of two, Shaw opened a GoFundMe page. In a sign of how low we have sunk, GoFundMe put her fundraiser under review the very next day, February 20. Shaw wrote on Twitter, which had not yet canceled her account, that she thought GoFundMe was motivated by ideological reasons.

This is not how Americans are supposed to live. Shaw's courage is admirable, but the system that is making her suffer in this manner has become abominable. If the government, the schools, and the corporations are not stopped, we will soon become the Land of the Cowed. This is why it is so important that Rufo on January 20—Inauguration Day and the day the new president revoked the ban on trainings—announced the formation of a coalition of law firms and legal foundations called Stop Critical Race Theory "with the specific goal of fighting Critical Race Theory in the courts." A statement said that "Critical race theory-based programs—which perpetuate racial stereotypes, compel discriminatory speech, and create hostile working environments—violate the Civil Rights Act of 1964 and the United States Constitution."[26] Rufo says he hopes that the victories sure to come in the courts will have a ripple effect throughout "every school, government agency and private employer in the nation."

State governments are also getting involved, and many legislators spread throughout this land are calling Rufo, myself, and many others seeking help on how best to stop CRT trainings and the curricula described in the last chapter. The type of law fare the coalition promises, and the state actions being replicated throughout the land, will help create the political climate needed for Americans to regain their voice, and for Shaw not to have to stand alone.

The same type of activism must be brought to the shareholder meetings of companies that spend shareholder money on BLM GNF, M4BL, BLM at School, or any of their tentacles. Part of the reason corporate America has thrown in the towel in the fight against woke culture has to do with buying peace from activist shareholders. Who says conservatives and liberals who understand what is happening can't adopt the same practice? If corporations, local government agencies, and school districts might abstain from blatantly racist "anti-racist trainings" and from equally flagrant curricula for fear of barratry and other litigation, who's to say they won't do the same when it comes to their philanthropy? Conservatives, too, can engineer shareholder petitions, disrupt shareholder meetings, and join proxy fights to force corporations to stop putting their employees through Cultural Revolution struggle sessions and to stop acceding to all the dictates of the woke—in other words, put fear into the hearts of a C-suite. And this time, these activists would actually be helping the bottom line of profits rather than demanding that corporations engage in activities inimical to their self-interests and that of the free market that sustains them.

AND IT DOESN'T EVEN WORK

The postulates and remedies that CRT and BLM propose are not just unconstitutional and immoral but will also severely diminish the ability of individual Americans to improve their chances of success in life. As Rufo wrote in a Heritage paper in early 2021, when he was a visiting scholar,

> Unfortunately, despite the superficial appeal of "fighting racism," these policies will do little to alleviate poverty and inequality in the real world. As scholars such as Ron Haskins, Robert Rector, Isabel Sawhill, and others have demonstrated, the real drivers of American poverty—for all racial groups—are the so-called

"background variables" of family structure, educational attainment, and workforce participation.

There is a reason for this. These policy approaches are not supposed to uplift a single life, only to tear down the existing system. As we saw in the last chapter, the principles of Black Lives Matter at School include calls to be "free from patriarchal practices," and for the "disruption of Western nuclear family dynamics and a return to the 'collective village,'" which should remind us of Marcuse's desire to have the "disintegration of the institutions in which the private interpersonal relations have been organized, particularly the monogamic and patriarchal family." This is all the recognition we need of what all research shows, that a strong, intact family is the most important pillar underpinning society, which is why the family's destruction is always the goal of those who seek to destroy society. Given the devastation of the 72 percent out-of-wedlock birth rate among African Americans, and all the evidence that growing up without a father can lead to poverty, unemployment, criminality, and incarceration, BLM's support for undermining the family is nothing if not perverse.

Black Lives Matter similarly targets educational achievement, which, along with family formation, is one of the necessary requirements of success. Included in the December 10, 2020, list of ten demands that the Black Lives Matter Steering Committee said the Biden/Harris Administration had to accomplish within its first one hundred days was a panoply of requirements that would make educational achievement harder. The very first, in fact, was a call to end the tracking of students, which BLM called "the modern-day segregation inherently fuels equity gaps and creates disparate access to resources that are largely stratified along divisions of race and class [sic]."[27] The letter also called for an end to "high stakes standardized testing" because it said the tests are used "to sort and label Black students as inferior." This was quite an extraordinarily racist statement in itself, but the letter said ominously that candidate Biden had already promised the steering committee in December 2019 that he would end such testing—which he constitutionally lacks the power to do. The letter also called for the ending of law enforcement at schools, which, as has already been noted, would have deleterious consequences for learning; and for Culturally Responsive Teaching methods, which are a waste of limited resources and have a record of failure.[28] In other words, BLM at School's educational demands have nothing to do with educational attainment and everything to do with indoctrinating young minds into Marxist ideas and sexual habits already described in the last chapter.

As for workplace participation, another sine qua non of success, BLM and its CRT ideology militates against garnering the habits conducive to it. The trainer Glenn Singleton, for example, told the *New York Times Magazine*'s Daniel Bergner that valuing "written communication over other forms" is "a hallmark of whiteness." Another such "hallmark" of being white is "scientific, linear thinking. Cause and effect . . . There's this whole group of people who are named the scientists. That's where you get into this whole idea that if it's not codified in scientific thought that it can't be valid." Another trainer, Marcus Moore, listed among white traits "the King's English' rules," "objective, rational, linear thinking" and "quantitative emphasis," "work before play," "plan for future," "adherence to rigid time schedules" and punctuality, or, as Moore called it, an obsession with "mechanical time."

The policy package of BLM and CRT is, in other words, a recipe for failure, so much so that one must wonder if, because failure is necessary for revolution, it is all done on purpose. The point is not workplace participation, nor is it rising incomes, nor educational attainment, and not even diversity—the point is change! Angela Davis made this clear when she spoke to University of Virginia students in 2018 and told them, "Diversity without changing the structure, without calling for structural formation, simply brings those who were previously excluded into a process that continues to be as racist, as misogynist as it was before."[29] Again, we are reminded of O'Brien's quip to Winston.

SO WHAT TO DO?

If we want to prove that black lives matter to us, then the thing to do is to address the causes of the disparities that do exist in education, in income, in wealth—in far too many areas of life. Our political leader, when she comes along to speak truth to power, must address herself not just to the realities stated above, but also to the realities of the existing gaps between the races. As Professor Loury said, "Socially mediated behavioral issues lie at the root of today's racial inequality problem. They are real and must be faced squarely if we are to grasp why racial disparities persist." Loury derides the leftist activists who blame any and all disparities on "white supremacy," "implicit bias," or "anti-black racism." Those activists, he says, are "daring you to disagree with them. They are threatening to 'cancel' you if you do not accept their account: You must be a 'racist.'" But that, adds Loury, is merely "a debater's trick." He is right, and our politicians should ignore such tactics. He continues,

> Nobody wants to be cancelled. But we should all want to stay in touch with reality. Common sense and much evidence suggest that, on the whole, people are not being arrested, convicted, and sentenced because of their race. Those in prison are, in the main, those who have broken the law—who have hurt others, or stolen things, or otherwise violated the basic behavioral norms which make civil society possible. Seeing prisons as a racist conspiracy to confine black people is an absurd proposition. No serious person could believe it.[30]

Sure, all the things we have seen in this chapter and in this book require some courage to say, let alone write. The leader that emerges will have to not only make the case laid out above but also bring together many different tribes within conservatism that are now warring with one another. Bringing under one tent small-government types and a new type of conservative who wants to use government to protect the "common good" will not be easy. But the threat of domestic Marxism, to which this book has tried to alert the American public, should help create the same fusion that we saw take place in the 1950s because of the external Soviet threat. We should welcome, too, liberals who understand the immediacy of the moment. As Bion Bartning of the Foundation Against Intolerance and Racism, which is doing great work against the advance of critical race theory, puts it, this moment calls for "a movement." Our political leader should state the fact that, unless we do reverse the damage that has already been done, all of our lives will become much poorer—so, no, there is no alternative to taking a stand.

None of this is to say that Americans should underestimate the enormity of the challenge we face. Those who have read this book up to this point will understand full well what we face, and why so many others want to sue for peace. Yet Americans should also take heart from the fact that we have defeated communism and fascism before. It took guts, the willingness to put in the long hours to fully size up the Soviet threat, unity among the conservative tribes (fusionism), and the willingness to stick it out for the long haul. It also took the right kind of leader, one who was not in the least interested in containment or détente, much less coexistence. That leader was Ronald Reagan, a Midwestern Happy Warrior with a preternaturally sunny personality but nerves of steel, and all the right instincts about communism. The Soviet Union lasted until the country elected Reagan. We can, again, find the right person who takes the encroachment of communism, this time domestic, seriously, and is unperturbed by the opposition he or she will encounter.

The United States, a country that took me in as an immigrant, is worth fighting for. No, given everything written here, it shouldn't take too much courage to tell our critics that, as chairman of the Claremont Institute Thomas Klingenstein said in remarks in 2020, "Absolutely, black lives matter. They just don't matter to you."[31]

ACKNOWLEDGMENTS

Many people have helped in the conception of this book. Because resistance to the forces I describe in this book will ultimately require a movement, I have consulted with and read people across the political spectrum. There are, therefore, many people to thank.

For starters, I want to thank my family. A book always takes time away from those who love you and want to spend time with you—or need you to take them to practice, the store, or simply to listen to them. I thank my wife and children for giving me time to put these ideas down. I also want to thank my sister Lucy, to whom this book is dedicated, for her love and support for lo these many decades.

I want to thank Kay Coles James and Kim Holmes, two veteran leaders of The Heritage Foundation, and until recently its President and Executive Vice President, respectively, for giving this project their support. Dr. Holmes has, in addition, been not only a leader but also an esteemed colleague for many years, one who has helped shaped my ideas and those of many others. James Carafano has been a greater supporter of my work, including this book, and I'm deeply grateful to have him as a boss. I also want to thank Roger Kimball, Sam Schneider, and Lauren Miklos at Encounter Books for encouraging me to write this book, and for their support. My editor, Nancy Evans of Wilsted and Taylor Publishing Services, did a stellar job in a very short period of time.

I am especially indebted to three colleagues with whom I often coauthor essays, papers, and op-eds: Jonathan Butcher, Lindsey

Burke, and Andrew Olivastro. Their constant counsel, feedback, and, in this particular manuscript, their edits and advice, have been invaluable. So has their friendship been. My work often reflects their analysis.

I also want to thank my colleagues and friends Rob Bluey, Danielle Bonnesen, Marguerite Bowling, John Cooper, Breanna Deutsch, Katie Gorka, Emilie Kao, Walter Lohman, John Malcolm, Lora Ries, Angela Sailor, Brett Schaefer, Greg Scott, Katrina Trinko, Hans von Spakovsky, Bridgett Wagner, and many others on whose professional advice I often rely. Special thanks also go to two former colleagues who are now academics at Hillsdale College, Matthew Spalding and David Azerrad, from whose analysis of the issues tackled in this book, and friendship, I have long been fortunate to benefit.

I would be remiss not to mention the indefatigable professionals at the Capital Research Center, especially Scott Walter, Jake Klein, Robert Stilson, and Kristen Eastlick. I describe the CRC as "indispensable" in this book for a reason—nobody covers the sinews of the hard left's philanthropy like they do. Two fellow writers who understand well the advances that Marxism is making in this country and overseas, James Simpson and Trevor Loudon, also deserve my praise and gratitude.

Finally, there are many other professionals on whose advice, editing, and encouragement I have relied as I wrote this book. Because they are fearful of what it could do to their careers or businesses, they have asked me not to name them. They know who they are and how grateful I am to them. That they feared reprisals, in the Land of the Free, is a statement of where we are in this country at the present moment, and all the more reason why I had to write this book.

Lastly, I know I must have left out friends and colleagues who helped me during the process of writing this book. I apologize to them in advance for the thoughtless omission.

NOTES

INTRODUCTION

1 ABC News provided a transcript of his remarks the next day, which you can find here: Julia Jacobo, "This Is What Trump Told Supporters Before Many Stormed Capitol Hill," ABC News, July 7, 2021, https://abcnews.go.com/Politics/trump-told-supporters-stormed-capitol-hill/story?id=75110558.

2 Mike Gonzalez, "It Didn't Start on January 6: Brief History of Terrorist Violence at Capitol," The Heritage Foundation, February 16, 2021, https://www.heritage.org/crime-and-justice/commentary/it-didnt-start-jan-6-brief-history-terrorist-violence-capitol.

3 Stephen Groves and Lisa Mascaro, "Judge in Chauvin Trial Calls Waters' Comments 'Abhorrent,'" The Associated Press, https://apnews.com/article/maxine-waters-comments-derek-chauvin-trial-c7813707962c9f723c75db54605bad2c.

4 NPR, "Retired Army Lt. Gen. Analyzes the Violent Riot at the Capitol," interview transcript, January 7, 2021, https://www.npr.org/2021/01/17/957779141/retired-u-s-army-lieutenant-general-analyzes-the-violent-riot-at-the-capitol.

5 Insurance Information Institute, "Facts + Statistics: Civil Disorder," https://www.iii.org/fact-statistic/facts-statistics-civil-disorders; Noah Manskar, "Riots Following George Floyd's Death May Cost Insurance Companies up to $2B," The New York Post, September 16, 2020, https://nypost.com/2020/09/16/riots-following-george-floyds-death-could-cost-up-to-2b/; and Jemima McEvoy, "Fourteen Days of Protests, 19 Dead," Forbes, June 8, 2020, https://www.forbes.com/sites/jemimamcevoy/2020/06/08/14-days-of-protests-19-dead/?sh=7bad05ac4de4.

6 David Kilcullen, "America in 2020: 'Insurrection' or 'Incipient Insurgency'?" Foundation for the Defense of Democracies, June 23, 2020, https://www.fdd.org/analysis/2020/06/23/us-insurrection-or-incipient-insurgency/.

7 Central Intelligence Agency, *Guide to the Analysis of Insurgency* (2012), 6–7, Homeland Security Digital Library, https://www.hsdl.org/?abstract&did=713599.

8 Heather Mac Donald, "Trump's Exit," *City Journal*, January 8, 2021, https://www.city-journal.org/trumps-exit.

9 U.S. Crisis Monitor, "Demonstrations and Political Violence in America: New Data for Summer 2020," ACLED," https://acleddata.com/2020/09/03/demonstrations-political-violence-in-america-new-data-for-summer-2020/ (accessed December 3, 2020).

10 CIA, *Guide to the Analysis of Insurgency*, 10.

11 Tom Kertscher, "Is Black Lives Matter a Marxist Movement?" PolitiFact, July 21, 2020, https://www.politifact.com/article/2020/jul/21/black-lives-matter-marxist-movement/.

12 David Remnick, "An American Uprising," *The New Yorker*, May 31, 2020, https://www.newyorker.com/news/daily-comment/an-american-uprising-george-floyd-minneapolis-protests?mbid=social_twitter&utm_source=twitter&utm_brand=tny&utm_social-type=owned&utm_medium=social.

13 Mayor Ted Wheeler, City of Portland, letter to President Trump, August 28, 2020, https://www.portland.gov/sites/default/files/2020-08/8.28.20-letter-to-president-trump.pdf.

14 Bryan Burrough, *Days of Rage: America's Radical Underground, the FBI, and the Forgotten Age of Revolutionary Violence* (New York: Penguin Press, 2015), 68.

15 Justice John Marshall Harlan's dissent in *Plessy v. Ferguson,* 163 U.S. 537 (1896), available at https://chnm.gmu.edu/courses/nclc375/harlan.html.

16 "Angela Davis and BLM Co-Founder Alicia Garza in Conversation Across Generations," *Democracy Now!* January 23, 2017, https://www.youtube.com/watch?v=_gqGVni8Oec.

17 Yaron Steinbuch, "Black Lives Matter Co-Founder Describes Herself as a Trained Marxist," *The New York Post*, June 25, 2020, https://nypost.com/2020/06/25/blm-co-founder-describes-herself-as-trained-marxist/.

18 California Cultures, UC San Diego, *Growing Activism: Labor/Community Strategy Center*, UCTV, April 30, 2007, https://www.uctv.tv/shows/Growing-Activism-Labor-Community-Strategy-Center-12261.

19 Congressional Black Caucus, letter to Director Christopher Wray, Federal Bureau of Investigation, October 13, 2017, https://cbc.house.gov/uploadedfiles/cbc_rm_thompson_cummings_conyers_letter_to_fbi_re_intel_assessment.pdf.

20 Office of Senator Cory Booker, "VIDEO: In Response to Booker Questioning, FBI Director Announces Agency No Longer Using Baseless 'Black Identity Extremists' Label," June 23, 2020, https://www.booker.senate.gov/news/press/video-in-response-to-booker-questioning-fbi-director-announces-agency-no-longer-using-baseless-and-ldquoblack-identity-extremists-and-rdquo-label.

21 Aristotle, *Nicomachean Ethics*, Book VI, http://people.bu.edu/wwildman/WeirdWildWeb/courses/wphil/readings/wphil_rdg09_nichomacheanethics_entire.htm.

CHAPTER 1. THE FOUNDING V. SLAVERY

1 Frederick Douglass, *My Bondage and My Freedom* (London: Partridge and Oakey, 1855), chapter 17, https://etc.usf.edu/lit2go/45/my-bondage-and-my-freedom/1482/chapter-17-the-last-flogging/.

2 C. Bradley Thompson, *America's Revolutionary Mind* (New York: Encounter Books, 2019), 362.

3 Harry Jaffa, "Calhoun versus Madison," Claremont, California, 2001, https://www.loc.gov/loc/madison/jaffa-paper.html.

4 "James Buchanan," https://www.tulane.edu/~sumter/Buchanan.html.

5 W. D. Weatherford, *The Negro from Africa to America* (George H. Doran Company, 1924), 368, https://www.google.com/books/edition/The_Negro_from_Africa_to_America/dq4TAAAAYAAJ?hl=en&gbpv=1&dq=%22assem blies+of+slaves,+free+negroes,+mulattoes+and+mestizoes%22+%22ment al+instruction%22+south+carolina+1800&pg=PA368&printsec=frontcover. Capitalization per the original.

6 Christopher Frank Lee, "Establishing a Republic: The South Carolina Assembly, 1783–1800" (PhD diss., University of Virginia, 1986), 296, file:///C:/Users/gonzalezm/Downloads/X001276655.pdf.

7 "Historic Resource Study" (Tuskegee Institute, National Historic Site, 2019), 2-2, http://npshistory.com/publications/tuin/hrs-2019.pdf.

8 Alabama's 1833 Slave Code, in *A Digest of the Laws of the State of Alabama* (1833), https://archives.alabama.gov/cornerstone/slavecode1833/title_page.html.

9 Chief Justice Roger Taney, *Dred Scott, Plaintiff in Error, v. John F. A. Sandford*, https://www.law.cornell.edu/supremecourt/text/60/393.

10 Ibid.

11 Abraham Lincoln, "Document: Speech on the Dred Scott Decision," June 26, 1857, https://teachingamericanhistory.org/library/document/speech-on-the-dred-scott-decision/.

12 "Justice Curtis Dissenting," American History: From Revolution to Reconstruction, http://www.let.rug.nl/usa/documents/1826-1850/dred-scott-case/justice-curtis-dissenting.php.

13 David Azerrad, "What the Constitution Really Says About Race and Slavery," The Heritage Foundation, December 28, 2015, https://www.heritage.org/the-constitution/commentary/what-the-constitution-really-says-about-race-and-slavery.

14 Quoted as direct speech in Peter A. Dorsey, *Slavery as Metaphor in Revolutionary America* (Knoxville, Tenn.: The University of Tennessee Press, 2009), 214, and as reported speech by François Furstenberg in "Atlantic Slavery, Atlantic Freedom: George Washington, Slavery and Trans-Atlantic Abolitionist Networks," *The William & Mary Quarterly* 68, no. 2, 280, from where the "Time, patience…" quote comes.

15 Sean Wilentz, "Constitutionally, Slavery Is No National Institution," *The New York Times*, September 16, 2015, https://www.nytimes.com/2015/09/16/opinion/constitutionally-slavery-is-no-national-institution.html.

16 *Collected Works of Abraham Lincoln*, vol. 3, Third Debate with Stephen A. Douglas, https://quod.lib.umich.edu/l/lincoln/lincoln3/1:17?rgn=div1;view=fulltext.

17 Bushrod Washington, "#BLM Founders: Support the Constitution and You're a Racist!," February 26, 2016, https://thefederalistpapers.org/us/blm-founders-support-the-constitution-and-youre-a-racist.

18 "Alicia Garza: Call of Service Lecture, 2015," http://pbha.org/stories/alicia-garza-call-of-service-lecture-2015/.

19 Black Lives Matter Week of Action in Schools, DC Area Educators for Social Justice, December 19, 2018, https://www.dcareaeducators4socialjustice.org/news/kenmore.

20 Carla Bell, "Black Lives Matter at School Week: A Complex Time of Learning," Seattleschild.com, March 2019, https://www.seattleschild.com/black-lives-matter-at-school-week-a-complex-important-time-of-learning/.

21 Nikole Hannah-Jones, "Our Democracy's Founding Ideals Were False When They Were Written. Black Americans Have Fought to Make Them True," *The New York Times Magazine*, August 14, 2019, https://www.nytimes.com/interactive/2019/08/14/magazine/black-history-american-democracy.html.

22 Ibram X. Kendi, *How to Be an Antiracist* (New York: One World, an Imprint of Random House, 2019), 10 and 32.

23 The author was a member of the Commission.

24 For a fuller discussion on the farm bill, see Mike Gonzalez, "The Left's New Constitution," *City Journal*, March 15, 2021, https://www.city-journal.org/the-lefts-new-constitution.

25 See Charles R. Kesler, *Crisis of the Two Constitutions* (New York: Encounter Books, 2021), for a full discussion of this problem.

26 Ibram X. Kendi, *Stamped from the Beginning* (Nation Books, 2016), 116.

27 Azerrad, "What the Constitution Really Says."

28 Frederick Douglass, "What to the Slave is the Fourth of July?," 1852, https://liberalarts.utexas.edu/coretexts/_files/resources/texts/c/1852%20Douglass%20July%204.pdf.

29 Video of Garza's speech at the Left Forum panel, No Justice, No Peace: Confronting the Crises of Capitalism & Democracy, http://othervoicesotherchoices.blogspot.com/search/label/Alicia%20Garza.

30 Julia Carrie Wong, "The Bay Area Roots of Black Lives Matter," *SF Weekly*, November 11, 2015, https://www.sfweekly.com/news/the-bay-area-roots-of-black-lives-matter/.

31 Damon Root, "Frederick Douglass on Capitalism, Slavery and the 'Arrant Nonsense' of Socialism," *Reason*, August 28, 2016, https://reason.

com/2016/08/28/frederick-douglass-on-capitalism-slavery/. Timothy Sandefur also includes most of these quotations in *Frederick Douglass: Self-Made Man* (Washington, DC: Cato Institute, 2018), 74.

32 John C. Calhoun, "Speech on the Oregon Bill," June 27, 1848, https://teachingamericanhistory.org/library/document/oregon-bill-speech/.

33 Ibid.

34 Ibid.

35 The Negro Law of South Carolina, Section Two, Genealogy Trails, History Group, http://genealogytrails.com/scar/negro_law.htm.

36 Lee, "Establishing a Republic," 294.

37 Ibid., 295.

38 David W. Dangerfield, "Hard Rows to Hoe: Free Black Farmers in Antebellum South Carolina," PhD diss., University of South Carolina, August 9, 2014, https://scholarcommons.sc.edu/cgi/viewcontent.cgi?article=3778&context=etd, quoting Robert Olwell, *Masters, Slaves, and Subjects: The Culture of Power in the South Carolina Low Country, 1740–1790* (Ithaca: Cornell University Press, 1998), 25 and 282.

39 Lincoln, "Document: Speech on the Dred Scott Decision."

40 See the case of New York in 1788 in John P. Kaminski's essay in *The Reluctant Pillar: New York and the Adoption of the Federal Constitution* (Troy, NY: Russell Sage College, 1985), https://files.eric.ed.gov/fulltext/ED345999.pdf.

41 Lincoln, "Document: Speech on the Dred Scott Decision."

42 Article 6, Transcript of the Northwest Ordinance, Ourdocuments.gov, https://www.ourdocuments.gov/doc.php?flash=false&doc=8&page=transcript.

43 Calhoun, "Speech on the Oregon Bill."

44 Peter W. Wood, *1620: A Critical Response to the 1619 Project* (New York: Encounter Books, 2020), 3.

45 Ibid., 44.

46 Historical Documents, Colonial Laws, https://www.pbs.org/wgbh/aia/part1/1h315.html.

47 Wood, *1620*, 14.

48 Justice John Marshall Harlan's dissent in *Plessy v. Ferguson*, 163 U.S. 537 (1896), available at https://chnm.gmu.edu/courses/nclc375/harlan.html.

49 For an example of demands for unequal treatment, see the demands for "individualized treatment—context—that pays attention to minorities' lives" in Richard Delgado, *Critical Race Theory: An Introduction* (New York: New York University Press, 2017), 65.

50 The figures on lynchings are provided by the Tuskegee Institute: https://web.archive.org/web/20100629081241/http://www.law.umkc.edu/faculty/projects/ftrials/shipp/lynchingsstate.html.

CHAPTER 2. THE SOVIETS' FAILED INFILTRATION

1   Partially quoted by Damon Root in "Frederick Douglass on Capitalism, Slavery and the 'Arrant Nonsense' of Socialism," *Reason*, August 28, 2016, https://reason.com/2016/08/28/frederick-douglass-on-capitalism-slavery/. From Carl J. Guarneri, *The Utopian Alternative: Fourierism in Nineteenth-Century America* (Ithaca and London: Cornell University Press, 1991), 255.

2   Karl Marx, "Theories of Surplus Value," 1863, https://www.marxists.org/archive/marx/works/1863/theories-surplus-value/ch07.htm.

3   Conversation between Glenn Loury, John McWhorter, and Shelby and Eli Steele, transcribed and published by Quillette on November 19, 2020, https://quillette.com/2020/11/19/victimhood-or-development/.

4   Quoted by Harold Cruse, *The Crisis of the Negro Intellectual* (New York: New York Review of Books, 1967), 34.

5   Ibid., 9.

6   Ibid., 10.

7   Theodore Draper, *American Communism and Soviet Russia* (New York: Viking Press, 1957), 325.

8   Robert Belano, "Langston Hughes Reflects on the Promise of the Soviet Union," Left Voice, February 18, 2020, https://www.leftvoice.org/langston-hughes-reflects-on-the-promise-of-the-soviet-union.

9   *The Collected Works of Langston Hughes: Essays on Art, Race, Politics, and World Affairs* (Columbia: University of Missouri Press, 2001), 74.

10 Claude McKay, quoted by Joy Gleason Carew in "Translating Whose Vision?: Claude McKay, Langston Hughes, Paul Robeson and the Soviet Experiment," *Intercultural Communications Studies* (University of Louisville), 23, no. 2 (2014): 4, https://www.s3-live.kent.edu/s3fs-root/s3fs-public/file/Joy-Gleason-Carew.pdf.

11 Ibid.

12 Ibid.

13 Ibid.

14 Cruse, *Crisis of the Negro Intellectual*, 6.

15 Britannica, "Universal Negro Improvement Association," https://www.britannica.com/topic/Universal-Negro-Improvement-Association.

16 Shawn Carter, "The Economic Philosophy of Marcus Garvey," *The Western Journal of Black Studies* 26, no. 1 (2002): 3.

17 Marcus Garvey, "Explanation of the Objects of the Universal Negro Improvement Association (1921)," The American Yawp Reader, https://www.americanyawp.com/reader/22-the-new-era/marcus-garvey-explanation-of-the-objects-of-the-universal-negro-improvement-association-1921/.

18 Stephen Cooper, "The Case for a Posthumous Pardon of Marcus Garvey," *The Hill*, October 13, 2016, https://thehill.com/blogs/pundits-blog/crime/300847-the-case-for-a-posthumous-pardon-of-marcus-garvey.

19 "Alliances," *The Wire*, https://www.imdb.com/title/tt0763098/characters/nm0835120.

20 Cooper, "Case for a Posthumous Pardon of Marcus Garvey."

21 Shawn Carter, quoting from A. Jacques-Garvey, *The Philosophy and Opinions of Marcus Garvey* (New York: Atheneum, 1969).

22 Ibid.

23 Ibid.

24 Bryan Burrough, *Days of Rage: America's Radical Underground, the FBI, and the Forgotten Age of Revolutionary Violence* (New York: Penguin Press, 2015), 34.

25 "Lessons from Fidel: Black Lives Matter and the Transition of El Comandante," November 27, 2016, https://medium.com/@BlackLivesMatterNetwork/lessons-from-fidel-black-lives-matter-and-the-transition-of-el-comandante-c11ee5e51fbo#.gclgjnrw1.

26 Draper, *American Communism and Soviet Russia*, 163.

27 Ryan Miniot, *The Black Left's War on Marcus Garvey and Garveyism* (Simmons College, 2010), https://beatleyweb.simmons.edu/scholar/files/original/fbca6e9c15e516168f538fa9993d3c40.pdf.

28 Draper, *American Communism and Soviet Russia*, 330, 331.

29 Ibid., 331.

30 Ibid., 332.

31 Marcus Garvey, *Message to the People: The Course of African Philosophy* (Dover Publications, 2020), 99, https://www.google.com/books/edition/Message_to_the_People/_K3qDwAAQBAJ?hl=en&gbpv=1&bsq=communists.

32 Draper, *American Communism and Soviet Russia*, 323.

33 Ibid.

34 A good definition came in a 1958 FBI report, "The Communist Party and the Negro, 1953–1956," which stated, "The term 'Black Belt' as used by communists refers to the portion of the southern United States containing a large concentration of the Negro population"; https://www.eisenhowerlibrary.gov/sites/default/files/research/online-documents/civil-rights-eisenhower-administration/1956-10-communist-party-and-the negro.pdf.

35 Quoted by Charles R. Holm, in "Black Radicals and Marxist Internationalism," MA thesis (University of Nebraska, 2014), 108, https://digitalcommons.unl.edu/cgi/viewcontent.cgi?article=1071&context=historydiss.

36 Editorial quoted by Draper, *American Communism and Soviet Russia*.

37 FBI report, "The Communist Party and the Negro, 1953–1956," https://www.eisenhowerlibrary.gov/sites/default/files/research/online-documents/civil-rights-eisenhower-administration/1956-10-communist-party-and-the-negro.pdf.

38 Quoted by Sean Braswell, "When the Soviet Union Tried to Woo Black America," https://www.ozy.com/true-and-stories/when-the-soviet-union-tried-to-woo-black-america/62517/.

39 Draper, *American Communism and Soviet Russia*.

40 FBI report, "The Communist Party and the Negro, 1953–1956."

41 Ibid., ii.

42 M. Stanton Evans and Herbert Romerstein, *Stalin's Secret Agents* (New York: Threshold Editions, Simon & Schuster, 2012), 4, 5.

CHAPTER 3. THEN THE 1960S HAPPENED

1 Figure provided by Bryan Burrough in *Days of Rage: America's Radical Underground, the FBI, and the Forgotten Age of Revolutionary Violence* (New York: Penguin Press, 2015), 5.

2 For a discussion of how the Office of Management and Budget created the Hispanic and Asian American categories for government use, see Mike Gonzalez, *The Plot to Change America* (New York: Encounter Books, 2020), 48.

3 Herbert Marcuse, *One-Dimensional Man: Studies in the Ideology of Advanced Industrial Society* (Boston: Beacon Press, 1991), 256–257, quoted in Gonzalez, *Plot to Change America*, 134.

4 For examples of two Weathermen recanting their past violence, see Daniel J. Wakin, "Quieter Lives for 60's Militants, But Intensity of Beliefs Hasn't Faded," *The New York Times*, August 24, 2003, https://www.nytimes.com/2003/08/24/nyregion/quieter-lives-for-60-s-militants-but-intensity-of-beliefs-hasn-t-faded.html.

5 Figure reported by Burrough, *Days of Rage*, 7.

6 "'White Guilt' and the End of the Civil Rights Era," NPR interview, May 5, 2006, https://www.npr.org/templates/story/story.php?storyId=5385701.

7 Shelby Steele, "The Right and the Moral High Ground," *The Wall Street Journal*, March 31, 2019, https://www.wsj.com/articles/the-right-and-the-moral-high-ground-11554057729.

8 Shelby Steele, *Shame: How America's Past Sins Have Polarized Our Country* (New York: Basic Books, 2015), 33, quoted in Joshua Mitchell, *American Awakening* (New York: Encounter Books, 2020), 44.

9 Burrough, *Days of Rage*, 57.

10 Charles Hamilton, "An Advocate of Black Power Defines It," *The New York Times*, April 14, 1968, https://timesmachine.nytimes.com/timesmachine/1968/04/14/91225005.html?pageNumber=286.

11 See the author's treatment of this period in Mike Gonzalez, "We Might Get Fooled Again," *The Wall Street Journal*, July 9, 2020, https://www.wsj.com/articles/we-might-get-fooled-again-11594336612.

12 Mitchell, *American Awakening*, 44.

13 PBS, "Marcus Garvey: Look for Me in the Whirlwind: Earl and Louise Little," https://www.pbs.org/wgbh/americanexperience/features/garvey-little/.

14 Ray Smith, "Malcolm X: You Show Me a Socialist, I'll Show You a Bloodsucker," *Socialist Appeal*, February 23, 2015, https://www.socialist.net/malcolm-x-you-show-me-a-capitalist-i-ll-show-you-a-bloodsucker.htm.

15 Deneen L. Brown, "Martin Luther King Met Malcolm X. Just Once," *The Washington Post*, January 14, 2018, https://www.washingtonpost.com/news/

retropolis/wp/2018/01/14/martin-luther-king-jr-met-malcolm-x-just-once-the-photo-still-haunts-us-with-what-was-lost/.

16   Quoted by Burrough, *Days of Rage*, 35.

17   "Farrakhan Regrets Role in Malcolm X's Death," *The Washington Post*, March 11, 2000, https://www.washingtonpost.com/archive/politics/2000/05/11/farrakhan-regrets-role-in-malcolm-xs-death/f8880174-939c-40f6-b1e0-e0f79e6673e0/.

18   "Patrisse Cullors: Malcolm Revisited," October 2, 2020, https://www.redcat.org/event/patrisse-cullors-malcolm-revisited.

19   Conversation between Glenn Loury, John McWhorter, and Shelby and Eli Steele, transcribed and published by Quillette on November 19, 2020, https://quillette.com/2020/11/19/victimhood-or-development/.

20   Burrough, *Days of Rage*, 37.

21   Digital Gateway, "1966, Stokely Carmichael Elected as SNCC Chair," https://snccdigital.org/events/stokely-carmichael-elected-snccs-chair/#:~:text=After%20a%20late%20night%20of,the%20morning%2C%20Carmichael%20won%20handily.

22   Testimony of Stokely Carmichael, March 25, 1970, Appendix, 21, https://www.google.com/books/edition/Testimony_of_Stokely_Carmichael/Ux83AQAAIAAJ?hl=en&gbpv=1&bsq=%22because%20at%20that%20time%20Martin%20Luther%20King%20was%20the%20central%20figure%22.

23   David Remnick, "An American Uprising," *The New Yorker*, May 31, 2020, https://www.newyorker.com/news/daily-comment/an-american-uprising-george-floyd-minneapolis-protests?mbid=social_twitter&utm_source=twitter&utm_brand=tny&utm_social-type=owned&utm_medium=social.

24   Burrough, *Days of Rage*, 39.

25   Ibid.

26   Randall Kennedy, "Reflections on Black Power," in *Reassessing the Sixties: Debating the Political and Cultural Legacy*, edited by Stephen Macedo (New York: W. W. Norton, 1997), 240, 242.

27   David Azerrad, "The Promises and Perils of Identity Politics," The Heritage Foundation, January 23, 2019, 21.

28   Stokely Carmichael and Charles V. Hamilton, *Black Power: The Politics of Liberation in America* (New York: Vintage Books, 1967), 45.

29   "Fidel Castro Speech on July 26 Anniversary," http://lanic.utexas.edu/project/castro/db/1967/19670726.html.

30   "Stokely Carmichael, 1941–1998," https://www.encyclopedia.com/people/social-sciences-and-law/social-reformers/stokely-carmichael.

31   See, for example, Daniela Charris's paper for Franklin and Marshall's Junto Society, "#BlackLivesMatter and Black Power: A Black Feminist Outlook," https://www.fandm.edu/uploads/files/76299744321824579-charris-junto.pdf.

32   Victoria M. Massie, "67 Former Civil Rights Era Activists Endorse Black

Lives Matter," Vox, August 9, 2016, https://www.vox.com/2016/8/9/12411214/civil-rights-black-lives-matter-endorsement.

33 Essay by Eldridge Cleaver, quoted in Burrough, *Days of Rage*, 46.

34 Burrough, *Days of Rage*, 51.

35 Ibid., 178, 173.

36 Dennis A. Pluchinsky, *Anti-American Terrorism: From Eisenhower to Trump* (London and New York: World Scientific Publishing, 2020), 99.

37 Coordinating Committee, the Black Liberation Army, "Message to the Black Movement: A Political Statement from the Black Underground," ii, https://archive.lib.msu.edu/AFS/dmc/radicalism/public/all/messageblackmovement/AAL.pdf?CFID=327481&CFTOKEN=39064116.

38 Figure for the dead from the NYC Fraternal Order of Police, https://web.archive.org/web/20060102131029/http://www.nysfop.org/events/kathy_boudin.htm. Armstrong Williams and others put it higher, at at least thirteen: "What Do Groups Including Antifa and Black Lives Matter Hope to Accomplish?," September 22, 2020, https://katu.com/news/armstrong-army-strong/what-do-groups-including-antifa-and-black-lives-matter-hope-to-accomplish.

39 Jone Johnson Lewis, "Biography of Angela Davis, Political Activist and Academic," ThoughtCo., November 9, 2020, https://www.thoughtco.com/angela-davis-biography-3528285; and "Angela Davis," National Archives, African American Heritage, https://www.archives.gov/research/african-americans/individuals/angela-davis.

40 "Oral Histories: Angela Davis," C-SPAN, April 15, 2009, https://www.c-span.org/video/?328898-1/angela-davis-oral-history-interview.

41 Elinor Langer, "Autobiography as an Act of Political Communication," *The New York Times*, October 27, 1974, https://archive.nytimes.com/www.nytimes.com/books/98/03/08/home/davis-autobio.html.

42 Johnson Lewis, "Biography of Angela Davis, Political Activist and Academic."

43 Ibid.

44 "Oral Histories: Angela Davis," C-SPAN.

45 For a look at the charges against Davis, see Earl Caldwell, "A Shotgun That Miss Davis Purchased Is Linked to the Fatal Shooting of Judge," *The New York Times*, April 18, 1972, https://www.nytimes.com/1972/04/18/archives/a-shotgun-that-miss-davis-purchased-is-linked-to-the-fatal-shooting.html.

46 Philip Hager, "Five Factors Noted in Angela Davis's Verdict," *The Los Angeles Times*, June 6, 1972, https://documents.latimes.com/5-factors-noted-angela-davis-innocent-verdict/.

47 See Mike Gonzalez, "Angela Davis and the Distortion of Diversity," The Heritage Foundation, May 4, 2018, https://www.heritage.org/civil-society/commentary/angela-davis-and-the-distortion-diversity.

48 Burrough, *Days of Rage*, 474, 475.

49 Ibid., 238.

50 Ibid.

51 For descriptions of Rosenberg's charges and trial, see Catherine Lucey, "From Radical to Life of Service," March 7, 2011, *The Philadelphia Inquirer*, https://www.inquirer.com/philly/hp/news_update/20110307_From_radical_to___life_of_service_.html; and Hollie McKay, "Behind Susan Rosenberg and the Roots of Domestic Extremism," Fox News, November 17, 2020, https://www.foxnews.com/us/susan-rosenberg-left-wing-domestic-extremism-roots.

52 "Port Huron Statement. Introduction, Agenda for a Generation," http://www2.iath.virginia.edu/sixties/HTML_docs/Resources/Primary/Manifestos/SDS_Port_Huron.html.

53 For the original draft, see https://www.sds-1960s.org/PortHuronStatement-draft.htm.

54 Burrough, *Days of Rage*, 59, 60.

55 Ibid., 65.

56 "You Don't Need a Weatherman to Know Which Way the Wind Blows," June 18, 1969, https://www.sds-1960s.org/sds_wuo/weather/weatherman_document.txt.

57 Coordinating Committee, the Black Liberation Army, "Message to the Black Movement: A Political Statement from the Black Underground," https://archive.lib.msu.edu/AFS/dmc/radicalism/public/all/messageblackmovement/AAL.pdf?CFID=327481&CFTOKEN=39064116.

CHAPTER 4. BLM

1 This exchange is transcribed from the January 27, 2017, episode of *Democracy Now!*, "Angela Davis and BLM Co-Founder Alicia Garza in Conversation Across Generations," https://www.youtube.com/watch?v=_gqGVni8Oec.

2 Aristotle, *Nicomachean Ethics*, Book VI, http://people.bu.edu/wwildman/WeirdWildWeb/courses/wphil/readings/wphil_rdg09_nichomacheanethics_entire.htm.

3 For full disclosure, the author was a member of the White House 1776 Commission. Please see my response to Biden's action, "Biden's Disbanding of 1776 Commission Shows Left's War on U.S. History," The Heritage Foundation, January 20, 2021, https://www.heritage.org/american-founders/commentary/bidens-disbanding-1776-commission-shows-lefts-war-us-history.

4 Jemima McEvoy, "'We Don't Want Biden' Eight Arrested in Portland After Anti-Fascist Demonstrators Vandalize Democratic Party HQ," *Forbes*, January 21, 2021, https://www.forbes.com/sites/jemimamcevoy/2021/01/21/we-dont-want-biden-eight-arrested-in-portland-after-anti-fascist-demonstrators-vandalize-democratic-party-hq/?sh=2095e4972a50.

5 Larry Buchanan, Quoctrung Bui, and Jugal K. Patel, "Black Lives Matter May Be the Largest Movement in U.S. History," *The New York Times*, July 3, 2020, https://www.nytimes.com/interactive/2020/07/03/us/george-floyd-protests-crowd-size.html.

6 "Black Lives Matter: 2020 Impact Report," 7, https://blacklivesmatter.com/wp-content/uploads/2021/02/blm-2020-impact-report.pdf.

7 U.S. Crisis Monitor, https://acleddata.com/2020/09/03/demonstrations-political-violence-in-america-new-data-for-summer-2020/.

8 Jenna Wortham, "A 'Glorious, Poetic Rage,'" *The New York Times*, June 5, 2020, https://www.nytimes.com/2020/06/05/sunday-review/black-lives-matter-protests-floyd.html?auth=login-google.

9 Andrea Castillo, "How Two Black Women in L.A. Helped Build Black Lives Matter from Hashtag to Global Movement," *Los Angeles Times*, June 21, 2020, https://www.latimes.com/california/story/2020-06-21/black-lives-matter-los-angeles-patrisse-cullors-melina-abdullah.

10 For two news reports out of many describing these changes, see Rebecca Torrence, "It's Bigger Than Us," *The Chronicle*, September 17, 2020, https://www.dukechronicle.com/article/2020/09/duke-university-abolish-fraternity-sorority-panhel-fight-greek-life; and Corey Kilgannon, "Columbia Marching Band Shuts Itself Down over Offensive Behavior," *The New York Times*, September 15, 2020, https://www.nytimes.com/2020/09/15/nyregion/columbia-marching-band-shutdown.html.

11 Tom Kertscher, "Is Black Lives Matter a Marxist Movement?," PolitiFact, July 21, 2020, https://www.politifact.com/article/2020/jul/21/black-lives-matter-marxist-movement/.

12 Patrisse Cullors and asha bandele, *When They Call You a Terrorist: A Black Lives Matter Memoir* (St. Martin's Press, 2017), 1.

13 #BlogHer15, Assata Chant, July 21, 2015, https://www.youtube.com/watch?v=dUZDZaWNOFg#action=share.

14 This biographical language can be found everywhere, including in the entry for Opal Tometi in SpeakerBooking, https://www.speakerbookingagency.com/talent/opal-tometi.

15 Micha Frazer-Carroll, "What I Learned from Founding Black Lives Matter," Dazed, December 19, 2019, https://www.dazeddigital.com/politics/article/47167/1/opal-tometi-what-i-learned-from-founding-black-lives-matter.

16 Opal Tometi, "Black Lives Matter Network Denounces U.S. 'Continuing Intervention' in Venezuela," December 26, 2015, https://venezuelanalysis.com/analysis/11789.

17 Rosa-Luxemburg-Stiftung, Interview with Opal Tometi, https://www.youtube.com/watch?v=ho_v_iN-JM8.

18 Cullors and bandele, *When They Call You a Terrorist*.

19 Ibid.

20 The Eric Mann talk at UCSD can be seen in the video *Growing Activism: Labor/Community Strategy Center*, February 8, 2008, https://www.youtube.com/watch?v=BO6MR2s4aos.

21 Video of the event can be seen at https://www.youtube.com/watch?v=uoCHEgqKwD4.

22 Patrisse Cullors, "Abolition and Reparations: Histories of Resistance,

Transformative Justice, and Accountability," *Harvard Law Review*, April 10, 2019, https://harvardlawreview.org/2019/04/abolition-and-reparations-histories-of-resistance-transformative-justice-and-accountability/.

23 Left Forum 2015—Saturday Evening Event, May 30, 2015, http://othervoicesotherchoices.blogspot.com/search/label/Alicia%20Garza.

24 Julia Carrie Wong, "The Bay Area Roots of Black Lives Matter," *SF Weekly*, November 11, 2015, https://www.sfweekly.com/news/the-bay-area-roots-of-black-lives-matter/.

25 Peter Byrne, "SOUL Trainers," *SF Weekly*, October 16, 2002, https://www.sfweekly.com/news/soul-trainers/.

26 James Simpson, "Reds Exploiting Blacks, the Roots of Black Lives Matter," January 12, 2016, https://www.aim.org/special-report/reds-exploiting-blacks-the-roots-of-black-lives-matter/. And indeed, there are plenty of examples of SOUL and FRSO teaming up, as can be seen in this Center for Political Education, Marxism 101 Resources announcement (where the National Domestic Alliance, another Garza group, is also involved): https://politicaleducation.org/program/2017-2/marxism-101-resources/; or, "What Is Going to Get Revolution out of the Air and onto the Ground," https://collectiveliberation.org/our-work-2/study-and-struggle/.

27 That LeftRoots is aligned with the FRSO can be seen from the way it quotes directly from it in LeftRoots, "From the Base: Revolutionary Left Organizing in the U.S.," https://leftroots.net/from-the-base/.

28 Scott Walter, "Radical Lives Matter," Capital Research Center, November 18, 2020, https://capitalresearch.org/article/radical-lives-matter/.

29 The Marxist-Leninist, A Communist Website, "Fight Back at the U.S. Social Forum," June 17, 2010, https://marxistleninist.wordpress.com/2010/06/17/fight-back-at-the-u-s-social-forum/#more-5863.

30 Interview with Giselle Fernandez, June 23, 2020, "Black Lives Matter Co-Founder Melina Abdullah on Roots of Her Activism," Spectrum News, https://spectrumnews1.com/ca/la-west/la-stories/2020/06/23/black-lives-matter-co-founder-melina-abdullah-on-roots-of her-activism#.

31 John Riemann's writings can be perused here: https://oaklandsocialist.com/category/john-riemanns-personal-blog/.

32 Michael Hrebeniak, "Guenter Reimann: Casting a Critical Eye on Capitalism," *The Guardian*, February 28, 2005, https://www.theguardian.com/news/2005/mar/01/guardianobituaries.germany.

33 "Black Lives Matter Leader's Campaign to Cancel Capitalism Shaped by Marxist Upbringing," *The Daily Wire*, July 2, 2020, https://www.truenewshub.com/dailywire/black-lives-matter-leaders-campaign-to-cancel-capitalism-shaped-by-marxist-upbringing/.

34 Sharon McNary, "Black Lives Matter-LA Leader Explains 'Very Deliberate Choice' to Demonstrate in Upscale Neighborhoods," LAist, May 31, 2020, https://laist.com/2020/05/31/melina-abdullah-black-lives-matter-la-protest-police-violence-george-floyd.php.

35 Simpson, "Reds Exploiting Blacks, the Roots of Black Lives Matter."

36 Frazer-Carroll, "#Blacklives Matter Co-Founder Opal Tometi."

37 Byron York, "Cindy Sheehan's Radical Strategist," *National Review*, August 29, 2005, https://www.nationalreview.com/2005/08/cindy-sheehans-radical-strategist-byron-york/.

38 Aston Bunn, "Them Against the World," *The New York Times*, November 16, 2003, https://www.nytimes.com/2003/11/16/magazine/them-against-the-world-part-2.html.

39 Julia Wong, "As Ferguson 'Weekend of Resistance' Begins, Organizers Weigh How to Turn a Moment into a Movement," *In These Times*, October 10, 2014, https://inthesetimes.com/article/from-a-moment-to-a-movement.

40 Facebook page of allied group Solidarity, https://www.facebook.com/SolidarityUS/posts/10152269738612325.

41 "Herstory," Black Lives Matter Global Network, https://blacklivesmatter.com/herstory/.

42 This is the date given by M4BL's website, https://m4bl.org/about-us/. The number of one hundred organizations comes from an article in late December 2020, though of course it continues to grow: see Dylan Matthews, "A Criminal Justice Expert's Guide to Donating Effectively Right Now," Vox, December 21, 2020, https://www.vox.com/future-perfect/21729124/how-to-donate-to-black-lives-matter-charity. M4BL's own page is erratic when it comes to the number of organizations in its network. Its ActBlue funding page has the largest number seen anywhere, 150: https://secure.actblue.com/donate/movement-4-black-lives-1.

43 The Black Lives Matter Global Network Foundation, discussed below, also claims Color of Change and M4BL as partner organizations: https://blacklivesmatter.com/partners/#:~:text=Color%20Of%20Change&text=We%20help%20people%20respond%20effectively,for%20Black%20people%20in%20America. A fuller list of M4BL organizations is given by Giving Compass: https://givingcompass.org/fund/the-movement-for-black-lives-fund.

44 Julia Travers, "The Movement for Black Lives Is on the Rise, and Funders Are Paying Attention," Inside Philanthropy, July 9, 2020, https://www.insidephilanthropy.com/home/2020/7/9/the-movement-for-black-lives-is-on-the-rise-and-funders-are-paying-attention.

45 Aleem Maqbool, "Black Lives Matter: From Social Media Post to Global Movement," BBC, July 9, 2020, https://www.bbc.com/news/world-us-canada-53273381; and Daniel Funke, "How the Black Lives Matter Global Network Is Set Up," PolitiFact, June 17, 2020, https://www.politifact.com/factchecks/2020/jun/17/candace-owens/how-black-lives-matter-global-network-set/.

46 Patrisse Cullors, "Why I'm Transitioning Out of My Role as Executive Director of BLM," May 27, 2021, https://www.youtube.com/watch?app=desktop&v=K-6vwtWQVjg.

47 Isabel Vincent, "Inside BLM co-founder Patrisse Khan-Cullors' Million-Dollar Real Estate Buying Binge," *The New York Post*, April 10, 2021, https://

nypost.com/2021/04/10/inside-blm-co-founder-patrisse-khan-cullors-real-estate-buying-binge/.

48 Patrisse Cullors, "What Is Abolition and Am I an Abolitionist?" February 22, 2021, https://www.youtube.com/watch?v=-RbFhM32YN.

49 Black Lives Matter Global Action Foundation 2020 Impact Report, https://blacklivesmatter.com/wp-content/uploads/2021/02/blm-2020-impact-report.pdf.

50 Laura Barron-Lopez, "Why the Black Lives Matter Movement Does Not Want a Singular Leader," Politico, July 22, 2020, https://www.politico.com/news/2020/07/22/black-lives-matter-movement-leader-377369; and Melina Abdullah's GoFundMe page, https://www.gofundme.com/f/h2tqv-black-lives-matter-los-angeles.

51 Andrew Olivastro and Mike Gonzalez, "The Agenda of Black Lives Matter Is Far Different from the Slogan," *The New York Post,* July 1, 2020, https://nypost.com/2020/07/01/the-agenda-of-black-lives-matter-is-far-different-from-the-slogan/.

52 Natalie Finn, "How Black Lives Matter Began," E! Online, June 9, 2020, https://www.eonline.com/news/1158910/how-black-lives-matter-began-meet-the-women-whose-hashtag-turned-into-a-global-movement.

53 Yoonj Kim, "Alicia Garza Is Bringing Black Power from the Streets to the Polls," MTV, July 10, 2020, http://www.mtv.com/news/3167574/alicia-garza-black-futures-lab/.

54 M4BL, About Us, https://m4bl.org/about-us/.

55 Dan Neumann, "Black Lives Matter Co-Founder: Maine Can Be a Leader in Dismantling White Nationalism," Beacon, June 28, 2019, https://mainebeacon.com/black-lives-matter-co-founder-maine-can-be-a-leader-in-dismantling-white-nationalism/.

56 Maya King, "Black Lives Matter Launches a Political Action Committee," Politico, October 9, 2020, https://www.politico.com/news/2020/10/09/black-lives-matter-pac-428403.

57 Doug Richards, "Political Messaging Aims to Drive Up Black Vote," 11alive.com, December 21, 2020, https://www.11alive.com/article/news/politics/elections/black-voter-messaging/85-246c807d-702f-48d5-ae1f-0a60beob64d1.

58 BLM 2020 Impact Report, 5, https://blacklivesmatter.com/wp-content/uploads/2021/02/blm-2020-impact-report.pdf.

59 Ibid.

60 Ibid., 34.

61 See Cullors's interview with Laura Flanders on *The Laura Flanders Show*, May 19, 2015, https://www.youtube.com/watch?v=W3KB27pdFoY; and Marc Lamont Hill's discussion with the Democratic Socialists of America, February 10, 2021, https://www.i24news.tv/en/news/international/americas/1612965439-blm-seeks-to-dismantle-the-zionist-project-admits-lamont-hill.

62 BLM 2020 Impact Report, 17, https://blacklivesmatter.com/wp-content/uploads/2021/02/blm-2020-impact-report.pdf.

CHAPTER 5. FOLLOW THE MONEY

1 Peter Byrne, "SOUL Trainers," *SF Weekly*, October 16, 2002, https://www.sfweekly.com/news/soul-trainers/.

2 Yuval Levin, *A Time to Build* (New York: Basic Books, 2020), 111.

3 From ActBlue's "About" page, https://secure.actblue.com/about.

4 This article/diagram explains it well: https://capitalresearch.org/article/actblue-the-lefts-favorite-dark-money-machine/.

5 Aaron Morrison, "Black Lives Matter Network Establishes $12 Million Grant Fund," The Associated Press, June 17, 2020, https://apnews.com/article/1d5d0 9286d910bc84c48ffe2d3a111197.

6 Thousand Currents' 2019 financials, 15, https://thousandcurrents.org/wp-content/uploads/2020/12/Thousand-Currents-FY19-Audit.pdf.

7 Black Lives Matter Global Action Foundation 2020 Impact Report, https://blacklivesmatter.com/wp-content/uploads/2021/02/blm-2020-impact-report.pdf.

8 David Burton and Mike Gonzalez, "Nasdaq's Diversity Rule Is Discriminatory and Immoral," *The Washington Examiner*, December 14, 2020, https://www.washingtonexaminer.com/opinion/nasdaqs-diversity-rule-is-discriminatory-and-immoral.

9 Fred Lucas, "These 18 Corporations Gave Money to Radical Black Lives Matter Group," *The Daily Signal*, July 7, 2020, https://www.dailysignal.com/2020/07/07/these-18-corporations-gave-money-to-black-lives-matter-group/.

10 Spreadsheet presented by The Plug, https://docs.google.com/spreadsheets/d/1OZx-_tm3PPyx6-ZJAST1xxOJRfn7KfYDjDT6JedrTfs/edit#gid=0.

11 Saranac Hale Spencer, "False Claims on Corporate Donations to Black Lives Matter," FactCheck.org, August 25, 2020, https://www.factcheck.org/2020/08/false-claims-on-corporate-donations-to-black-lives-matter/.

12 Deja Thomas and Juliana Menasce Horowitz, "Support for Black Lives Matter Has Decreased Since June but Remains Strong Among Black Americans," Pew Research Center, September 16, 2020, https://www.pewresearch.org/fact-tank/2020/09/16/support-for-black-lives-matter-has-decreased-since-june-but-remains-strong-among-black-americans/.

13 Andrew Olivastro and Mike Gonzalez, "Like the Soviets, Black Lives Matter Purges Its History," *The Daily Signal*, September 23, 2020, https://www.heritage.org/progressivism/commentary/the-soviets-black-lives-matter-purges-its-history.

14 Patrisse Cullors, "Seven Years of Growth: BLM's Co-Founder and Incoming Executive Director Reflects on the Movement," September 11, 2020, https://blacklivesmatter.com/seven-years-of-growth-blms-co-founder-and-incoming-executive-director-reflects-on-the-movement/.

15 Merle Hoffman, "America's Most Dangerous Woman," *On the Issues Magazine*, vol. 13, 1989, https://www.ontheissuesmagazine.com/1989vol13/rosenberg.php.

16 Sean Cooper, "Is Warren Buffett the Wallet Behind Black Lives Matter?," Tablet Magazine, October 6, 2020, https://www.tabletmag.com/sections/news/articles/warren-buffett-black-lives-matter.

17 "IDEX and Black Lives Matter Announce Global Partnership," https://pdf.pr.com/press-release/pr-686434.pdf.

18 NoVo Foundation's 990 form, published by ProPublica, https://projects.propublica.org/nonprofits/organizations/470824753/201913189349100246/full.

19 These numbers, and more, can be seen on InfluenceWatch's page on Tides, https://www.influencewatch.org/non-profit/tides-foundation/#:~:text=Funding-,Financial%20Overview,to%20other%20organizations%20in%202018. Because Tides is an entire nexus of multiple nonprofits, InfluenceWatch also has an overview at https://www.influencewatch.org/organization/tides-nexus/.

20 Astead W. Herndon, "George Soros's Foundation Pours $220 Million into Racial Equality Push," *The New York Times*, July 13, 2020, https://www.nytimes.com/2020/07/13/us/politics/george-soros-racial-justice-organizations.html.

21 Brook Kelly-Green and Luna Yasui, "Why Black Lives Matter to Philanthropy," The Ford Foundation, July 19, 2016, https://www.fordfoundation.org/just-matters/equals-change-blog/posts/why-black-lives-matter-to-philanthropy/.

22 Ellen McGirt, "Who Is Funding Black Lives Matter?" Yahoo!Finance, August 8, 2016, https://finance.yahoo.com/news/funding-black-lives-matter-220006041.html?soc_src=social-sh&soc_trk=tw.

23 Julia Travers, "The Movement for Black Lives Is on the Rise, and Funders Are Paying Attention," Inside Philanthropy, July 9, 2020, https://www.insidephilanthropy.com/home/2020/7/9/the-movement-for-black-lives-is-on-the-rise-and-funders-are-paying-attention.

24 For example, the website of the Alliance for Global Justice has reprinted Communist Party propaganda praising the gulag state of North Korea. AfGJ version here: https://afgj.org/an-interview-with-north-koreans; Communist Party website version here: https://www.workers.org/2013/04/8171/.

25 Alliance for Global Justice, Our History, https://afgj.org/about/our-history.

26 Ibid.

27 David Hogberg, "Communists Funding the Resistance: The Alliance for Global Justice," Capital Research Center, August 29, 2017, https://capitalresearch.org/article/communists-funding-the-resistance-the-alliance-for-global-justice/.

28 Travers, "The Movement for Black Lives Is on the Rise."

29 The Archive of the League for Revolutionary Struggle, a Marxist-Leninist organization, https://unityarchiveproject.org/interview/fay-wong/.

30 See, for example, the Spring/Summer 1987 issue of the League's periodical, *East Wind: Politics and Culture of Asians in the U.S.*, https://www.marxists.org/history/erol/periodicals/east-wind/east-wind-6.pdf.

31 LeftRoots journal, *Out to Win* 1 (February 2019): 16, https://journal.leftroots. net/downloads/out-to-win_eng_fin.pdf.

32 See Foy's identification as an FRSO member on the board of directors of Causa Justa/Just Cause, https://cjjc.org/es/acerca-de-nosotros/board-of-directors/.

33 "Asian Americans Solidarity Statement and Articles in Support of #blacklivesmatter," Seeding Change, December 11, 2014, https://www. seeding-change.org/asiansforblacklives/.

34 "We Choose Resistance: Listen to the Call on Black and Asian Solidarity," Seeding Change, December 18, 2014, https://www.seeding-change.org/ wechooseresistance-listen/.

35 "An Open Letter to Community: A Call for Unity and Solidarity in the Face of Violence," May 29, 2020, https://caalmn.org/api4georgefloyd/.

36 "Common Counsel Is on the Move," https://www.commoncounsel.org/ common-counsel-is-on-the-move/.

37 Listen to the Red Nation Podcast: "A Critical Look at the U.S. Imperialist 'Pivot' to China in a Time of Pandemic," posted on May 26, 2020, one day after George Floyd's death: https://directory.libsyn.com/episode/index/ id/14573543/tdest_id/1617341.

38 "Letter of Resignation by Henry Ford II," Philanthropy Roundtable, https:// www.philanthropyroundtable.org/home/resources/donor-intent/donor-intent-resource-library/when-philanthropy-goes-wrong/the-ford-foundation-and-safe-guarding-donor-intent/letter-of-resignation-by-henry-ford-ii.

39 Travers, "The Movement for Black Lives Is on the Rise."

CHAPTER 6. HOW ANTIFA BECAME THE SAFE SPACE

1 David Garrow, "The FBI and Martin Luther King," *The Atlantic*, July/August 2002, https://www.theatlantic.com/magazine/archive/2002/07/the-fbi-and-martin-luther-king/302537/.

2 Federal Bureau of Investigation Intelligence Assessment, "U//FOUO: Black Identity Extremists Motivated to Target Law Enforcement Officers," August 3, 2017, https://www.politico.com/f/?id=0000015f-11c2-d01e-a35f-f7c641380000.

3 Monica Davey and Manny Fernandez, "Security in Ferguson Is Tightened After Night of Unrest," *The New York Times*, November 25, 2014, https://www. nytimes.com/2014/11/26/us/ferguson-missouri-violence.html.

4 Travis Campbell, "Black Lives Matter's Effect on Police Lethal Use of Force," SSRN, May 13, 2021, p. 23, https://papers.ssrn.com/sol3/papers.cfm?abstract_ id=3767097.

5 Jerusalem Demsas, "The Effects of Black Lives Matter Protests," Vox, April 9, 2021, https://www.vox.com/22360290/black-lives-matter-protest-crime-ferguson-effects-murder.

6 Unclassified Supplemental Information, November 21, 2014, https://www. documentcloud.org/documents/4412917-FBI-Intelligence-Report-Tracking-Black-Lives.html.

7   George Joseph and Murtaza Hussain, "FBI Tracked an Activist Involved with Black Lives Matter as They Traveled Across the U.S., Documents Show," *The Intercept*, March 19, 2018, https://theintercept.com/2018/03/19/black-lives-matter-fbi-surveillance/.

8   Michael German, "The Law Is Designed to Punish Whistleblowers Like Me," *The Washington Post*, October 11, 2019, https://www.washingtonpost.com/outlook/the-law-is-designed-to-punish-whistleblowers-like-me/2019/10/10/9eefe4da-eb71-11e9-9c6d-436a0df4f31d_story.html.

9   FBI Chicago Official Report, https://www.documentcloud.org/documents/4412923-FBI-Intelligence-Report-on-Surveillance-of-Cars.html.

10 Email chain, https://www.documentcloud.org/documents/4412971-FBI-Document-on-Staking-Out-Location-Related-to.html.

11 Lee Fang, "Why Was an FBI Joint Terrorism Task Force Tracking a Black Lives Matter Protest?," *The Intercept*, March 12, 2015, https://theintercept.com/2015/03/12/fbi-appeared-use-informant-track-black-lives-matter-protest/.

12 Feliks Garcia, "Black Lives Matter Activists Say FBI Told Them Not to Protest GOP Convention," *The Independent*, July 14, 2016, https://www.independent.co.uk/news/world/americas/black-lives-matter-activists-fbi-republican-convention-cleveland-samuel-sinyangwe-johnetta-elzie-a7137806.html.

13 James Comey, "Hard Truths: Law Enforcement and Race," February 12, 2015, https://www.fbi.gov/news/speeches/hard-truths-law-enforcement-and-race.

14 Email with subject line: "Language from OGC Red Collecting Info Touching on Protests," July 8, 2016, https://www.aljazeera.com/mritems/Documents/201 7/11/28/81a951f0088c4bda9a34d6f3239e947c_100.pdf.

15 Sweta Vohra, "Documents Show US Monitoring of Black Lives Matter," *Al Jazeera*, November 28, 2017, https://www.aljazeera.com/news/2017/11/28/documents-show-us-monitoring-of-black-lives-matter.

16 FBI Chicago Official Report, 3.

17 Aamer Madhani, "Black Lives Matter: Don't Blame Movement for Dallas Police Ambush," *USA Today*, July 8, 2016, https://www.usatoday.com/story/news/2016/07/08/black-lives-matter-dont-blame-movement-dallas-police-ambush/86866014/.

18 FBI Chicago Official Report, 4.

19 Ibid., 5, 6.

20 Alice Speri, "Fear of a Black Homeland," *The Intercept*, March 23, 2019, https://theintercept.com/2019/03/23/black-identity-extremist-fbi-domestic-terrorism/.

21 Southern Poverty Law Center, "The New Black Panther Party," https://www.splcenter.org/fighting-hate/extremist-files/group/new-black-panther-party.

22 Jana Winter and Sharon Weinberger, "The FBI's New Terrorist Threat, 'Black Identity Extremists,'" *Foreign Policy*, October 6, 2017, https://foreignpolicy.com/2017/10/06/the-fbi-has-identified-a-new-domestic-terrorist-threat-and-its-black-identity-extremists/.

23 Congressional Black Caucus letter to Director Wray, October 13, 2017.

24 Speri, "Fear of a Black Homeland."

25 Cory Booker press release: "In Response to Booker Questioning, FBI Director Announces Agency No Longer Using Baseless 'Black Identity Extremists' Label," https://www.booker.senate.gov/news/press/video-in-response-to-booker-questioning-fbi-director-announces-agency-no-longer-using-baseless-and-ldquoblack-identity-extremists-and-rdquo-label.

26 Masood Farivar, "Hundreds of Domestic Terrorism Investigations Opened Since Start of George Floyd Protests, Official Says," VOA News, August 4, 2020, https://www.voanews.com/usa/race-america/hundreds-domestic-terrorism-investigations-opened-start-george-floyd-protests.

27 Rachel E. Barkow, "Three Lessons for Criminal Law Reformers from Locking Up Our Own," *California Law Review* 107, no. 6 (2019): 1968.

28 "The Rachael Rollins Policy Memo," Appendix D (D-1), http://files.suffolkdistrictattorney.com/The-Rachael-Rollins-Policy-Memo.pdf.

29 Cully Stimson and Zak Smith, "George Gascon: A Rogue Prosecutor Whose Extreme Policies Undermine the Rule of Law and Make Los Angeles Less Safe," The Heritage Foundation, January 28, 2021, https://www.heritage.org/crime-and-justice/report/george-gascon-rogue-prosecutor-whose-extreme-policies-undermine-the-rule.

30 Allan Smith, "Parents Guilty of Murder and Raised by Radicals, Chesa Boudin Is San Francisco's Next District Attorney," NBC News, December 16, 2019, https://www.nbcnews.com/politics/elections/parents-guilty-murder-raised-radicals-chesa-boudin-san-francisco-s-n1101071.

31 "Open Society Foundations Announce $220 Million for Building Power in Black Communities," July 13, 2020, https://www.opensocietyfoundations.org/newsroom/open-society-foundations-announce-220-million-for-building-power-in-black-communities.

32 Kerry Picket, "Kamala Harris Pushed Bail Fund That Helped Murder and Rape Suspects Get Out of Jail While Awaiting Trial," *Washington Examiner*, October 1, 2020, https://www.washingtonexaminer.com/news/kamala-harris-pushed-bail-fund-that-helped-murder-and-rape-suspects-get-out-of-jail-while-awaiting-trial.

33 Lora Ries and Zack Smith, "Portland's Rogue DA in Inaction: 543 Cases of Injustice," *The Daily Signal*, October 16, 2020, https://www.heritage.org/crime-and-justice/commentary/portlands-rogue-da-inaction-543-cases-injustice.

34 Joel Finkelstein et al., "Network Enabled Anarchy," A Contagion and Ideology Report, August 2020, http://ncri.io/wp-content/uploads/NCRI-White-Paper-Network-Enabled-Anarchy.pdf.

35 The "Capitol Hill Autonomous Zone" that BLM activists established in Seattle in June 2020.

36 Finkelstein et al., "Network Enabled Anarchy."

37 Ibid.

38 Michael German, "The FBI Targets a New Generation of Black Activists," The Brennan Center for Justice, June 26, 2020, https://www.brennancenter.org/our-work/analysis-opinion/fbi-targets-new-generation-black-activists.

39 Mike Levine, "Trump Vows to Designate Antifa a Terrorist Group. Here's Why DOJ Officials Call that 'Highly Problematic,'" ABC News, June 1, 2020, https://abcnews.go.com/Politics/trump-vows-designate-antifa-terrorist-group-heres-doj/story?id=70999186.

40 S.Res.279—116th Congress (2019–2020), Congress.gov, https://www.congress.gov/bill/116th-congress/senate-resolution/279.

41 The Torch Network website, https://torchantifa.org/about/.

42 Thomas Fuller, Alan Feuer, and Serge F. Kovaleski, "'Antifa' Grows as Left-Wing Faction Set to, Literally, Fight the Far Right," *The New York Times*, August 17, 2017, https://www.nytimes.com/2017/08/17/us/antifa-left-wing-faction-far-right.html.

43 Andy Ngo, *Unmasked* (New York: Hachette, 2021).

44 Mark Hemingway, "Roots of Antifa: This Idea Has Violent Consequences," Real Clear Investigations, October 30, 2020, https://www.realclearinvestigations.com/articles/2020/10/30/roots_of_antifa_this_idea_has_violent_consequences_125818.html.

45 "Points of Unity," https://torchantifa.org/points-of-unity/.

46 Antifa website, Anti-Racist Action, ARA Network, https://antiracistaction.org/about/.

47 Hemingway, "Roots of Antifa."

48 CampusActivism.org, http://www.campusactivism.org/displayevent-2778.htm.

49 Hemingway, "Roots of Antifa."

50 Ibid.

51 Justin Kaufmann, "Bill Ayers Compares Weather Underground Days to Black Lives Matters Era," June 23, 2020, https://www.wbez.org/stories/bill-ayers-compares-weather-underground-days-to-black-lives-matters-era/f4a4064a-9642-4667-a200-a2de2277f35f.

CHAPTER 7. SCHOOLING THE REVOLUTION

1 Quoted in Martin Jay, *The Dialectical Imagination* (Boston and Toronto: Little, Brown and Company, 1973), 19.

2 Ibid., 44.

3 Ibid., 4 and 5.

4 Max Horkheimer, *Critical Theory: Selected Essays* (New York: The Continuum Publishing Company, 2002), 246, http://blogs.law.columbia.edu/critique1313/files/2019/09/Horkheimer-Traditional-and-Critical-Theory-2.pdf.

5 Herbert Marcuse, *Eros and Civilization: A Philosophical Inquiry into Freud* (New York: Routledge, 1959), 201.

6 Karl Marx and Friedrich Engels, *The Manifesto of the Communist Party*, edited and annotated by Friedrich Engels (Chicago: Charles H. Kerr & Company, 1906), 39, https://www.google.com/books/edition/Manifesto_of_the_Communist_Party/s2iEeCJAlusC?hl=en&gbpv=1&bsq=abolition%20of%20the%20family.

7 Herbert Marcuse, *One-Dimensional Man: Studies in the Ideology of Advanced Industrial Society* (Boston: Beacon Press, 1991), 256–257.

8 Ibid., 9.

9 Cornell Law School, "Critical Legal Theory," https://www.law.cornell.edu/wex/critical_legal_theory.

10 See #2019ASA Presidential Session: Intersectionality and Critical Race Theory, https://www.youtube.com/watch?v=elaIUgX-zZE.

11 Kimberlé Crenshaw, "Mapping the Margins: Intersectionality, Identity Politics, and Violence Against Women of Color," *Stanford Law Review* 43, no. 6 (July 1991): 1296, https://is.muni.cz/el/1423/jaro2017/SPR470/um/68138626/Crenshaw_1991.txt.

12 Combahee River Collective Statement, https://americanstudies.yale.edu/sites/default/files/files/Keyword%20Coalition_Readings.pdf.

13 Derrick A. Bell, "Who's Afraid of Critical Race Theory?," *University of Illinois Law Review* 1995, no. 4 (1995): 893 and 899, https://sph.umd.edu/sites/default/files/files/Bell_Whos%20Afraid%20of%20CRT_1995UIllLRev893.pdf.

14 Ibid., 902.

15 Ibid., 901.

16 Richard Delgado and Jean Stefancic, *Critical Race Theory: An Introduction*, 3rd ed. (New York: New York University Press, 2017), 3.

17 Daniel Bergner, "'White Fragility' Is Everywhere, But Does Antiracism Training Work?," *The New York Times Magazine*, July 15, 2020, https://www.nytimes.com/2020/07/15/magazine/white-fragility-robin-diangelo.html.

18 Mike Gonzalez, "Angela Davis and the Distortion of Diversity," *The Daily Signal*, May 4, 2018, https://www.heritage.org/civil-society/commentary/angela-davis-and-the-distortion-diversity.

19 Quoted in Sol Stern's masterful takedown of the former terrorist, "The Bomber as School Reformer," *City Journal*, October 6, 2008, https://www.city-journal.org/html/bomber-school-reformer-10465.html. Original in Bill Ayers, "World Education Forum," November 7, 2006, https://billayers.org/2006/11/.

20 Victor Zitta, *Georg Lukács' Marxism, Alienation, Dialectics, Revolution* (Berlin: Springer, 2016), 106, quoted in Stephen R. Soukup, *The Dictatorship of Woke Capital* (New York: Encounter Books, 2021), 37, 38.

21 This information comes from the "About" page of the Black Lives Matter at School site: https://www.blacklivesmatteratschool.com/about.html.

22 National Black Lives Matter at School Week of Action Starter Kit, https://docs.google.com/document/d/1kjnmt8y-7d0_8y6eVxRG_OeGv5Sy4yHudDIpmiaoLFg/edit.

23 "The Heartbeat of Racism Is Denial," November 16, 2020, https://www.blacklivesmatteratschool.com/updates-and-info.

24 "About" page, https://www.blacklivesmatteratschool.com/about.html.

25 "Endorsement" page, https://www.blacklivesmatteratschool.com/endorsements.html.

26 Christopher Rogers, "National Black Lives Matter at School Steering Committee Statement on Attacks Against CRT, BLM@School and the 1619

Project," Medium, September 16, 2020, https://medium.com/national-blm-week-of-action-in-schools/national-black-lives-matter-at-school-steering-committee-statement-on-attacks-against-crt-9b122913b15f.

27 Teaching for Change, *Beyond Heroes and Holidays*, https://www.teachingforchange.org/wp-content/uploads/2012/01/BHH_Opening_Intro.pdf.

28 Learning for Justice, "A Framework for Anti-Bias Education," https://www.learningforjustice.org/frameworks/social-justice-standards.

29 "Unit 4, Probability and Statistics, Checklist and Rubric," https://docs.google.com/document/d/1BTJostYqGuxoauuP0057x1bGOCov_h3C/edit.

30 National Black Lives Matter at School Week of Action Starter Kit, https://docs.google.com/document/d/1kjnmt8y-7d0_8y6eVxRG_OeGv5Sy4yHudDIpmiaoLFg/edit.

31 DC Area Educators for Social Justice, "Black Lives Matter 12 Guiding Principles," https://www.dcareaeducators4socialjustice.org/black-lives-matter/13-guiding-principles.

32 Restorative Justice Colorado, "Restorative Justice Practices," https://www.rjcolorado.org/restorative-justice/#:~:text=Restorative%20justice%20practices%20are%20about,of%20balance%20through%20harmful%20actions.

33 "An Open Letter to President Elect Biden and Vice-President Elect Harris," December 10, 2020," https://www.blacklivesmatteratschool.com/updates-and-info.

CHAPTER 8. CONCLUSION

1 David Azerrad, "The Promises and Perils of Identity Politics," The Heritage Foundation, January 23, 2019, 22.

2 Jesenia Santana, "Ally or Co-Conspirator?," https://movetoendviolence.org/blog/ally-co-conspirator-means-act-insolidarity/.

3 Anti-Racism Research Guides, "Why Co-Conspirators?," https://researchguides.library.tufts.edu/AntiRacismResourceGuide/WhyCoConspirators.

4 Alicia Garza, "How to Be an Ally," December 21, 2020, https://www.youtube.com/watch?v=5QJmmPt9f3s.

5 Jessica Powell and Amber Kelly, "Accomplices in the Academy in the Age of Black Lives Matter," *Journal of Critical Thought and Praxis* (Iowa State University) 6, no. 2 (2017): 45.

6 Neil Genzlinger, "Noel Ignatiev, 78, Persistent Voice Against White Privilege, Dies," *The New York Times*, November 14, 2019, https://www.nytimes.com/2019/11/14/books/noel-ignatiev-dead.html.

7 Noel Ignatin (a penname he often used) and Ted Allen, "The White Blindspot," The Sojourner Truth Organization, 1967, http://www.sojournertruth.net/whiteblindspot.html.

8 Genzlinger, "Noel Ignatiev."

9 As Sol Stern put it in 2008, "Calling Bill Ayers a school reformer is a bit like calling Joseph Stalin an agricultural reformer." See "The Bomber as School

Reformer," *City Journal*, October 6, 2008, https://www.city-journal.org/html/bomber-school-reformer-10465.html.

10 Powell and Kelly, "Accomplices in the Academy," 52.

11 Ivan Fernando, "Progressive Professor Urges White Male Students to Commit Suicide During Class," Diversity Chronicles, November 18, 2013, https://diversitychronicle.wordpress.com/2013/11/18/progressive-professor-urges-white-male-students-to-commit-suicide-during-class/.

12 Anthony Kim, "Milton Friedman at 101: We Need His Ideas Now More Than Ever," *The Daily Signal*, July 31, 2013, https://www.dailysignal.com/2013/07/31/milton-friedman-at-101-we-need-his-ideas-now-more-than-ever/.

13 John Gramlich, "What the Data Says (And Doesn't Say) About Crime in the United States," Pew Research, November 20, 2020, https://www.pewresearch.org/fact-tank/2020/11/20/facts-about-crime-in-the-u-s/.

14 Ibid.

15 Ann Carson, "Prisoners in 2019," Bureau of Justice Statistics, October 2020, https://www.bjs.gov/content/pub/pdf/p19.pdf.

16 Glenn Loury, "Unspeakable Truths About Racial Inequalities in America," Quillette, February 11, 2021, https://quillette.com/2021/02/10/unspeakable-truths-about-racial-inequality-in-america/.

17 Lois James, David Klinger, and Bryan J. Vila, "Ethnic and Racial Bias in Decisions to Shoot Seen Through a Stronger Lens," *Journal of Experimental Criminology* 10, no. 3 (September 2014): 328, 329, https://www.researchgate.net/publication/269354127_Racial_and_ethnic_bias_in_decisions_to_shoot_seen_through_a_stronger_lens_Experimental_results_from_high-fidelity_laboratory_simulations/link/55a536ba08ae00cf99c952ef/download.

18 Chris Isidore, "Black Unemployment Falls to a Record Low," CNN Business, September 6, 2019, https://www.cnn.com/2019/09/06/economy/black-unemployment-rate/index.html.

19 Alan Berube, "Black Household Income Is Rising Across the United States," Brookings Institution, October 3, 2019, https://www.brookings.edu/blog/the-avenue/2019/10/03/black-household-income-is-rising-across-the-united-states/.

20 Daniel Bergner, "'White Fragility' Is Everywhere, But Does Antiracism Training Work?," *The New York Times Magazine*, July 15, 2020, https://www.nytimes.com/2020/07/15/magazine/white-fragility-robin-diangelo.html.

21 Virginia Allen, "Legal Coalition to Sue to Stop Fed's 'Critical Race Theory' Training," *The Daily Signal*, February 1, 2021, https://www.dailysignal.com/2021/02/01/legal-coalition-to-sue-to-stop-feds-critical-race-theory-training/.

22 Christopher F. Rufo, "The New Segregation," October 19, 2020, https://christopherrufo.com/the-new-segregation/.

23 Christopher F. Rufo, "Gone Crazy," *City Journal*, February 18, 2021, https://www.city-journal.org/east-side-community-school-tells-parents-to-become-white-traitors.

24 This Twitter user has since made her tweet private.

25 Bari Weiss, "Whistleblower at Smith College Resigns over Racism," Bari Weiss Substack, October 19, 2021, https://bariweiss.substack.com/p/whistleblower-at-smith-college-resigns.

26 Stop Critical Race Theory, https://twitter.com/realchrisrufo/status/1352033792458776578/photo/1.

27 "An Open Letter to President Elect Biden and Vice-President Elect Harris," December 10, 2020, https://www.blacklivesmatteratschool.com/updates-and-info.

28 See my January 17, 2017, article in *The Washington Post*, "Montgomery County's Wrong Track on Culturally Diverse Education," https://www.washingtonpost.com/opinions/montgomery-countys-wrong-tack-on-culturally-diverse-education/2017/01/20/ae613906-de67-11e6-acdf-14da832ae861_story.html.

29 Mike Gonzalez, "Angela Davis and the Distortion of Diversity," *The Daily Signal*, May 4, 2018, https://www.heritage.org/civil-society/commentary/angela-davis-and-the-distortion-diversity.

30 Loury, "Unspeakable Truths About Racial Inequalities in America."

31 "Claremont Institute Chairman Thomas Klingenstein: Trump 2020: A Man vs. a Movement," Real Clear Politics, October 13,, 2020, https://www.realclearpolitics.com/video/2020/10/13/claremont_institute_chairman_thomas_klingenstein_trump_2020_a_man_vs_a_movement.html.

INDEX